Praise for Eros and Revolution

"Both inciting and insightful, the essays in Eros and Revolution nurture hidden histories while besting opponents with daring ripostes. In the end, everything that Katsiaficas writes is a love letter, and no other movement-based scholar conveys struggle's lessons with such grace and such force."
— **AK Thompson**, author of *Black Bloc, White Riot*

"This splendid book brings together some of George Katsiaficas"s most important essays... Read as a collection, the pieces are sometimes provocative, sometimes inspiring, but never depressing or dull. Anyone who cares about democracy should read this book."
— **Andrej Grubačić**, author of *Wobblies and Zapatistas*, and *Living at the Edges of Capitalism: Adventures in Exile and Mutual Aid*

"George Katsiaficas brings a distinctive blend of scholarly rigour and activist commitment to all his writings. His subject matter spans the globe, and is consistently inspired by personal involvement in the histories he analyzes."
— **Victor Wallis**, author of *Socialist Practice: Histories and Theories*

"Collected in this volume are the fruits of a lifetime of penetrating insights, remarkable escapades, and an abiding love for humanity... From the Black Panthers to the Black Bloc, Philadelphia to Berlin, to the sequential uprisings across Asia in the 1980s-90s, and later to the alter-globalization and anti-war mobilizations and eventually the Arab Spring and Occupy Wall Street, Katsiaficas centers the instinctual human need for freedom... His 'eros effect' seeks to rescue the revolutionary value of spontaneity, to put human emotion at the center of our capacity for renewal and rebellion."
— **Chris Carlsson**, San Francisco historian, author, photographer, bicycling grandfather. His new novel, *When Shells Crumble*, is forthcoming

Eros *and* Revolution

GEORGE KATSIAFICAS

FOREWORD

Paul Messersmith-Glavin

EPILOGUE

Dimitrios Roussopoulos

Montréal • New York • London

Black Rose Books No. WW437

Library and Archives Canada Cataloguing in Publication

Title: Eros and revolution / George Katsiaficas ; foreword, Paul Messersmith-Glavin ; epilogue, Dimitrios Roussopoulos.
Other titles: Essays. Selections
Names: Katsiaficas, George N., 1949- author. | Messersmith-Glavin, Paul. | Roussopoulos, Dimitrios I.
Description: Some essays previously published. | Includes bibliographical references.
Identifiers: Canadiana (print) 20230528252 | Canadiana (ebook) 20230535291 | ISBN 9781551648118 (hardcover) | ISBN 9781551648095 (softcover) | ISBN 9781551648132 (PDF)
Subjects: LCSH: Social movements. | LCSH: Social history.
Classification: LCC HM881 .K38 2024 | DDC 303.48/4—dc23

Design by Associés Libres

C.P. 42002, Succ. Roy,
Montréal, Quebec H2W 2T3
CANADA
www.blackrosebooks.com

ORDERING INFORMATION

CANADA/US

University of Toronto Press
5201 Dufferin Street
Toronto, ON
M3H 5T8

1-800-565-9523

utpbooks@utpress.utoronto.ca

UK/INTERNATIONAL

Central Books
Freshwater Road
Dagenham
RM8 1RX

+44 20 8525 8800

contactus@centralbooks.com

TABLE OF CONTENTS

Paris, May 1968, Atelier of Revolutionary Artists

ACKNOWLEDGEMENTS

George Katsiaficas

I OWE THE PUBLICATION of this book to two revolutionary comrades, Alejandra Pinto and Dimitrios Roussopoulos. Ale took it upon herself to translate some of my essays and published them in Chile under the same title as this book. It was no coincidence that her initiative came on the heels of the historic uprising from 2019–2020. When I went to Chile for the book's publication, Ale had organized a series of events, each of which had a unique character that convinced me of the continuing relevance of my ideas to emergent insurgencies.

Later that year, as Dimitri and I sat at a taverna in Greece recounting our experiences since last we had met, he immediately agreed to publish the Chilean book in English "sight unseen." While this collection differs slightly from the Spanish anthology, it remains essentially the same.

I should add my gratitude for the respect shown me by my Greek publisher, Panayiotis Kalamaras, who released his own anthology of my essays in 2019. Paul Messersmith-Glavin has remained my comrade and friend through years of struggles. I am humbled by his high estimation of the value of my work. I owe a special debt to Era Purnama Sari, whose dedication to struggle inspires me every day.

The importance of Eros to my life and work can be traced to Herbert Marcuse, my friend and teacher during our years together in San Diego in the 1970s.

GK
www.eroseffect.com
Jakarta, Indonesia
August 1, 2023

FOREWORD

Paul Messersmith-Glavin

FOR THOSE OF US radicalized in the 1980s and 1990s, George Katsiaficas has served as a bridge to previous generations of revolutionary thinkers and organizers. Katsiaficas provides a connection to the ideas of his teacher and friend, Herbert Marcuse—the most inspiring member of the Frankfurt School of Marxist intellectuals who fled Nazi Germany. He also connects us to the Black Panthers, with whom he organized mobilizations in solidarity, as well as many of the insurrectionary and tumultuous counter cultural and politically radical movements of the 1960s and 1970s. He links us not only to previous movements and thinkers, but also to struggles elsewhere in the world: the German autonomous movement, in particular, within which he was immersed for a period in the 1980s, and later to Asian uprisings, as in Korea, where he lived for five years. This type of international and intergenerational movement-building is as important as it is rare—as is Katsiaficas himself.

As a young organizer, inspired by Katsiaficas' writings on the German Autonomen and after reading *The Imagination of the New Left*, his book on the global movements of 1968, I drove all night to Boston with a comrade to meet him for the first time. He invited myself, as well as my traveling companion, over to his apartment so we could drink beer while talking about life and politics late into the night. What struck me upon encountering him was how personable he is: open, relaxed, welcoming. Getting to know him felt to me like hanging out with a cool uncle, someone with more life experience, who nevertheless treats you as a peer by respecting your opinions and showing interest in your ideas and dreams. We immediately became friends.

Katsiaficas' role is what activist-scholar Chris Dixon refers to as part of cultivating a long view to revolutionary organizing, "This multi-generational perspective can help us to find continuity and community in our efforts."[1] Dixon's lessons resonate with those coming out of years of struggle in the German autonomous movement. There, according to a long-time organizer, they learned the need for "*Verbindlichkeit und Kontinuität* (commitment and continuity)," to address the all-to-common problems of a "lack of personal continuity, … no transmission of lessons and experiences from the older to the younger people, or from one generation to the next."[2] Too often, people get involved in political organizing for a period, but in time become disillusioned or burnt out for any number of reasons. They then drop out of movement work, taking whatever insights or lessons they learned with them. The resulting lack of personal continuity in the movement is exacerbated by the absence of sustained organizing structures.

George Katsiaficas and other organizing veterans' focus on long-term movement work helps prevent the endless reinvention of wheels, nurturing a movement that has both historical memory and informed strategy. As Dixon points out, "Sustained efforts to transform the world need ways of reproducing themselves and need contributions from people throughout their lives. … This means building movements capable of welcoming and holding children, aging people, and caregivers."[3]

George Katsiaficas first become politically active in the anti-Vietnam War movement in 1969. He was imprisoned during its high point in May 1970, becoming the sole person ever to graduate from the Massachusetts Institute of Technology while in solitary confinement. Under the mentorship of Marcuse—who taught Katsiaficas to take the study of ideas seriously—he developed his theoretical perspectives and historical understandings. From working with Marcuse and thinking through his years of research on the worldwide events of 1968, Katsiaficas began developing his concept of the "Eros effect" to help explain seemingly spontaneous uprisings. The concept of the Eros effect helps one understand not only the events of 1968, but subsequently other historical moments, such as the successively unfolding Arab Spring, occupations of squares in Spain and Greece, and the Occupy movement in the US. It also helps account for one of the largest social movements in US history, the movement for Black lives that emerged in 2013 in Ferguson, Missouri, coming back with a renewed fury across the US in 2020 after the police murdered George Floyd. As Katsiaficas explains, "When the Eros effect is activated, humans' love for and solidarity with each other suddenly replace previously dominant values and norms. …Moments of the Eros effect reveal movements' aspirations and visions as embodied in actions of millions of people, a far more significant dimension than statements of leaders, organizations, or parties." [4]

Despite his working in the Marxist tradition, this sounded like anarchism to those of us new to political organizing and social theory. The framework of the Eros effect helps account for a fuller range of the human experience and myriad ways societies change than those that only focus on, or reduce social phenomenon simply to economic, political, or material levels. As we have seen with the rise of authoritarian and neo-fascist movements around the world, emotions play a significant role in motivating political action. Though, as Katsiaficas points out, "Rather than portraying emotions as linked to reaction, the notion of the Eros effect seeks to bring them into the realm of positive revolutionary resources whose mobilization can result in significant social transformation."[5] Katsiaficas has documented countless examples of people collectively striving to actualize genuine freedom throughout modern history,

People in Prague, Czech Republic respond to the 1968 Russian invasion

basing his theory in Marcuse's later writings on "political Eros." Marcuse grounded his ideas not only in Marx, but in that of psychoanalyst Sigmund Freud. In Marcuse's reading of Freud, humans develop "through the activity of two original basic instincts: the *life* instinct (sexuality, which Freud for the most part now calls *Eros*) and the *death* instinct, the destructive instinct."[6] For Marcuse, human instincts are mutable, and modern society can be viewed as a struggle between the drive towards life, exemplified by liberatory social movements such as the 1960s counter-culture, and the drive towards death as embodied in the hellfire and destruction unleased by the US against the people of Vietnam, Iraq, and Afganistan, or the total war of Putin's Russia against the people of Ukraine.

Marcuse's intellectual work, as well as that of his fellow Frankfurt School theorists, such as Theodore Adorno and Max Horkheimer, was in part a response to the rise of Nazism, a reaction to the genocidal Auschwitz concentration camp, and these events' bleak implications for humanity. Equally important to Marcuse was to explore how people could work towards the very antithesis of the Nazi genocidal project: to collectively create a liberated and free society, one in which class and other hierarchies are abolished, and people are free to pursue their highest aspirations. Much of Marcuse's work, and that of the Frankfurt School in general, revolved around this tension between examining the horrors of contemporary life—be they Nazism or the vicissitudes of capitalist consumer society—and the struggle to create something better. Marcuse reached the height of his popularity with the international student movements in the late 1960s and early 1970s, speaking to large crowds after publishing works such as *Reason and Revolution, One-Dimensional Man*, and later, *An Essay on Liberation* and *Counterrevolution and Revolt*. Alongside other notable figures with whom Marcuse either taught or was acquainted, such as Angela Davis, the German student leader Rudi Dutschke, and Susan Sontag, Katsiaficas was one of the young people Marcuse conspired with, and who took his urgent message to heart.

Katsiaficas' work and political direction has also been shaped by his ties to on-the-ground struggles and his participation in uprisings, while being guided by Marcuse's thinking. Katsiaficas was close to and worked with the Black Panthers on the East Coast and he attended the Panthers' Revolutionary People's Constitutional Convention in Philadelphia, what he refers to as the high point of the 1960s movements.[7] He immersed himself in the youth counterculture of the era, and he was involved in organizing a series of anti-Vietnam War protests. The FBI referred to him in their files as a "New Left/anarchist," and he was classified "Priority 1 ADEX," indicating that he was to be immediately arrested in the event of a "national emergency." He left Boston in the early 1970s after continual arrests and police harassment, and moved to San Diego, where Marcuse was living and teaching.

After the San Diego commune where he lived was shot up by the FBI-organized Secret Army Organization (SAO), and believing in the possibility of organizing a revolutionary base in Ocean Beach, California, Katsiaficas cofounded the Red House, a new commune built upon political agitation and establishing counter-institutions. He and his comrades at the Red House were influenced by Grace Lee and James Boggs, who had once collaborated with CLR James and who organized in Detroit. Ocean Beach became a center of organizing and soon drew further attention from the FBI.

As the revolutionary movements of the period receded, Katsiaficas returned to Boston and began teaching at Wentworth Institute of Technology—an inner-city working-class college. In the 1980s, he lived with and worked together with comrades involved in the Autonomen movement in Germany, writing about his experiences in places like *Z Magazine*. These writings on the Autonomen—with their revolutionary politics, squatted housing, cultural spaces, and street militancy, including black bloc tactics—were hugely influential for many anarchists and other North American radicals at that time.

Katsiaficas' work with the Autonomen was subsequently transformed into his *The Subversion of Politics: European Autonomous Social Movements and the Decolonization of Everyday Life*. In that work, he traces the autonomous lineage from the movements of 1968, through the Italian Autonomia and women's movement, antinuclear mobilizations, and the Red Zoras—an autonomous part of the decentralized armed successor to the Red Army Fraction made up solely by women influenced by anti-imperialism and feminism—to the confrontational tactics and politics of the Autonomen, while fleshing out the general theory of autonomy and its expression in several European countries. The politics and tactics of the Autonomen resonated with young radicals in North America in the 1980s and 1990s, and their tactic of the black bloc has now been an aspect of oppositional protest from the shutdown of the World Trade Organization (WTO) meetings in Seattle in 1999, the Trump Inauguration protests in Washington, DC in 2016, the uprising for Black lives during 2020, to the ongoing fight against fascism.

Katsiaficas has consistently challenged Eurocentric and traditional academic approaches to social theory. When writing about movements, his vision is not restricted to the West. His book on the 1960s, *The Imagination of the New Left: A Global Analysis of 1968*, represents the movements of the time as global, not confined only to examining events in North America and Europe and not solely to white students in the US, but prominently featuring people of color. Katsiaficas subsequently spent five years in Korea studying Asian social movements and uprisings, writing about them in his two-volume *Asia's Unknown Uprisings*. These two volumes uncover the Eros effect present within the wave of people's movements in ten Asian countries, including China, Thailand, and Tibet, among others.

Katsiaficas has been a movement participant and dedicated organizer who goes beyond serving as just an observer to being a militant researcher, someone who lives amongst and collaborates with the people he writes about, seeing his research and writing as part of movement organizing. As he reflects, "… My own activist orientation means that I refuse to bifurcate theory from practice. For me, the praxis of thousands of people contains analysis within itself. Actions speak louder than words. By theorizing peoples' actions, I facilitate their speaking for themselves. History is made and freedom is defined in the streets by hundreds of thousands of people—and in the case of the 2020 Black Lives Matter uprising—by tens of millions."[8]

*   *   *

At a national Greens Gathering in the sleepy, hippy college town of Eugene, Oregon in 1989, George Katsiaficas, an organizer from India named Bharat Pantankar, and I sat on the steps outside the University of Oregon auditorium where decisions were being made via popular assembly. This was when the Greens in the US were largely focused on grassroots organizing around social and environmental issues and promoting direct democracy, inspired by *die Grünen* (the Greens) in what was then West Germany, though careerists interested in national electoral politics were already caucusing. I was in my twenties and was part of the Youth Greens and the Left Green

Network, both of whom identified with the so-called *die Grünen Fundis,* such as Jutta Ditforth, and other extra-electoral social movement organizers involved in the German Greens. We were very influenced by the work of Murray Bookchin.

At the time in the US, radical organizing mostly focused on Central America solidarity, anti-nuclear power and weapons, and ACT UP's work around the AIDS crisis. We embraced the Greens at the time because we saw them bringing disparate movements together by locating common causes of the world's problems in the capitalist social and economic system, patriarchy, and nation-states, among other institutions. Examining the root causes rather than simply fighting various symptoms helped us better make sense of the world, enabling us to think strategically about ways to create something different. Like many oppositional movements, there were both revolutionary and reformist wings in the Greens; also, like many oppositional movements, those two wings spent a good deal of time trying to counter one another's strategies and ideas.

In this context, Katsiaficas, Pantankar, and I were catching up and talking about various debates going on between the advocates of a national and electoral Green Party and those of us pushing a bottom-up, social movement perspective. The three of us were the only ones who showed up for a workshop on actions. I was going to be moving to New York that year and somewhat jokingly said, "We should shut down Wall Street for the twentieth anniversary of Earth Day!" which was coming up the following spring. As it turned out, it wasn't a joke. Katsiaficas loved the idea, and made me a deal: if he raised it during his keynote talk that night, and it was well received, I would have to make sure it happened. He did propose the idea, drawing explicit connections between capitalism and ecological destruction and singing the praises of direct action, even suggesting chaining abandoned cars to light poles and other tactics to blockade streets and shut down Wall Street. He received a standing ovation. I was on the hook.

A year later, several thousand people showed up before dawn in the financial district the Monday morning after the twentieth Earth Day celebration in New York City.[9] Six hundred NYPD cops showed up even earlier, effectively shutting Wall Street down for us, and the Wall Street Action was front page news on papers across the US. The Youth Greens, working with the Love and Rage Revolutionary Anarchist Federation and other radical organizers, formed a black bloc to shut down Broadway, the main boulevard leading south to Wall Street. It was Katsiaficas' writing about the Autonomen's use of this tactic that inspired us. A black bloc would also be organized for the following year's march in Washington, DC against the first Gulf War. That bloc had several hundred participants from around North America, throwing paint bombs at the Justice Department building, breaking windows, and spray-painting anarchist symbols on World Bank headquarters during a breakaway march, all the while unarresting any comrades grabbed by police, pulling them back into the safety of the bloc. It was the most militant, fun, and creative part of the huge march in opposition to the Gulf War that warm day.

In his life and writings, Katsiaficas has been a catalyst for actions such as these. His theory of the Eros effect helps us "comprehend social movements as the logical progress in history that unfolds within the praxis of thousands—and sometimes millions—of people as they rise up to change their lives. The inner logic in seemingly spontaneous actions during moments of crisis—particularly in events like general strikes, uprisings, insurrections, and revolutions—constitutes the concrete realization of liberty in history." Thus, "The concept of the Eros effect is a means of rescuing the revolutionary value of spontaneity."[10]

Spontaneity exists in rhizomatic relationship to various forms of organization. Affinity groups organizing on larger scales by sending mandated delegates to decision-making spokescouncils; cadre groups of organizers with shared politics agitating within social movements; dual-power confederations of neighborhood and workplace assemblies and counter-institutions; revolutionary organizations; tactical teams making on-the-spot practical decisions amidst protests and uprisings: all have a role to play amidst the outpouring of people driven to the streets or compelled to take over their workplaces.

The importance of spontaneity, of the unexpected happening, is a source of optimism to those of us who aspire to and struggle for a better life. This is the most important aspect of the Eros effect. In times of despair, I remind myself and others of the many times over the last few decades when the unexpected happens: the Zapatistas emerge out of the Lacandon Jungle in Chiapas, Mexico and announce to the world their Indigenous opposition to further capitalist extraction and exploitation; the Black Lives Matter movement explodes in Ferguson, Missouri, cultivated through generations of Black struggle and resistance, ignited in response to the murders of Trayvon Martin and Michael Brown. And recently, the relentless courage of women and other young people in Iran rebelling against the severe repression of the Mullahs. Katsiaficas has documented countless international examples of people rising up with joyful militancy, changing themselves and social realities in the process.

George Katsiaficas inspires hope. Hope—for a good life, to live more freely and cooperatively—motivates people to take risks, to be daring. Katsiaficas embodies the belief that radical ideas can lead to radical action; that if we can think and imagine our way out of the dystopia we have been born into, perhaps collectively, we can do the work to change it and create something new.

NOTES

1   Chris Dixon, "Cultivating a Long View," *Upping the Anti* 23, May 21, 2023.

2   Paul O'Banion, "Autonomous Antifa: From the Autonomen to Post-Antifa in Germany – An Interview with Bender, a German Comrade," *It's Going Down*, November 20, 2017.

3   Dixon, 2023.

4   George Katsiaficas, "Eros and Revolution," *Radical Philosophy Review* 16, n. 2 (2013), pp. 492–93.

5.   Katsiaficas, "Eros," p. 494.

6   Herbert Marcuse, "Freedom and Freud's Theory of Instincts," *Five Lectures* (Boston: Beacon Press, 1970), p. 6.

7   George Katsiaficas, "Organization and Movement: The Case of the Black Panther Party and the Revolutionary People's Constitutional Convention of 1970," *Liberation, Imagination, and the Black Panther Party: A New Look at the Panthers and their Legacy*, eds. Kathleen Cleaver and George Katsiaficas (New York: Routledge, 2001), pp. 141–55.

8   George Katsiaficas, "A Response to 'Spontaneous Combustion' from George Katsiaficas," *Perspectives on Anarchist Theory* 33 (2023), pp. 68–69.

9   George Katsiaficas and Paul Messersmith-Glavin, "Why Wall Street? The Case for Green Direct Action," *Remaking Radicalism: A Grassroots Documentary Reader of the United States, 1973-2001*, eds. Emily K. Hobson and Dan Berger (Athens, GA: University of Georgia Press, 2020), pp. 388–90.

10   Katsiaficas, "Eros," pp. 493–94.

Paul Messersmith-Glavin is a longtime anarchist organizer living in the Pacific Northwest of the US. He is a Chinese medicine practitioner and member of the Perspectives on Anarchist Theory *collective and the Mutual Aid Acupuncture Collective. His writing has appeared in* The Philosophy of the Beats *(The University Press of Kentucky, 2012) and* Remaking Radicalism: A Grassroots Documentary Reader of the United States, 1973–2001 *(University of Georgia Press, 2020). He edited and wrote the forward to* Imperiled Life: Revolution Against Climate Catastrophe *(IAS/AK Press, 2012) and served as the Institute for Anarchist Studies' editor for* No Pasaran! Antifascist Dispatches from a World in Crisis *(IAS/AK Press, 2022).*

The World-Historical Character of 1968

The nature of Spirit may be understood by a glance at its direct opposite—Matter. As the essence of Matter is Gravity, so, on the other hand, we may affirm that the substance, the essence of Spirit is Freedom.
—G.W.F. HEGEL

WORLDWIDE EPISODES of revolt in 1968 have generally been analyzed from within their own national contexts, but only in reference to the global constellation of forces and to each other can these movements be understood in theory as they occurred in practice. Particularly since World War II, it is increasingly difficult to analyze social movements from within the confines of a nation-state. The events that catalyze social movements are often international ones. The May 1970 nationwide university strike in the United States is remembered mainly because of the killings at Kent State and Jackson State Universities, but it was enacted in opposition to the US invasion of Cambodia as well as to repression of the Black Panther Party.

International connections between movements in 1968 were often synchronic, as television, radio, and newspapers relayed news of events as they occurred. In May 1968, when a student revolt led to a general strike of over nine million workers in France, there were significant demonstrations of solidarity in Mexico City, Berlin, Tokyo, Buenos Aires, Berkeley, and Belgrade, and students and workers in both Spain and Uruguay attempted general strikes of their own. Massive student strikes in Italy forced Prime Minister Aldo Moro and his cabinet to resign; Germany experienced its worst political crisis since World War II; and a student strike at the University of Dakar, Senegal, led to a general strike of workers. These are instances of what sociologists have called "contagion effects" (and what I consider "eros effects"); they remain to this day understudied, a moment of neglect which stands in inverse proportion to their significance.

It was not by chance alone that the Tet offensive in Vietnam occurred in the same year as the Prague Spring, the May events in France, the student rebellion in West Germany, the assassination of Martin Luther King Jr., the takeover of Columbia University, riots at the Democratic National Convention in Chicago, and the pre-Olympic massacre in Mexico City. These events were related to one another, and a synchronic analysis of world social movements in 1968 validates Hegel's proposition that history moves from east to west. Global oppositional forces converged in a pattern of mutual amplification: "The whole world was watching," and with each act of the unfolding drama, new strata of social actors entered the arena of history, until finally an internationally synchronized insurgency against war and all forms of oppression emerged. In 1968 and 1970, crises of revolutionary proportions were reached in France and the US These climactic points involved intense struggles between uprisings and reaction, a pivot around which protests ultimately lost momentum as "repressive tolerance" shed its benign appearance.

Looking back half a century later, we can say that 1968 signaled an enormous historical transition. The world today is changing faster than ever before in a dizzying process seemingly without outline. Yet 1968 gave us unusual clarity. As one observer put it:

> History does not usually suit the convenience of people who like to divide it into neat periods, but there are times when it seems to have pity on them. The year 1968 almost looks as though it had been designed to serve as some sort of signpost. There is hardly any region of the world in which it is not marked by spectacular and dramatic events which were to have profound repercussions on the history of the country in which they occurred and, as often as not, globally. This is true of the developed and industrialized capitalist countries, of the socialist world, and of the so-called "third world"; of both the eastern and western, the northern and southern hemispheres.[1]

Prior to 1968, no one knew and few could have guessed what was in store for world history. Without warning, worldwide movements spontaneously erupted. At the beginning of the year, President Charles de Gaulle hailed France as an "infallible beacon for the world," but within months the country teetered on the brink of revolution. If he had known what kind of beacon France would be in 1968, he might never have delivered his New Year's Address. After weathering the revolutionary crisis two years later in the United States, President Richard Nixon (popularly known as Tricky Dick) in his State of the Union address in January 1971 called for a "New American Revolution . . . as profound, as far-reaching, as exciting as that first revolution almost 200 years ago."[2] While some people scratched their hands in bewilderment, many more understood Nixon's Orwellian universe to mean "peace" was war, and "revolution" was counterrevolutionary repression.

Without warning, global turmoil of 1968 erupted against both capitalism and real-world socialism, against authoritarian power and patriarchal authority. The New Left opposed both state "socialism" and American "democracy." In its best moments, the movement challenged the entire universe of capitalist patriarchy—and in doing so, gave future generations an enduring vision of freedom. Although 1968 is often used as shorthand for the New Left, insurgencies were not confined to one year. The 1955 bus boycott in Montgomery, which catapulted Martin Luther King to national attention, did not consider itself a "New Left" movement, but in essential aspects, it certainly was. The 1980 Gwangju People's Uprising (which ultimately brought parliamentary rule to South Korea) took place long after the New Left was supposed to have died, but it too carried New Left features. There was a self-described "New Left" in France as early as 1957, and a "New Left" insurrection in Sri Lanka in 1971.

Despite its brief appearance in history, the New Left regenerated dormant traditions of self-government and international solidarity. In Europe and the United States, after decades of cultural conformity, the possibility of revolution once again was widely discussed—and acted upon. At the same time, the meaning of revolution was enlarged to include questions of power in everyday life as well as the quality of power won by past revolutions. If the idea of revolution in an industrialized society was inconceivable for three decades prior to 1968, the kind of revolution prefigured in the emergent praxis of the movement was unlike previous ones. The goal of revolution was redefined to be decentralization and self-management of power and resources—destruction, not seizure, of militarized nation-states embedded in an international web of war and corporate machinations.

By enunciating the desire for a new world society based on cooperative sharing of international resources (not national or individual aggregation), on a communalism based upon enlarged social autonomy and greater individual freedom (not their suppression), and a way of life based on a new harmony with nature (not its accelerating exploitation), the New Left defined a unique stage in the aspirations of revolutionary movements. A new set of values was born in the movement's international and interracial solidarity, in its rejection of middle-class values like the accumulation of wealth and power, in its fight against stupefying routines and ingrained patterns of patriarchal domination, and in its attempt to reconstruct everyday life, not according to tradition or scientific rationality but through a liberated sensibility. In crises generated by insurgencies in 1968 in France and 1970 in the United States, these values were momentarily realized in spontaneously produced forms of dual power.

The tempo of modern history has been so rapid that what was new in 1968 seems to be as far away from us today as all the rest of history. Although no obvious trace of the movement seems to survive, once we review key events of 1968, it should become clear that, far from ending in failure, the New Left's very success contributed to its disappearance. To give just one example: in the 1960s, only a few people supported the right of South African blacks to rule their country. Today apartheid is a distant memory.

World-Historical Movements

Periods of crisis and turmoil on a global scale are relatively rare in history. Since the French and American Revolutions, it is possible to identify less than a handful of such periods of global eruptions: 1848–49, 1905–7, 1917–19, and 1968–70. In each of these periods, global upheavals were spontaneously generated. In a chain reaction of insurrections and revolts, new forms of power emerged in opposition to the established order, and new visions of the meaning of freedom were formulated in the actions of millions of people. Even when these movements were unsuccessful in seizing power, immense adjustments were necessitated both within and between nation-states, and the defeated movements offered revealing glimpses of the newly developed character of society and types of class struggles that would follow.

Throughout history, fresh outbreaks of revolution have been known to "conjure up the spirits of the past to their service and borrow from them names, battle cries, and costumes in order to present the new scene of world history in this time-honored disguise and this borrowed language."[3] The movements of 1968 were no exception: activists self-consciously acted in the tradition of past revolutions. Public statements issued by French insurgents during the May events invoked the memory of 1789, 1848, the 1871 Paris Commune, and the Russian soviets of 1905 and 1917. Outsiders confirmed what seemed like the collapse of time:

> In the Paris of May 1968, innumerable commentators, writing to celebrate or to deplore, proffered a vast range of mutually exclusive explanations and predictions. But for all of them, the sensibility of May triggered off a remembrance of things past. By way of Raymond Aron, himself in touch with Tocqueville, readers of *Le Figaro* remembered February 1848; by way of Henri Lefebvre, French students remembered the Proclamation of the Commune in March 1871, as did those who read Edgar Morin in *Le Monde*; French workers listened to elder militants who spoke of the occupation of factories in June 1936; and most adults, whether or not they had been in the Resistance, relived August 1944, the liberation of Paris.[4]

Such periods of the eros effect witness the basic assumptions and values of a social order (nationalism, hierarchy, and specialization) being challenged in theory and practice by new human standards. The capacity of millions of people to see beyond the social reality of their day—to imagine a better world and to fight for it—demonstrates a human characteristic that may be said to transcend time and space. During moments of the eros effect, universal interests become generalized at the same time as dominant values of society (national chauvinism, hierarchy, and domination) are negated. As Herbert Marcuse so clearly formulated it, humans have an instinctual need for freedom—something we grasp intuitively—and it is this vital need that is sublimated into a collective phenomenon during moments of the eros effect.[5]

Dimensions of the eros effect include the sudden and synchronous emergence of hundreds of thousands of people occupying public space; the simultaneous appearance of revolts in many places; the intuitive identification of hundreds of thousands of people with each other; their common belief in new values; and suspension of normal daily routines like competitive business practices, criminal behavior, and acquisitiveness. Though secular, such moments metaphorically resemble the religious transformation of the individual soul through the sacred baptism in the ocean of universal life and love. The integration of the sacred and the secular in such moments of "political Eros" (a term used by Herbert Marcuse) is an indication of the true potentiality of the human species, the "real history" which remains repressed and distorted within the confines of "prehistoric" powers and taboos.[6]

The reality of Paris at the end of May 1968 conformed less to the categories of existence preceding May (whether the former political legitimacy of the government, management's control of the workplaces, or the students' isolation from the "real world") than to the activated imaginations of millions of people who moved beyond a mere negation of the previous system by enacting new forms of social organization and new standards for the goal-determination of the whole system. Modes of thought, abolished in theory by empiricists and structuralists, emerged in a practical human effort to break out of antiquated categories of existence and establish nonfragmented modes of Being. Debate ceased as to whether human beings were capable of such universal notions as justice, liberty, and freedom. Rather, these abstractions, concretized in the actions of millions of people, became the popularly redefined reality.

The May events, like the Paris Commune, Gwangju Uprising, and other moments of revolutionary upheaval, established a new reality where living human energy and not things was predominant. From this perspective, they can be viewed as a taste of the joy of human life, which will be permanently unleashed with the advent of a new world system qualitatively different than anything that has ever existed. With the end of "prehistory" and the beginning of "human history," human imagination will be freed to take giant steps in constructing a better world. "All Power to the Imagination," written everywhere in May 1968, will become inscribed in the lives and institutions of future generations.[7]

Two years later, the United States underwent its most significant crisis since the Civil War. While a majority of workers did not join, a rupture even more acrimonious and violent than in France took place. US geographical size and the racial fragmentation of its citizens contributed to obscuring the magnitude of five months of climactic confrontations. Beginning in May with a university strike of more than four million people, a simultaneous battlefield revolt incapacitated the US military, the first Gay Pride marches openly dared to take public space, women organized a general strike, Latinos mobilized in the streets as never before, and a rainbow alliance of about ten thousand people responded to the call by Black Panthers and assembled in Philadelphia, despite police terror, to write a new constitution. Insurgents' visions of freedom are contained in their actions, yet the Black Panthers' Revolutionary Peoples' Constitutional Convention (RPCC) also gave explicit details of the conscious outline of a free society.

With hindsight, we may debate today whether May '68 and May–September '70 were revolutionary crises, prerevolutionary situations, or simply "moments of madness," but in both cases self-understood revolutionary movements involving hundreds of thousands of people mobilized millions of supporters who decisively fought to overthrow the Establishment. In the US, unlike France, the forces of order used murderous force to crush the insurgency. Historically speaking, it has often been the case that a particular nation has experienced social upheavals at the same time as order reigned elsewhere. Coups d'etat, putsches, and armed takeovers of power within the confines of a particular nation are to be expected. In 1968 (and 1848 and 1905), there were seldom successful seizures of power despite the movement's global character. Nonetheless, social convulsions in these periods profoundly redirected world cultures and political trajectories. Spontaneous chain reactions of uprisings, strikes, rebellions, and revolutionary movements signaled massive proliferation of movement ideas and aspirations, a crucial aspect of their world-historical character.[8]

Some epochs of class struggle are world-historical and others are not, a distinction noted by Antonio Gramsci, who used the terms "organic" (relatively permanent) and "conjunctural" (occasional, immediate, almost accidental) to describe the difference.[9] The apparent climax and disappearance of the New Left led many observers to conclude it conformed to what Gramsci called conjunctural, arising as a unique product of the post–World War II baby boom, the injustice of Jim Crow segregation, or the prolonged intensity of the war in Vietnam. In the twenty-first century, with international acceptance of feminism's goal of gender equality, a global consensus against racism, and growing insurgencies against capitalist inequality and environmental devastation, the organic character of 1968 is evident.

Even in failure, world-historical movements define new epochs in cultural, political, and economic dimensions of society. They present new ideas and values that become common sense as time passes. They qualitatively reformulate the meaning of freedom for millions of human beings. Massive and unexpected strife and international proliferation of new aspirations signal the beginning of epochal change. During the dramatic outbreak of revolts and reaction to them, new aspirations are passionately articulated and attacked, and progress occurs in weeks and months when previously it took decades and half centuries. History does not unfold in a linear direction or at an even pace. As Marcuse observed, "There is no even progress in the world: The appearance of every new condition involves a leap; the birth of the new is the death of the old."[10] He forgot to add that the birth of the new, after its period of celebration and youth, moves into maturity and then decays. In order to appreciate this, let us review what is meant by world history.

Hegel measured the development of world history through the emergence of individualized inward subjectivity.[11] Such a transposition of the individual for the species as agent and outcome of world history thoroughly conformed to the ideology of the ascendant bourgeoisie. Limitations of Hegel's outlook are apparent in his conclusion that history culminates in Germany and in his legitimation of the Prussian state.[12] In contrast to Hegel, it is my view that history is nothing but the development of the human species and is not measured through flowering of the individual in isolation from others (that is bourgeois history) but in the unfolding of human collectivities and of an individuality that surpasses bourgeois individualism. Moreover, what for Hegel was a dialectic of mind is analyzed here as a dialectic of praxis, of the consciousness in action of millions of people.

The history of modernity, from struggles for national independence and parliamentary democracy to liberation of oppressed classes and managed masses, follows a logic similar to that uncovered by Hegel, a dialectical framework within which potentialities of the human species as a species-being unfolds. The logic of world history carries an irony which "turns everything upside down," not only posing the new against the old, but simultaneously transforming what was once new and revolutionary into its opposite. In the past two hundred years, we see this in the history of the United States. From challenging and defeating the forces of "divine right," the world's first secular democratic state has long since degenerated, whether in bloodily invading Korea, Vietnam, Iraq, and Afghanistan or in abetting one of the world's last states founded on a notion of "divine right," a religious state whose technological weapons of genocide are provided by the United States to forestall the realization of its own ideal foundation: a secular, democratic state for people of all religions, but this time in Palestine.

But of course, to see the contradictory character of history, we only have to look at the important role of slave owners within the American Revolution of 1776, at the acceleration of genocide against Native Americans after it, and at US refusal to support the Haitian Revolution.[13] Is it surprising that the new republic annexed Texas in 1844 and northern Mexico four years later? Are we amazed by contemporary US support for the Saudi monarchy and for every variety of dictator "on our side"? So much for what can become of world-historical leaps when left adrift in the world of the "survival of the fittest." Let us return to their moments of joyful infancy, to the attempts made by human beings to leap beyond the dead weight of the past.

In the twentieth century, the essential indication of these leaps, the signal for a whole epoch of class struggles, was recognized to be the general strike. Such strikes are not cleverly orchestrated by a small group of conspirators or "world-historical individuals," but involve the spontaneous and conscious actions of millions of people. As Rosa Luxemburg pointed out:

> Political and economic strikes, mass strikes and partial strikes, demonstrative strikes and fighting strikes, general strikes of individual branches of industry and general strikes in individual towns, peaceful wage struggles and street massacres, barricade fighting—all these run through one another, run side by side, cross one another, flow in and over one another—it is ceaselessly moving, a changing sea of phenomena. . . . In a word, the mass strike . . . is not a crafty method discovered by subtle reasoning for the purpose of making the proletarian struggle more effective, but the method of motion of the proletarian mass, the phenomenal form of the proletarian struggle in the revolution.[14]

General strikes not only sum up new historical epochs of class struggle by revealing in utmost clarity the nature of the antagonists, they also indicate future directions of movements—their aspirations and goals, which, in the heat of historical struggle, emerge as popular wishes and intuitions. General strikes create a new reality, negating previous institutions, rupturing the hegemony of the existing order, and releasing seemingly boundless social energies that normally remain suppressed, repressed, and channeled into more "proper" outlets.

In contrast to what has become a commonplace alienation from politics, these moments are ones of the eroticization of politics, as portrayed by the May 1968 slogan, "The more I make revolution, the more I enjoy love."[15] Drudgery becomes play as imagination replaces practicality, and human competition and callousness are replaced by cooperation and dignity. During the Paris Commune of 1871, the streets were safe for the first time in years, even with no police of any kind. As one Communard said,

"We hear no longer of assassination, theft, and personal assault; it seems, indeed, as if the police had dragged along with it to Versailles all its conservative friends."[16] The 1980 Gwangju Commune was an "absolute community of love" based upon "the act of recognizing a value larger than individual life."[17] The liberation of life instincts in these moments creates unique qualities of social life. In 1848, 1905, and 1968, for example, anti-anti-Semitism was a recurrent public theme, and international solidarity momentarily outweighed patriotic sentiments.[18]

Such spontaneous leaps are certainly products of long-term social processes in which organized groups and conscious individuals prepare groundwork, but when political struggles come to involve tens and hundreds of thousands of people, it is possible to glimpse a rare historical occurrence: the emergence of the eros effect, the massive awakening of the instinctual human need for justice and for freedom. When the eros effect occurs, it becomes clear that the fabric of the status quo has been torn, and the forms of social control have been ruptured. This break becomes clear when established patterns of interaction are negated, and new and better ones are created. In essence, general strikes (and revolutions) are the emergence of humans as a species-being, the negation of the age-old "survival of the fittest" through a process by which nature becomes history (Aufhebung der Naturwüchsigkeit).[19]

The international impact of revolutionary movements that succeed in seizing state power is widely recognized. Few people would question the profound and long-lasting repercussions of revolutions in 1776 in the United States, 1789 in France, or 1917 in Russia. The ruptures of social order in 1848, 1905, and 1968 may not have toppled the dominant institutions, but they marked the emergence of new values, ideas, and aspirations that became consolidated as time passed. These intense periods of class struggle were important to the self-formation of the human species; they dramatically changed human beings. The new realities created by the eros effect changed the conversations. They were not limited to elite regime change, but transformed entire populations, revealing new needs and higher aspirations of millions of people.

Experiences accumulated from political praxis are a significant historical legacy that imbues future struggles with a higher consciousness. Whether in intuitive terms, directly intergenerational, or obtained from the study of history, human beings are transformed by social movements, and the self-formation of the species remains the innermost meaning of history. If history teaches us anything, it reveals the process through which the human species becomes conscious of its own development, an awareness that takes shape with utmost clarity during moments of the eros effect.

Thomas Jefferson observed this phenomenon in his analysis of the global impact of the American Revolution:

As yet that light (of liberty) has dawned on the middling classes only of the men of Europe. The Kings and the rabble, of equal importance, have not yet received its beams, but it continues to spread, and . . . it can no more recede than the sun return on his course. A first attempt to recover the right of self-government may fail, so may a second, a third, etc. But as a younger and more instructed race comes on, the sentiment becomes more and more intuitive, and a fourth, a fifth, or some subsequent one of the ever-renewed attempts will ultimately succeed.[20]

American revolutionaries of Jefferson's day were hemispheric. Beginning in 1776, the brothers Catari protested uninterruptedly against the abuses of authorities in Chayanta (now part of Bolivia). On November 16, 1780, Tupac Amaru proclaimed liberty of slaves during an uprising joined by Creoles, Spanish, Africans, Mestizos, and Native Americans.[21] Riding his famous white horse, Amaru led an insurrectionary army of as many as twenty thousand fighters in fourteen provinces. He exhorted his compatriots to realize that they were "all born in our lands and from the same natural origin, all of whom have been oppressed by European tyranny."[22] By the time the rebellion reached its zenith, it affected a generalized uprising from Buenos Aires to Chile, Quito, New Granada, and Venezuela.

Far from being the result of any single event, abolition of European colonialism and feudalism was a process that required centuries of struggle. Uprisings and revolutions accelerated the birth of a new social formation as part of a process that occurred on many levels. In retrospect, we can observe today that 1848, 1905, and 1968 marked the first acts of the emergence of new social classes on the stage of world history. Despite defeat in their first experiences in the class struggle, these "failed" movements had their moments of success—even if incomplete—in subsequent epochs. Within the context of the world system's escalating spiral of expansion, fresh social movements take up where previous ones leave off. The "failed" social movements of 1848, 1905, and 1968 connected the emergent subjectivity of millions of people over more than a century. The world-historical movements of the working class of 1848, the landless peasantry of 1905, and the new working class of 1968 provide a glimpse of the essential forces that have produced—and are products of—the movement of history. Although each of these periods of upheaval revitalized social movements, differing economic conditions precipitated the storms. The revolutions of 1848 were preceded by the prolonged economic slump of 1825–48, and the movements of 1905 were also preceded by severe hardships following the worldwide slump of 1873–96.[23] The two decades prior to 1968, however, were ones of immense global economic expansion before the world economic downturn of the 1970s.

Despite differing precipitating conditions and historical epochs, striking similarities can be found in cultural contestation of rules governing everyday life in 1848, 1905, and 1968. As initially pointed out by Alexis de Tocqueville, the first revolution against boredom was in 1848. He makes it quite clear that in the established political life, "there reigned nothing but languor, impotence, immobility, boredom" and that "the nation was bored listening to them."[24] When he turned to the poet Lamartine, Tocqueville commented, "He is the only man, I believe, who always seemed to be ready to turn the world upsidedown to divert himself." If 1848 was, at least partially, a revolution against boredom, the May events in France were even more so. As the Situationists put it: "We do not want to exchange a world in which it is possible to die of starvation for one in which it is possible to die from boredom." Shortly before May 1968, the front page of *Le Monde* ran the headline "France s'ennuie! " and Godard's film *Weekend* had expressed a similar message. In the United States, Abbie Hoffman's *Revolution for the Hell of It!* sold out as quickly as it was printed.

Leading up to the cataclysmic events of 1848 in Vienna, Jesuit priests were handed control of nearly all the high schools, and when they forbade the old and joyous custom of nude bathing in the river, the first sparks of student protest began to fly. From these small beginnings emerged the revolutionary student brigade that became the government in Vienna for months.[25] In 1968, at Nanterre University on the outskirts of Paris, a few men who had spent the night in the women's dormitory to protest sexual segregation and parietal hours were chased by police into a crowded lecture hall where scores of students were then mercilessly beaten. So began the escalating spiral of the May events.

Berlin in 1848 had a reputation of being gay in every way. Berliners adored picnics, bonfires, parades, and festivals, but one of the many prohibitions included a ban on workers smoking in the public gardens, the Tiergarten. After the first round of barricade fighting in March, a crowd carried some of the 230 dead civilians to the palace, and someone called out loudly for the king to come and see the flower-covered corpses. His Majesty appeared on the balcony and took his hat off at the sight of the dead while the queen fainted. In this delicate moment, Prince Lichnowsky addressed the crowd, telling them their demands were granted. No one moved. Suddenly someone called out, "Smoking too?" "Yes, smoking too." "Even in the Tiergarten?" "You may smoke in the Tiergarten, gentlemen." With that, the crowd dispersed. The fact that another Prussian, Prinz zu Hohenlohe-Ingelfingen, questioned whether it was tobacco or some other concoction that workers were smoking provides another aspect of cultural affinity between the movements of 1848 and 1968. Such parallels might be regarded as trivial ones, but their significance should not be disregarded unless one refuses to contemplate the need of the established order to control leisure time and the aspirations of popular movements to transform everyday life. Precisely because these movements were rooted in the popular need to transform power structures in everyday life are they "world-historical." The birth of the women's movement in 1848, its revival after 1905, and its reemergence in 1968 are further indications of the "organic" awakening in these years.

1848, 1905, 1968: Historical Overview

These three world-historical movements emerged at different historical conjunctures, and they were composed of differing social classes. Although many groups participated in the revolutions of 1848, these events marked the entrance of the working class on the stage of world history. On February 22–24, 1848, the workers of Paris rose up and toppled the monarchy, sending the king into exile and sparking a continent-wide movement for democratic rights, the end of the monarchies, and economic justice. The French uprising had an enormous international impact in part because of the country's new telegraph system.[26] In March, a bloody uprising in Vienna defeated the army and led to a new constitution.

As the fighting spread to Berlin, Bavaria, Baden, and Saxony, the King of Prussia formed a new government and promised a democratic constitution. In Sicily, the Bourbon dynasty was overthrown, and the revolt spread to Naples, Milan, Venice, and Piedmont. The Poles rose against their Prussian rulers, and two nights of bloody barricade fighting broke out in Prague. Altogether there were some fifty revolutions in Europe in 1848 (counting the small German and Italian States and Austrian provinces), and these movements converged in their demands for republics and in their tactic of building barricades for urban warfare.

In June 1848, a new round of insurrections began when the working class of Paris seized control of the city. In four days of bloody barricade fighting, thousands of people were killed. After the revolt, the army held more than fifteen thousand prisoners, many of whom were later executed. Despite their defeat, the workers of Paris catalyzed a new wave of armed insurrections in Berlin, Vienna, and Frankfurt, and vast movements emerged among the peasantry. A revolutionary army appeared in Hungary, where Lajos Kossuth eloquently exhorted people to rise up for self-government and social revolution. The pope fled Rome as the republican movement won control from the French army. If the Hungarian revolutionary army had been able to reach the insurgents in Vienna, a Europe-wide revolution might have consolidated. Instead, counterrevolution reigned as order was brutally restored. The Holy Alliance (fashioned by Metternich in the wake of Napoleon) may not have been shattered in 1848, but Metternich himself was forced to flee Vienna, and greater liberties were won within the confines of existing states.

Rebellion in 1848 swept the distant island of Sri Lanka (then Ceylon), and British imperialism was also opposed in the Punjab. Sri Lankans were aware of the uprisings in India and around the world. One British observer noted that: "intelligence from Europe arrived of the revolution in France . . . and the disturbances in other European countries . . . and almost simultaneously with that there arrived intelligence of disasters to our Army in India. . . . I am assured by intelligent Kandyans that those two circumstances had a very material affect on the minds of the Kandyans . . . and improper use of those circumstances was made by the local press."[27] For the first time in Sri Lanka, in 1848, rural protesters united with the urban intelligentsia. Although the revolt was mercilessly crushed, the system of compulsory labor was brought to an end, and the colonial governor was recalled to England. The controversial poll tax levied on Buddhist monks was also withdrawn.

From 1845 to 1864, in a fusion of Christianity and Eastern philosophies, the Taiping rebellion led to civil war in China in which some twenty million people were killed. Ruling a vast liberated territory from their capital in Nanjing for eleven years, the Taiping were ultimately defeated by the Manchu Qing Dynasty. Although defeated, Taiping notions of communal property and complete equality of men and women subsequently reappeared. Only after World War I would the Kaiser, the Czar, and the Hapsburgs be permanently dethroned, but after the storms of 1848, modern political parties, trade unions, and democratic rights emerged as bourgeois society was consolidated.

The defeats of the insurrectionary governments of 1848 throughout Europe led to a period of stagnation for revolutionary movements. As Austria and Germany became more autocratic, more than one million Germans emigrated. For Immanuel Wallerstein's, 1848's failed revolutions created a Left ideology that broke decisively with feudal conservatism and centrist liberalism, thereby paving the way for a long-term socialist organizing project that culminated in the 1917 Russian Revolution.[28] Although challenged in the streets in 1848, centrist liberalism went on to become the dominant "geoculture of the world-system" founded on formal democracy (based on universal suffrage within nation-states) and material improvements for the vast majority of citizens.

In the twenty-five years after 1848, free enterprise experienced some of its most dynamic years. For the first time, industrialization took root in France, Austria, Hungary, Poland, and Russia. Germany quickly developed into a major industrial country. New economic masters whose program of industrialization necessitated freeing the slaves conquered the United States. During this period, there was another wave of global expansion of European powers: the Syrian expedition (1860); Anglo-French war against China; French conquest of Indochina (1863); Maximilian's dispatch to Mexico; and conquest of Algeria and Senegal. There were also wars between capitalist powers, notably those in the Crimea and the Franco-Prussian War (which precipitated the Paris Commune).

Global expansionism after 1848 accelerated accumulation of vast wealth in industrialized nations, and concomitant harnessing of science to production and new mass production techniques (that is, the Second Industrial Revolution) further intensified the system's tendency toward global expansion. The whole world became divided into oppressor and oppressed nations as "free trade" led to imperialist conquest.

Nearly seventy years after the emergence of the working class as a class for itself, the peasants and natives of the periphery, increasingly denied land and liberty by the expanding imperial system, emerged as a force in their own right. At the beginning of the twentieth century, global networks of communication and transportation were limited compared to today, but nonetheless they helped synchronize world movements even more than in 1848. Beginning with Korea (1894), Cuba (1895), and the Philippines (1897), uprisings and movements for national independence appeared throughout the world. From 1904 to 1907, significant social movements erupted in India, Indochina, Madagascar, Angola, Portuguese Guinea, Egypt, Crete, Albania, Serbia, Poland, Guatemala, and Peru. A protracted guerrilla war against German colonial rule in Namibia cost the lives of one hundred thousand Africans, and the Zulus in Natal rose against their British rulers.

The 1905 defeat of Russia, a great European power, by Japan, then a small Asian sovereignty, helped precipitate this global wave of revolutionary activity. At one end of Asia, Sun Yat-sen declared, "We regarded the Russian defeat by Japan as the defeat of the West by the East." Similarly, Jawaharlal Nehru described how "Japanese victories stirred up my enthusiasm. . . . Nationalistic ideas filled my mind. I mused of Indian freedom."[29] At the other end of Asia, a British diplomat in Constantinople reported to London that the Japanese victory made every fiber in Turkish political life tingle with excitement. Three years later, the Young Turk revolt led to an insurrection in Salonika, and a constitutional government was quickly won for the entire Ottoman Empire. In China, the 1911 nationalist revolution led to the end of the Manchu dynasty and the emergence of modern Chinese political parties. Korean "righteous armies" rose against their Japanese rulers.

Popular movements erupted among miners and railroad workers in Germany, England, France, and the United States, and among farm workers in Italy and Galicia. The praxis of the working-class movement from 1900 to 1905 was a demonstration of the historically new tactic of the general strike. In this period, there were general strikes in Russia, Bohemia, Spain, Sweden, and Italy, strikes modeled on the first general strike of 1877 in St. Louis, Missouri. Between 1900 and 1905, there were massive strikes by miners in Pennsylvania (1900), Colorado (1903–4), Austria (1900), and France (1902); a general strike of all production workers in Barcelona (1902); and strikes for universal voting rights in Sweden (1902), Belgium (1902), Prague (1905), Galicia (1905), and Austria (1905). Although no movement came to power, organizations of farm workers in Italy and Galicia were strengthened; the Wobblies (Industrial Workers of the World) came to life in the United States; and in Belgium, Austria, and Sweden, universal suffrage was enacted.[30]

In Persia, general strikes and the emergence of soviets (organs of dual power or anjomans) precipitated a constitutional revolution that ultimately deposed the Qajar dynasty. In the course of these struggles, Persian women played an integral role. Organized into secret societies, masked women carried out armed actions while others published feminist newspapers and organized discussion groups. Although these actions achieved only minimal legal change in the status of women, there was a more significant transformation of the social attitude toward women, a change that established the cornerstone for future feminist movements there.[31]

Further to the north, in Russia, the mighty Czar was nearly overthrown. The massacre of hundreds of peaceful marchers in St. Petersburg on Bloody Sunday (January 22, 1905) precipitated a general strike coordinated by spontaneously formed soviets. Only after thousands of workers were killed during months of strikes did the movement temporarily abate. The revolution of 1905 transformed Russian politics by illuminating the brutality of Czarist rule at the same time as it indicated the popular movement's strength. As previously disenfranchised workers and humble peasants found themselves rallying the country to their cause, women of Russia became activated: "There had been no specifically feminist movement in Russia before this time, but there were obvious feminist implications in the idea of universal suffrage. And they encouraged the faint beginnings of a movement that now began to pick up a following."[32]

Although the movement did not seize power, the Czar was forced to grant limited democratic reforms, the Duma (Russian Parliament) was created, and Russian workers won a shorter working day and the right to organize. The spontaneously generated movement of 1905 permanently changed the common sense of Russia, and over the next twelve years, there was a growing wave of strikes that culminated in the reappearance of soviets and overthrow of the Czar in 1917. Russia's defeat in World War I left a vacuum of power. Eight months later, the Bolsheviks seized the state amid an uprising they orchestrated. The Bolsheviks' success helped to catalyze council movements in Germany, Austria, and Hungary, movements of workers and peasants which led to the end of the Austrian and German empires, even though the insurgents were unable to remain in power. From the March 1, 1919, Korean independence uprising to the May 4 movement in China, from the Egyptian revolt to massive strikes in the United States and Great Britain, international repercussions of the Russian Revolution were enormous.

In the decades following 1917, the working class and its peasant allies were successful in a host of countries as the locus of revolutionary movements shifted away from Europe to the world system's periphery. Within industrialized societies, overproduction led to a worldwide depression beginning in 1929, and working-class movements were temporarily revived in the Popular Front government in France, the Spanish Republic, the San Francisco General Strike, the battle of Minneapolis, and the great sit-in movements and factory occupations. Of course, the Comintern (or Third Communist International) played an overdetermining role in many popular struggles of the 1930s. More often than not, it defused vital energies of insurgent movements. Although the generation of the Abraham Lincoln Brigade demonstrated remarkable proletarian internationalism, it was nearly extinguished in the struggle against the fascism that filled the political void in old Central European empires. In the United States and Western Europe, struggles of the 1930s won trade unions new legitimacy, and the working class emerged from these struggles with a new sense of dignity. As one participant explained, he was "fortunate enough to be caught up in a great movement of millions of people, [which] literally changed not only the course of the workingman ... but also the nature of the relationship between the workingman and the boss, for all time."[33]

In the first half of the twentieth century, although social movements came to power in Russia and China, global expansion of capitalism accelerated in the other half of the world. The origins of the world economy date well before the twentieth century, but in the latter half of this century, transnational corporations have centralized the world's productive capacity under their supervision. Monopoly production has moved from a national to an international level, and modern technology has revolutionized production through cybernetic control.

In 1968, the Third Industrial Revolution announced itself with the publication of the Double Helix (which revolutionized knowledge of DNA), marketing of the first microcomputer, and Apollo 8's rounding the moon. Modern space-age production, made possible by global centralization of resources and modern technology, has engendered an increasingly complex division of labor, and, in 1968, new oppositional forces emerged in the most developed capitalist countries: the new working class (technicians, employed professionals, off-line office workers, service workers, and students). As the First Industrial Revolution produced the working class and the Second a landless peasantry, so the Third created the new working class. The rapid growth of universities necessitated by high technology, internationalized division of

The Development of World-Historical Social Movements

	1778–1789	1848	1905	1917	1968
Ascendant Revolutionary class(es)	Bourgeoisie	Urban proletariat	Rural proletariat	Urban and rural working class	New working class
Emergent organization	Representative assemblies	Insurrectionary parliaments and political parties	Soviets/ councils	Vanguard party	Action committees/ collectives
Vision/ aspirations	Formal democracy; liberty, equality, fraternity	Economic democracy; trade unions; democratic constitutions	Universal suffrage; unions; freedom from empires	Socialism as the "dictatorship of the proletariat"; land, bread and peace	Self-management, all power to the people/ imagination
Tactics	Revolutionary war	Popular insurrections	General strike	Organized seizure of power	Contestation of public space/ everyday life

labor, and consolidation of consumer society all converged to create the new working class. In 1968, their aspirations for a decentralized and self-managed global society transcended previous calls for liberty, equality, and fraternity in 1789; for jobs, trade unions, and employment security in 1848; and for land, peace, bread, and voting rights from 1905 to 1917.

The New Left enriched traditions of revolutionary organization and tactics: from insurrectionary parliaments and barricade fighting in 1848; to soviets and general strikes in 1905; to vanguard parties and insurrections in 1917; and finally to decentralized, self-managed councils and popular contestation of public space in 1968. The New Left merger of culture and politics created situations in which contestation of public space was neither an armed insurrection nor a military assault for control of territory. Aspirations of the New Left in the advanced industrialized countries were decidedly not a dictatorship of the proletariat, but "Power to the People" and "All Power to the Imagination." In 1968, issues raised by the movement, like racism and patriarchy, were species issues, and at the same time, a new "we" was concretely defined in self-management which sprang up at the levels of campus, factory, and neighborhood. The chart above summarizes the New Left's relationship to previous world-historical movements.

The New Left: A Global Definition

Unlike the centrally organized Communist International, the New Left's international political unity was not mandated from above but grew out of the needs and aspirations of popular movements around the world. That is why the New Left can simultaneously be regarded as one insurgency and many social movements.

Despite attempts to construe the New Left as tied to the Soviet Union, Communist parties globally opposed the movement.[34] For its part, the New Left did not regard Communist parties as friends. As an observer in Italy put it:

> The fight of the New Left in Italy is taking place on two fronts: on one side against conservative forces and on the other against the traditional Left. One often gets the impression that the conflict with the Old Left is the predominant element in the choice of criteria for action by the New Left, since the target they set for themselves is to "unmask" the traditional Left as being "non-Left," as aiming at no more than an infiltration of the capitalist system in order to reform it; this they regard as a non-alternative, in fact as strictly organic and functional to the authoritarian and repressive system.[35]

Italy was not the only place where emergent movements opposed Soviet Communism. In 1953, 1956, 1968, and 1970, uprisings that erupted in Eastern Europe against Soviet regimes displayed remarkable similarities to their counterparts in the West. In some cases, they self-consciously identified themselves as New Left,[36] and in almost all cases, activists in the West spontaneously welcomed them as part of a larger international movement.

Despite their international unity, it would be a mistake to equate all movements of 1968. Freedom from foreign domination and freedom from one's own government's attempts to dominate other nations may become the same struggle in the practicality of world events, but they are different freedoms, carrying within them different meanings. More importantly, movements in economically advanced societies must deal with qualitatively different objective conditions and with different immediate goals than those on the periphery of the world system. Despite obvious differences, participants did not act in isolation from one another. When Yippies brought panic to the New York stock exchange by throwing money on the floor, when Dutch Provos wreaked havoc on rush hour traffic in Amsterdam by releasing chickens into the streets, and when Strasbourg Situationists issued their manifesto denouncing boredom, they were using methods obviously different than those of liberation fighters in Vietnam. Despite their tactical differences, all these groups enunciated similar goals— a decentralized world with genuine human self-determination—and they increasingly acted in unison.

The Black Panther Party inspired the global movement. Pictured here are Kathleen Cleaver (left), first female member of the central committee, with Los Angeles party members in Oakland in 1968. Photo: Stephen Shames

Uneven development in the world system conditioned the diverse composition of the New Left as a world-historical movement. Vietnam was fighting for national liberation two centuries after the American colonies broke away from England. The Vietnamese modeled their struggle, at least in part, on that of the United States, even adopting word-for-word part of the US Declaration of Independence. Similarly, their organization was modeled on the Bolshevik Party. The global movement of 1968 was composed of many components: newly emergent social actors, as well as ones continuing unfinished struggles of previous epochs. The complete success of all these struggles would be a global revolution—the first truly world-historical revolution. Such a revolution would necessarily involve the radical transformation of the world system from within its core countries.[37] Successful twentieth-century revolutions, however, have been confined to the periphery of the world system, a situation that resulted in the disappearance of the idea of a world-historical revolution, at least until 1968. My analysis of social movements focuses on the core of the world system to illuminate the possibility of such a world-historical revolution.

Taken as a whole, the New Left was a global movement that sought to decentralize and redistribute world resources and power at a time when their centralization had never been greater. Of course, the movement developed within nation-states, not by people's own choosing but because of national organization of political power. Around

1968, however, the growing feeling among activists in Vietnam, Cuba, Latin America, Africa, and even in the United States and Europe was that they were all engaged in the same struggle. As Marcuse pointed out in that year: "The theoretical framework of revolution and subversive action has become a world framework. . . . Just as Vietnam is an integral part of the corporative capitalist system, so the national movements of liberation are an integral part of the potential socialist revolution. And the liberation movements in the Third World depend for their subversive power on the weakening of the capitalist metropolis."[38]

In the 1970s, international solidarity and coordination between radical movements in the core and periphery became even more intense than in 1968. Thousands of young Americans went to Cuba as part of Venceremos Brigades, helping cut sugarcane during the harvests, building schools and houses, and planting trees. In February 1972, the Indochinese liberation movements hosted a world conference in Paris, and representatives of solidarity groups from 84 countries attended. A carefully prepared global action calendar was formulated, and on March 31, the same day that worldwide demonstrations were to begin, a major offensive was launched in Vietnam that included the surprising appearance of tanks among the guerrillas. International coordination of the world movement had never been as conscious or well synchronized.

Since 1972, five other internationally synchronized mobilizations have taken place—all of them emanating from the grassroots:

1. Disarmament movements of the late 1970s and early 1980s, which helped to end the Cold War
2. Asian uprisings from 1986 to 1992, which overthrew eight entrenched dictatorships in six years
3. Turmoil in Eastern Europe that ended seven established Soviet governments
4. Alterglobalization mobilizations from Seattle 1999 to February 15, 2003
5. The Arab Spring, Spanish Indignados, Greek anarchists, and Occupy Wall Street in 2011

The New Left's world-historical character is revealed by insurgencies' recurrent patterns of independence from political parties, autonomous self-organization, direct democracy, and global solidarity. The global movement is increasingly self-conscious of its international synchronicity. In 1972, the Vietnamese revolution provided a centralized organizing group for the world antiwar offensive. Subsequent waves of protests emerged spontaneously from the grassroots without any central organization.

Rather than interpreting the New Left nationalistically, organizationally, or ideologically, I locate it in the praxis of millions of people. A universal definition of the New Left cannot merely be based on organizational ideology, that is, that it developed outside or in opposition to the "Old Left," nor can we clarify what it was in terms of specific organizations or theorists. The Student Nonviolent Coordinating Committee (SNCC), the Black Panther Party (BPP), the March 22 Movement in France, the Sozialistischer Deutscher Studentenbund (SDS) in Germany, and the Students for a Democratic Society (SDS) in the United States were all New Left organizations. Martin Luther King, Malcolm X, and Herbert Marcuse were New Left theorists, but the movement extended beyond these organizations and theorists. They were all part of but not equivalent to the movement.

The primary defining characteristics of the global New Left include:

(1) Opposition to racial, political, and patriarchal domination, as well as to economic exploitation.

The movement sought to overthrow the economic exploitation that the Old Left had opposed, but activists' antiauthoritarianism also opposed cultural and bureaucratic domination. Movements for national liberation and civil rights, the primary basis of global turmoil in 1968, ensured that racism (including within radical movements) would be a central concern. Women's liberation challenged patriarchal domination, and gay movements questioned established gender identities.

There may be an analogy between the development of Christianity and that of secular liberation. From this perspective, the New Left began a reinterpretation of the scope of freedom in much the same way that the Protestant Reformation redefined the individual's relationship to God by making the church an unnecessary vehicle for salvation and affirming the sanctity of individual subjectivity.

The universe of freedom spontaneously envisioned and practiced in 1968 included individual liberty within a framework of social justice and equality. New Left activists were concerned not only with economic and political issues, but also with domination in everyday life. Called into question were bureaucracy, economic exploitation, oppression of women, repression of children, homophobia, and racism—all aspects of capitalist patriarchy. Attempts to transform everyday life and to politicize taken-for-granted models of interaction, particularly in the practice of women's liberation, rest on a belief that economic and political structures are reproduced through the daily acceptance of predetermined patterns of life, a belief that stands in sharp contrast to the Old Left's economic determinism. Inner reworking of the psyche and human needs—the cultural revolution—lays the groundwork for a new type of revolution, one that does not culminate in the political sphere but that would move the realm of politics from the state to everyday life and transform politics from elite administration to self-management. Through its universal realization, politics would cease to exist as we know it today.

Nationalization of the economy and decision making do not define a free society as envisioned by the New Left. Forms of freedom in 1968 included decentralization of decision making, international sharing of resources, socialization of ecologically sustainable industry, worker and community self-management, and extension of democracy to all aspects of life. In slogan form, the New Left's "All Power to the People"—not the "Dictatorship of the Proletariat"—stood as a political guide to freedom.

All this should not be interpreted to mean that the New Left never reproduced racist, patriarchal, bureaucratic, or exploitative characteristics of the system from which it originated. As offspring of the society they opposed, the movement was stamped with birthmarks of the old order. Despite many shortcomings, when taken as a whole, the movement was profoundly universalistic in its consciousness of oppression, and its theory and practice attempted to transform all its forms.

(2) A concept of freedom as not only freedom from material deprivation but also freedom to create new human beings.

Compared with previous social movements, the New Left did not arise primarily in response to conditions of economic hardship but to political and cultural/psychological oppression. The need to change daily life was evident in Che Guevara's "new socialist person," and it applies equally well to Martin Luther King's "new Negro," the subsequent self-definition of Americans of African descent, the emergence of "Latino" and "Chicano" as ethnic markers rather than Hispanic or Spanish, and the new self-definitions of women, gay people, transgender people, and students. Asian Americans insisted they no longer wished to be called "Orientals."

The movement opposed "cultural imperialism" and "consumerism" at the same time as it sought to build people's culture: black culture, women's culture, Chicano culture, gay culture, and youth culture (as emergent countercultures became known). Insurgent cultures were based on new norms and values developed from a critique of generally accepted patterns of interaction. In retrospect, cultural precursors of the movement stand out—aesthetic and philosophical qualities that found popular embodiment in the 1960s. Existentialism and Godard films in France, the Kafka revival in Czechoslovakia, jazz, blues, rock, pop art, and the theory of the Frankfurt School all contributed to the creation of a social soul which became manifest in political form with the New Left.[39] The massive fusion of culture and politics defined the New Left's uniqueness. As a social movement the New Left represented the political emergence of many of the same human values and aspirations that gave rise to modern art and philosophy. Spontaneity, individual autonomy amid community, and the subversion of bureaucratic as well as economic domination were all values and ideals shared by artists and the movement.

By 1968, the art world's happenings, process art, action painting, kinetic art, pop art, op art, new realism, minimal art, environmental art, and Tachism had long challenged limits of what was considered possible. If sixties movements experimented with new forms of street protests and created communal spaces at be-ins and love fests, these innovative happenings were anticipated by artists already in the 1950s. Contemporary art's lack of coherence and frequent formless tendencies anticipated the New Left's rejection of organizational structure in favor of spontaneity and self-organization. While destroying boundaries between music and performance, Nam June Paik's humanization of technology paved the way for movement attempts to reconstitute social order beyond established borders. Conceptualism similarly questioned the boundaries of art. By prioritizing language over visual relevancy, it helped to create new vehicles for protest.[40]

Anticipating the subsequent merger of disparate political movements into a coherent whole, aesthetic streams of imaginative appropriation of technologies congealed under the name of Fluxus, which even before its 1962 Festum Fluxorum galvanized openness and cross-pollination of traditionally separate domains. Visual artist Joseph Beuys was attracted to Fluxus because he wanted "to create a theory that would go beyond the idea of actions and happenings." Musician Wolf Vostell was lured by "its way of looking at things that went from action music, to life music, thought music, de-collage music, and behavior music, and finally right down to invisible music."[41] Action poet Robert Filliou refused "to be colonized culturally by a self-styled race of specialists in painting, sculpture, poetry, music, etc. . . . This is what La Révolte des Médiocres is all about. With wonderful results in modern art, so far. Tomorrow could everybody revolt?" Long anathema to artists' creativity, nationalism was explicitly negated by international identities such as COBRA (an acronym for Copenhagen, Brussels, and Amsterdam). COBRA attempted to include Czechoslovakia but was prevented from doing so by Cold War politics.[42]

In contrast to rigid aesthetic formalism, postwar artists emphasized play, fun, imagination, and politics, creating new forms of expression that ran parallel to New Left innovations. Spontaneity, festivities, and play were deemed more important to human nature than work, thought, and vacation (a consumerist, individualized version of the festival). "European culture . . . is sick . . . [and] going to die," screamed the Situationists in 1961. They felt it would not be sufficient to have "a social and political revolution if this reorganization does not go hand-in-hand with a similar qualitative reshaping of culture."[43]

Autodestructive art completed the visual task of negating the dominant industrial system at the same time as it undermined the commodity form, which reified art as consumer objects. Dematerialization of the art object followed as another way to negate capitalist intrusions. In conjunction with the Spur Group, the Situationist International clashed with consumerism. They demanded utopia as a dialectical combination of art and life, with "professional amateurs" helping to make everyone an artist of their own life. They believed that "coffee cups can be more beautiful than fancy sculptures. A kiss in the morning can be more dramatic than a drama by Mr. Fancypants. The sloshing of my foot in my wet boot sounds more beautiful than fancy organ music."[44]

At the same time as the United States was the bête noire of world events— overthrowing governments, assassinating political leaders, and conducting genocidal wars—American culture had an undeniable magnetism and attraction. The contradiction between embracing the culture that gave the world nuclear bombs and protesting it did not prevent young British artists from created graphic designs and effective poster art for the antinuclear weapons movement, especially the Committee for Nuclear Disarmament, while emulating US-based artists' use of industrial materials, American pop culture, and abstract expressionism.[45] Collage artist Richard Hamilton attended an Easter protest march carrying a life-sized image of Marilyn Monroe.[46] When sculptor Anthony Caro was asked how his trip to America had affected his art, he replied, "I realized I had nothing to lose by throwing out History— here we are also steeped in it anyway. There's a fine-art quality about European art even when it's made from junk. America made me see that there are no barriers and no regulations—they simply aren't bound to traditional or conventional solutions in their art or anything else."[47] Through such actions, artists embodied the creation of a new planetary culture and liberated human beings.

As anticipated by Herbert Marcuse's *Eros and Civilization*, the body's liberation became a recurrent theme in visual arts and ultimately in radical politics as well. Marcuse called on us to "make the human body an instrument of pleasure rather than labor."[48] The body as art object was central to Yoko Ono's 1964 performance titled *Cut Piece*, in which she invited members of the audience to snip off her clothes. Ono's piece has been hailed as a forerunner to feminism, as was Shigeko Kubota's *Vagina Painting* a year later.[49] Attempts to bring the erotic to consciousness and to thematize the unconscious include Paik's performance pieces, especially his then-notorious 1967 Opera *Sextronique* (during which Charlotte Moorman was arrested as she played the cello in New York).

Marcuse's rethinking of humans' place in the cosmos found similar resonance. Beuys's performance of *How to Explain Pictures to a Dead Hare* came three years before the Yippies ran a pig for president in 1968. The Living Theatre included members of the audience in their performances, thereby helping to break down the distance between audience and actor, a transformation highly valued by both aesthetic and political movements. An early example of how to shatter viewers' distance from art (as insisted upon in the white cubes we call museums) can be found in Beuys's picking up an ax at Paik's *Exposition of Music—Electronic Television* and destroying one of Paik's pianos in 1963. The Situationist critique of the "Society of the Spectacle" followed in 1967.

As artists became politically active, the first demonstration at the Museum of Modern Art in New York took place on January 3, 1969, when sculptor Takis removed his own work. Later he broadcast the message: "Our group has become much bigger and taken the name of the Art Workers Coalition. Art workers! The time came to demystify the elite of the art rulers, directors of museums, and trustees."[50] With Takis's action, artists moved from constituting avant-gardes in the "autonomous" domain of culture to themselves joining protests. Little more than a year later, the New York Art Strike in 1970 seemed to affect the whole art world.

The counterculture that avant-garde artists helped to nurture and develop would, in turn, profoundly influence culture (and the art world) in the 1970s. Rock music and the rise of gay and feminist political cultures are sometimes seen as opposed to each other, but they all arose in the same period of time.[51]

(3) Extension of democracy and expansion of individual rights, not their constraint.

Strict principles of democracy were the norm, and bottom-up participatory democracy defined the process of interaction from the largest general assemblies to the smallest action committees. Although the media often focused on specific individuals, the movement generally avoided selecting leaders, and anyone with major responsibilities was often subject to immediate recall. Important positions of responsibility were rotated. Even among some armed movements in the Third World, extension of the democratic process occurred. In Vietnam, guerrilla units would, when possible, meet before their attacks to discuss tactics and options. In some cases, full-scale models of targets were constructed, and simulated attacks rehearsed with members rotated from one specific task to another until each could function best. Commanding officers for the actual attack were then democratically elected. Once the real attack was launched, of course, orders had to be followed without hesitation.[52] Among Tupamaro fighters in Uruguay, strict democratic decision making was also practiced.

Democratic process was manifest in self-management as represented in consensual decision making at general assemblies involving hundreds of people; in autonomy of black and women's liberation; in aspirations for self-determination for oppressed nations; in calls for community control of police and neighborhood development; and in self-management of factories, schools, and cities during New Left strikes. In contrast to monolithic Old Left organizations, many tendencies coexisted within New Left organizations, from Maoism to feminism, anarchism, democratic socialism, and common sense.

(4) Enlarged base of revolution.

At the same time as the movement sought to enlarge the scope of freedom, its praxis involved an enlarged constituency. Its historical experiences transcended a static model of class struggle developed from previous revolutions. The legacy of the New Left is enrichment of that tradition, a practical wealth often obscured by the Old Left's labor metaphysic and "base-superstructure" orthodoxy. In 1968, oppositional forces emerged whose existence could not be contained within the existing typology of class struggle modeled upon previous occurrences. In 1968, it was not predominantly the working class and their parties which rose to challenge the existing social order, but groups normally considered marginal: students, young people, national minorities, women, and the lumpenproletariat. By occupational categories, large numbers of factory workers helped lead workers' insurgencies as part of the overall movement (particularly in France, Poland, Czechoslovakia, and Italy), but the main oppositional constituencies originated in the urban underclass and the new working class. Particularly in France, the participation of the new working class in the radical movement was an important defining contour of the New Left, perhaps as important as the hostilities of the Old Left Communist Party. As the quantitative growth of the new working class has proceeded through intensification of world industrialization, so the practice of the New Left has demonstrated the "proletarian" aspect of these middle strata.

Part of the reason for the inability of the Left (including the "new Old Left"—the myriad assortment of "Marxist-Leninist" and anarchist groups that emerged in the 1970s) to comprehend the meaning of 1968 lies in the differing roles played by the middle strata, students, and the lumpenproletariat in other times and places. In 1848, the lumpenproletariat of Paris was wined and dined by Louis Napoleon Bonaparte so that it would fight for him against the proletariat. Indeed it was Napoleon III's ability to use these gangsters, thugs, and hoodlums to maintain order that eventually won him the mandate needed to rule France. More recently, in places like Guinea-Bissau, Algeria, Angola,and Greece, the lumpenproletariat has played reactionary roles as well.[53] In the 1960s, in the United States, when the civil rights movement entered its second phase by moving north, the black lumpenproletariat became the catalyst and leadership of the radical movement. Inspired by the example of Malcolm X, former criminals and drug addicts changed their lives and rebelled en masse against the conditions of their existence. During the 1980 Gwangju Uprising, lumpen were among the most dedicated freedom fighters.

The middle strata formed the social basis for the Nazi regime and played a distinctly reactionary role in Allende's Chile, but in the core of the world system in the 1960s, middle-class people—particularly women and young adults—were progressive forces. To be sure, there are economic reasons for the changing political role of the middle strata and for the enlarged base of revolution. In our rapidly changing world, farmers increasingly are made landless, proletarianized, and urbanized. Millions of office workers not directly involved in material production are increasingly seen (and see themselves) as part of the working class. Colonization of everyday life means the realm of the cash nexus has been enlarged to include production and consumption, work and leisure. Women's liberation arose concomitantly with massive entry of females onto the labor market. Universities have taken on an enlarged and more central role. When Clark Kerr compared the economic importance of the nation's universities in the last half of the twentieth century to that of automobiles in the early 1900s and railroads in the late 1800s, he made, if anything, an understatement.

In the 1960s, there were more students than farmers in the United States, more students than miners, and more people enrolled in formal studies than working in construction, transportation, or public utilities.[54] The new structural position of the universities within the modern world system gave rise to a student movement unlike ones of the past, a movement tied neither to "adult" nor "parent" organizations nor to the nation-state. Similarly, urbanization of African Americans and their central position in the inner cities, the military, and industry were conditions for the emergence of the black liberation movement.

(5) An emphasis on direct action.

Whether observed in the formation of the March 22 Movement at Nanterre or as early as the July 26 Movement in Cuba, the New Left was characterized by the belief that action in itself was a solution. Through direct action, activists believed that the movement would become quantitatively larger and qualitatively stronger. The actionism of the New Left was not merely a reversion to pure and simple spontaneity but a new method for the integration of theory and practice, a form of "conscious spontaneity." Sit-ins and building occupations, even teach-ins can be seen as a form of the "actionization" of theory.

The New Left's reliance on direct experience and the empirical evaluation of immediate events represented a negation of the Old Left's overemphasis on centralized organization and the primacy of the role of the "conscious element."

Although resulting in increased repression and premature armed struggle tendencies within the movement, the New Left's actionism did not culminate in attempted coups d'etat from above. The New Left continually maintained that society could be genuinely revolutionized only from the bottom up by the vast majority of people. Guerrillas in Guinea-Bissau actually delayed the seizure of state power in order to continue building popular power from below.[55] In the industrialized societies, New Left forms of action from sit-ins to university takeovers and freeway blockades were spontaneously developed in accordance with the military and political possibilities of 1968–1970.

In the epoch after 1968, popular movements have reproduced the New Left tactic of massive occupations of public space as a means of social transformation. This tactic's international diffusion can be seen in Oaxaca's Commune, Cairo's Tahrir Square, Istanbul's Taksim Square, Athens's Syntagma, and among Spanish Indignados. As cultural and economic integration of the world accelerates, the significance of the eros effect and the importance of synchronized insurgencies will only grow in importance. In 1848 and 1905, limited communication and economic ties existed, and movements were relatively undeveloped in their spatial and historical integration. Movements in 1968 exhibited remarkable international consciousness and interconnectedness, and their meteoric appearance and disintegration is a reflection of the rapid pace of change in the modern world. As a world-historical movement, the insurgency of 1968 forms the contours of subsequent insurgencies, which similarly will develop in unexpected, globally synchronized explosions.

NOTES

1.   Eric Hobsbawm, "1968—A Retrospect," *Marxism Today*, May 1978, 130.

2.   Richard Nixon, "26—Annual Message to the Congress on the State of the Union," *The American President Project*, January 22, 1971, http://www.presidency.ucsb.edu/ws/?pid=3110.

3.   Karl Marx, *The 18th Brumaire of Louis Napoleon* (New York: International Publishers, 1972), 15.

4.   Aristide R. Zolberg, "Moments of Madness," *Politics and Society* 2 (Winter 1972): 184.

5.   For Marcuse's inspired understanding of instinct and revolution, see *Essay on Liberation* (Boston: Beacon Press, 1969).

6.   A new anthology develops our understanding of erotic dimensions of social movements: Jason Del Gandio and A.K. Thompson, eds., *Spontaneous Combustion: The Eros Effect and Global Revolution* (Albany: SUNY Press, 2017).

7.   What the student movement expressed in the slogan "L'imagination au pouvoir" came to France from Vietnam. See Jean-Paul Sartre, *Between Existentialism and Marxism* (New York: Morrow Quill Paperbacks, 1979), 125.

8.   See Karl Marx, *The German Ideology* (New York: International Publishers, 1973), 56.

9.   Antonio Gramsci, *The Modern Prince* (New York: International Publishers, 1972), 165–66.

10. Herbert Marcuse, *Reason and Revolution* (Boston: Beacon Press, 1960), 141.

11. G.W.F. Hegel, *Philosophy of History* (New York: Colonial Press, 1899), 56.

12. Hegel, *Philosophy of History*, 108, 343.

13. See Gerald Horne's informative book *The Counter-Revolution of 1776: Slave Resistance and the Origins of the United States of America* (New York: New York University Press, 2016). His argument that the revolution of 1776 was an attempt to forestall British abolition of slavery in the colonies does not take into account Thomas Jefferson's rough draft of the Declaration of Independence, which blamed the king of England for slavery. Among the "injuries and usurpations" that the king was charged with perpetrating on the colonies, Jefferson included a "cruel war against human nature itself, violating its most sacred rights of life & liberty in the persons of a distant people who never offended him, captivating

& carrying them into slavery in another hemisphere, or to incur miserable death in their transportation thither. . . . He is now exciting those very people to rise in arms among us, and to purchase that liberty of which he has deprived them, by murdering the people on whom he also obtruded them: thus paying off former crimes committed against the liberties of one people, with crimes which he urges them to commit against the lives of another."

14. Rosa Luxemburg, *The Mass Strike* (New York: Harper and Row, 1971), 44–45. Georges Sorel described the general strike as "the myth in which Socialism is wholly comprised. . . . We thus obtain that intuition of Socialism which language cannot give us with perfect clearness—and we obtain it as a whole, perceived instantaneously." Georges Sorel, *Reflections on Violence* (New York: Collier Books, 1950), 127–28.

15. Alfred Willener, *The Action-Image of Society: On Cultural Politicization* (New York: Pantheon Books, 1970), 93.

16. *The Commune of 1871* (New York: New York Labor News, 1978), 7.

17. Choi Jungwoon, *The Gwangju Uprising: The Pivotal Democratic Movement That Changed the History of Modern Korea* (Paramus: Homa and Sekey Books, 2006), 85, 131.

18. Priscilla Robertson, *Revolutions of 1848: A Social History* (Princeton: Princeton University Press, 1952), 221, 269, 274, 289, 291, 300, 304, 391; Karl Marx, *The Revolutions of 1848–9* (New York: International Publishers, 1972), 108–9, 262; Sidney Harcave, *The Russian Revolution of 1905* (New York: Macmillan, 1964), 203.

19. Periods of revolutionary crisis bear little resemblance to crises produced by economic breakdowns. The latter have their roots in the irrational organization of the economy and the state, while general strikes and revolutions are essentially attempts to provide rational alternatives. A dialectical view of crisis includes both of these types, particularly since they commonly have a close relationship to each other. Traditional usage of the concept of crisis, however, generally denotes only economic dislocations like the Great Depression or the many financial meltdowns that characterize global capitalism. Economic crises are one type of social crisis and differ from crises produced by the eros effect. See the chapter in the 1987 edition titled "The Rationality of the New Left."

20. Thomas Jefferson, Letter to John Adams, September 4, 1823.

21. Daniel Valcarcel, *La Rebelión de Túpac Amaru* (Mexico: Fondo de Cultura Económica, 1965).

22. Valcarcel, *La Rebelión de Túpac Amaru*, 117–18.

23. Andr. Gunder Frank, *Crisis: In the Third World* (New York: Holmes and Meier, 1981).

24. Alexis de Tocqueville, *Souvenirs d'Alexis de Tocqueville* (Paris: Gallimard, 1942), 30.

25. Robertson, *Revolutions of 1848*, 81.

26. The momentum of that period originated in Greece, followed by Italy. On September 3, 1843, a popular uprising in Athens confronted the European kingdom imposed upon them little more than a decade after the overthrow of nearly four hundred years of Turkish domination. Greek soldiers marched on the palace with virtually the entire population of the city to demand constitutional rights. Eventually the popular movement's continuing insistence compelled King Otho to grant a constitution in March 1844.

27. Emerson Tennent as quoted in Kumari Jayawardena, *Perpetual Ferment* (Colombo: Social Scientists' Association, 2010), 144.

28. Immanuel Wallerstein, *Utopistics; or, Historical Choices of the 21st Century* (New York: The New Press, 1998), 17.

29. L.S. Stavrianos, *Global Rift: The Third World Comes of Age* (New York: William Morrow and Company, 1981), 389.

30. See Rosa Luxemburg, *Theory and Practice* (Detroit: News and Letters, 1980), 45; Richard Boyer and Herbert Morais, *Labor's Untold Story* (New York: United Electrical Press, 1974), 142–64.

31. Azar Tabari and Nabid Yaganeh, *In the Shadow of Islam* (London: Zed Press, 1962), 30.

32. Harcave, *The Russian Revolution of 1905*, 133.

33. Max Gordon, "The Communist Party and the New Left," *Socialist Revolution* 6 (January 1976): 19.

34. Klaus Mehnert, *Moscow and the New Left* (Berkeley: University of California Press, 1975), 41–42.

35. Valdo Spini, "The New Left in Italy," *Journal of Contemporary History* 7, no. 2 (January–April 1972): 51–71.

36. Mihailo Markov.c, "The New Left and the Cultural Revolution," in Mihailo Markov.c, *The Contemporary Marx: Essays in Humanist Communism* (Nottingham: Spokesman Books, 1974), 175.

37. Herbert Marcuse, *Counterrevolution and Revolt* (Boston: Beacon Press, 1972).

38. Herbert Marcuse, "Reexamination of the Concept of Revolution," *Diogenes*, no. 64 (Winter 1968): 17–27.

39. For a book-length study of this insight, see Willener, *The Action-Image of Society*.

40. *Global Conceptualism: Points of Origin 1950s–1980s* (New York: Queens Museum of Art, 1999).

41. Klaus Schrenk, ed., *Upheavals: Manifestoes, Manifestations* (Cologne: Dumont Verlag, 1984), 29.

42. Institute of Contemporary Art, Boston, *On the Passage of a Few People through a Rather Brief Moment in Time: The Situationist International 1957–1972* (Cambridge, MA: MIT Press, 1989), 63.

43. Quoted in Schrenk, *Upheavals, Manifestoes, Manifestations*, 142. 44. See Janet Jenkins, ed., *In the Spirit of Fluxus* (Minneapolis: Walker Art Center, 1993).

45. David Mellor, *The Sixties Art Scene in London* (London: Phaidon, 1993), 14–17.

46. Mellor, *The Sixties Art Scene in London*, 34.

47. *The Gazette* 1 (1961): 1.

48. Herbert Marcuse, "Political Preface" to *Eros and Civilization*, 19.

49. See John Hanhardt, ed., *The Worlds of Nam June Paik* (New York: Guggenheim Museum, 2003), 23.

50. Jeanne Siegel, ed., *Artworlds: Discourse on the 60s and 70s* (New York: Da Capo Press, 1992), 121.

51. See Robert Hewison, *Too Much: Art and Society in the Sixties 1960–75* (New York: Oxford University Press, 1987).

52. Wilfred Burchett, *Vietnam Will Win!* (New York: International Publishers, 1968).

53. Frantz Fanon, *The Wretched of the Earth* (New York: Grove Press, 1968), 136.

54. United States Office of Education, Projections of Educational Statistics to 1977– 1978 (Washington, DC: Government Printing Office, 1968).

55. James Boggs and Grace Lee Boggs, *Revolution and Evolution in the Twentieth Century* (New York: Monthly Review Press, 1976).

The Black Panthers' Place in History

ALTHOUGH WE like to think in linear terms, history has its own cunning that carries us along strange and mysterious paths. Long forgotten, "defeated" movements and their ideals sometimes emerge with a renewed popularity unpredictable only the blink of an eye before. Victors may define the history of an era in large type, but by ignoring the boldface script of textbooks and news programs, a better sense of the future may be gleaned from the margins. This essay reflects upon the margins of the present to consider the historical impact of the Black Panther Party—the most significant revolutionary organization in the US during the latter half of the twentieth century. Compared with the Congress of Racial Equality (CORE) or the National Association for the Advancement of Colored People (NAACP), the sixteen-year existence of the Black Panther Party seems brief indeed. While its revolutionary period lasted for less than half its life, the Black Panther Party gave organizational expression to a tendency in the movement that long predated the BPP: the idea that the entire system is corrupt and needs to be reconstructed. Dozens of groups dedicated to revolutionary change appeared in the US during the 1960s, but the BPP was the only one able to develop a massive following and to appeal to a broad constituency.

The Panthers' notoriety initially turned on their overt practice and explicit advocacy of armed self-defense. This dimension of the larger movement has systematically been deleted from history books and recollections of past struggles. Mississippi Freedom Summer of 1964, mythologized by sociologists and screenwriters alike for its non-violent resistance to racist terrorism, contained a militant theme of quiet self-defense woven throughout its history. How dozens of films, award-winning books, Hollywood scripts and intense media coverage all could ignore, overlook and distort this aspect of the resistance movement in Mississippi is itself worthy of study. No doubt such an analysis would reveal a great deal about the ways that prevailing ideologies deform the accounts of social movements, their emphasizing superficial characteristics and ignoring deeper connections to broader historical currents, suppressing in fact movements' appeals, ideals and actions. Even in portrayals of the Panthers trickling through the media gatekeepers and exhibited before millions of us in Hollywood accounts of the 1960s, militant actions are treated as episodic, whereby the fundamental break with the legitimacy and power of the established system which the Panthers represented is hidden from view.

The Panthers' influence spread far beyond the US borders and affected the entire global movement of the 1960s. As a global awakening of the need for freedom shook the planet, in at least six countries, organizations formed that modeled themselves on the BPP, and for its part, the BPP drew inspiration from several African, Latin American and Asian revolutions, and studied the work of Franz Fanon, Che Guevara, and Kwame Nkrumah. In nearly every country in the world in 1968, movements pressed for revolution. From Vietnam and China in the east to India, Czechoslovakia, Senegal, Syria, Mexico, Brazil and France, a globally united upsurge suddenly emerged—and everywhere the Panthers were intuitively (if not actually) tied into the fabric of feelings, images and actions. Once again, most histories of this period neglect a critical dimension of the movements: the international bonds and global imagination—how we inspired each other and went far beyond the patriotism propagandized by every government. Love for each other as human beings was a palpable wave that rolled over the whole planet. Nonetheless, the vast majority of histories (in every country) describe the sixties as a *national* phenomenon.

In the US, the archives of research libraries and availability of information surpasses the intellectual resources of any country in history, yet studies here consistently ignore the movement's global character and fundamental break in the late 1960s with the entire system. Written out of history books and largely ignored in most participants' narratives is the fact that from May to September 1970, the United States was in a prerevolutionary situation in which emergent revolutionary forces led by the BPP organized to transform totally the existing system. During this period, the largest strike in US history occurred. Over 4 million students and half a million faculty on the campuses demanded an end to the war in Indochina as well as freedom and peace for imprisoned Panthers. The events in the US from May to September 1970 were similar to the now-legendary French *evenements* of 1968 in which a student revolt precipitated a strike of ten million workers— posing a revolutionary situation. When the spiral of militant actions and massive resistance in the US reached its apex in 1970, the consciousness-in-action of millions of people called for the abolition of the existing system and the creation of one based on justice and peace. In place of patriotism, millions of Americans acted according to norms of international solidarity; instead of hierarchy and competition, equality and cooperation; rather than racial division, solidarity; as opposed to conformity and acquisition, free experimentation and altruism. People not only thought about revolution, they acted on their beliefs and convictions.

Recognizing this dynamic, the BPP called for a gathering of representatives of all radical constituencies in Philadelphia in September for a Revolutionary People's Constitutional Convention, and the vision produced there by the popular movement went a long way in reconceptualizing America. Although the police terrorized the Philadelphia Panthers and threatened to stop the convention, nearly 15,000 of us assembled to rewrite the constitution of the US. Led by the Panthers, an extraordinary alliance was forged, including the American Indian Movement, the Brown Berets, the Young Lords, I Wor Keun (an Asian-American revolutionary organization), women's liberation groups, former members of Students for Democratic Society (which had a membership of well over 70,000 at its high point), and the newly formed Gay Liberation Front. As I discuss in this essay, "Organization and Movement: The Case of the Black Panther Party and the Revolutionary People's Constitutional Convention," the outline of a freer society is visible in the proposals from the workshops, and the energy and enthusiasm of the popular movement made the Panther program of 1966 appear to be quite modest.

There are moments when history accomplishments more in days than at other times in years, and in this volatile period Huey Newton was released from a three-year imprisonment; 18-year-olds were granted the right to vote; the Chicano Moratorium was viciously attacked in Los Angeles; women called for a national strike and the symbol for feminism was born; troops in Vietnam mutinied and sometimes fragged their officers; and millions of Americans viewed themselves as revolutionaries and acted accordingly. The Army Math Research Center in Madison (where research used to capture and kill Che Guevara was conducted) was gutted by an explosion, and in California, Jonathan Jackson took over a courtroom, kidnapped a judge and demanded the liberation of his brother before a volley of gunfire killed him and two prisoners who had joined him.[1]

The Panthers were intricately connected to all the events of this period. When a group of us who had been arrested at Boston University (and savagely beaten inside a Boston police station) were arraigned in court, my most vivid memory is of Eric Mann, a leader of the local Weathermen, grimly informing us during a break in court's proceedings, that Fred Hampton had been murdered earlier that morning. By April 1970, after Bobby Seale had been severed from the Chicago 8 conspiracy trial and taken to New Haven, where he faced murder charges and the death penalty, many of us felt nothing was more important in our lives than banding together with those whose lives were also dedicated to the movement.

These were extraordinary times. Hundreds, sometimes thousands, of Vietnamese were killed everyday, and police repression in the US, already murderous, threatened to become sanctioned by the judicial system. Something had to be done to save Bobby Seale. When a few of the Panthers asked two of us they knew from Rosa Luxemburg SDS at MIT to speak for them at a movement meeting (since they rightfully felt that if they said what we were prepared to say, they would simply be arrested) we agreed. The April 15 anti-war moratorium, an event sure to draw tens of thousands of people was nearly upon us, and we thought that a "white riot" for Bobby Seale was our best shot at saving his life. When my good friend Peter Bohmer and I were introduced by the Panthers as brothers who had important things to say that people should pay attention to, we were immediately treated to everyone's rapt attention. Over the next few weeks, as a small group of us worked day and night to bring our project to fruition, the treatment we received at the hands of movement activists changed radically. As the date approached, people became hostile to our project—to the point of throwing us out of the movement offices and effectively ostracizing us from any gatherings. The night before the action, a delegation arrived at our Cambridge apartment in a final attempt to forestall any violence. I alone refused to agree, feeling among other things my commitment to free Bobby Seale and my conviction that radical street actions were one of our few avenues to have an impact.

The next day, at least 100,000 people gathered on the Boston Common for the antiwar moratorium. The radical contingent there, noted by their red, yellow and blue NLF flags, began to gather as Abbie Hoffman's time to speak approached. I had spoken with Abbie hours earlier and he agreed to help form the Bobby Seale brigade out of the diverse participants in the rally. When his turn finally came, he gave a magnificent speech, probably enhanced by his being high on LSD. Pointing at the John Hancock building, he screamed at the top of his lungs: "John Hancock wasn't a life insurance salesman. He was a revolutionary! Here we are in the cradle of liberty. Are you going to rock that cradle or are you going to cradle that rock?" The thunderous response left me assured that our action would succeed.

As the rally broke up, the Bobby Seale brigade assembled on Beacon Street. First hundreds, then thousands of us made ready to march across the river to Cambridge, and "do more than march and shout." We had made elaborate preparations to march across the Longfellow bridge and made sure the Cambridge police caught wind of them. As we began to march, rather than heading down Charles Street, however, we directed everyone to march down Beacon. I rode ahead on a motorcycle, checking for police roadblocks and activity. I rode back and forth, communicating with only two or three other people. As we turned the crowd over the Harvard bridge, it became apparent we were a huge gathering since we completely filled the bridge where the Charles River basin was at its widest. Busloads of Cambridge police dressed in riot gear were moving from the foot of the Longfellow bridge to Central Square, where they were setting up a blockade. Quickly driving to the various projects and informing people there of the march and impeding action at Harvard Square (to which they responded with boundless enthusiasm), I rode back to the march and roared through the crowd until I located a friendly attorney. With him on the back of my motorcycle, waving the permit gotten a week before, we rode ahead to the police line and convinced them we were a legal march and that we had no desire to have a riot in Central Square. Miraculously, the police lines parted as the march approached and we had made it to Harvard Square. The rest is history—the largest riot in the history of Cambridge, one that unfortunately resulted in many injuries and arrests, but one that also changed the fate of Bobby Seale. Before the end of the month, Kingman Brewster (president of Yale University, where protests were scheduled for May 1) had offered his most famous opinion, one with far-reaching implications and effects, when he said that he was skeptical that a black revolutionary could get a fair trial in America.

Today, more than half a century later, there remains ample grounds for such skepticism. To name just one example, Mumia Abu-Jamal remains locked up in Pennsylvania. As a seasoned member of the Black Panther Party in 1970, Abu-Jamal was one of the hosts and organizers of the RPCC. Unlike many sixties activists, he continues to write and organize today. Convicted under highly dubious conditions in 1982 for the killing of a Philadelphia policeman, Abu-Jamal's appeal for a new trial was ruled on by Albert Sabo, the same judge who had so arbitrarily presided over his trial. Sabo has sentenced more people to death (32—all but two of whom are racial minorities) than any other judge in the US. From death row, Abu-Jamal continued his work as an award-winning journalist, completed his master's degree, and is working on a PhD. He has received so much support from around the world that all his mail cannot fit into the cell in which he lives. Abu-Jamal traces a direct line from the original BPP to contemporary activism.

As Ward Churchill[2] and many others have amply documented, the BPP was so massively assaulted that at the end of 1971, it was "effectively destroyed" by the assassination of Fred Hampton and the murder of 27 other Panthers; the arbitrary arrest and persecution of hundreds of other BPP members; the FBI media campaign against the Party; the use of dozens of infiltrators; the neutralization of the Black Panther newspaper; the shutting down of breakfast for children programs; the generation of negative publicity through circulation of rumors that Party leaders were anti-Semitic, or embezzlers, or extortionists (depending on the audience). FBI counterintelligence programs undermined coalitions (as between the Panther and SNCC); exacerbated interorganizational tensions to the point of gunfire (as with the US organization); defamed and incapacitated key Panther supporters; coordinated military assaults on Panther headquarters around the country; and maliciously and falsely prosecuted leaders like Geronimo ji Jaga, Bobby Seale, the New York Panther 21, the Los Angeles 13, etc. By the end of 1969, some 30 Panthers were in jail facing the death penalty; another 40 were looking at life imprisonment; 55 were up on charges punishable by 30 years or more; and over 150 others had been forced underground. To complete the destruction of the BPP, the FBI fomented an internal split that tore the organization apart.

If not for the carefully orchestrated disintegration of the leadership of the Panthers, who knows where the revolutionary impetus they led could have taken us? Although it occurred some 50 years ago, little has been written about the split in the

Panthers. Anyone who has participated in such movements knows how quickly and loudly established voices are raised to denounce us, and how heavily we are called upon to struggle with the agony of defeats, recriminations, betrayals and acts of sabotage. In the glare of media spotlight and police surveillance, it is nearly impossible to find a space where free discussions of our failures can occur.

Few people see the Black Panther Party as error-free. We acknowledge the need for a broader discussion of many of the issues raised by their violent split. From within prison bars, Russell Shoats remarkably reconstructed details from the past to show how the Panther leadership in Oakland refused to acknowledge and take responsible leadership of the revolutionary upsurge. As a result of the sea change that so rapidly eviscerated the movement, Shoats—as well as hundreds of others like him—was left hanging out to dry as the revolutionary momentum was arrested, fractured, and finally collapsed.

In its day, the BPP improvised and innovated, inspired by and contributing to global revolutionary movements. In the face of overwhelming force wielded by armed government agents, the Panthers refused to surrender. A challenge facing us in upcoming struggles is to discuss painfully learned lessons of the past. Future activists will attempt to transform existing social orders, neither unduly glorifying the past nor falsely deprecating it. This essay anticipates the future emergence of movements with the universal vision of the BPP that will inspire and activate millions of people.

NOTES

1   Until his release in 2023, Ruchell Magee, the only survivor, spent nearly all of the intervening 53 years in solitary confinement.

2   See Ward Churchill and Jim Vander Wall, *Agents of Repression: The FBI's Secret War Against the Black Panther Party and the American Indian Movement* (Boston: South End Press, 1990).

Organization and Movement: The Black Panther Party and the Revolutionary Peoples' Constitutional Convention[1]

MILLIONS OF "ordinary" people pay with their lives for the decisive events that determine the outcome of world events. Their actions and thoughts enter into most histories, however, only as **objects** affected by momentous decisions leaders make, not as **subjects** of the social world upon which decision-makers depend. Historians typically study the writings of world leaders and construct meticulously researched biographies to shed light on momentous events, such as the creation of constitutions. Yet the notion that "people make history," long ago incorporated into contemporary conversations, seldom informs accounts of World War II , the Civil War or even grass-roots attempts to change outmoded patterns of everyday life—and certainly not writing constitutions.

Take the case of the civil rights movement. Biographies of Martin Luther King, Jr. or Malcolm X are the norm, not accounts of the millions who changed their lives and revolutionized society through sacrifice and struggle, transforming even Martin's and Malcolm's worldviews. Every child knows King's name, but how many Americans ever heard of Fred Hampton's assassination or know what COINTELPRO stands for? How many of us could say even one knowledgeable sentence about the massacres of students at Orangeburg, Jackson State or North Carolina A&T?

Even movements tends to regard the ideas of its leaders, political parties and organized groups as most significant. No less than conventional historians, radical analysts often seem unable to comprehend the intelligence of crowds that embody the popular imagination. There are many reasons for this blind spot, including the ease with which accounts of leaders and organizations can be constructed compared with the difficulties one encounters when seeking to comprehend single events in the ebb and flow of sporadic gatherings of nebulous groups—precisely those incidents thought to be little more than actions by random collections of people. Sometimes pivotal events are so shrouded in mystery that historians do not even agree as to whether the events in question even took place.[2]

History seldom cooperates by providing us with clear indications of participants' thinking during instances of "spontaneously conscious"[3] crowds. One such exceptional case is the Revolutionary People's Constitutional Convention (RPCC), a multicultural public gathering of between 10,000 and 15,000 people who answered the call by the Black Panther Party (BPP) and assembled in Philadelphia on the weekend of September 5, 1970. Arriving in the midst of police terror directed against the BPP, thousands of activists from around the country were determined to defend the Panthers. We also intended to redo what had been done in 1787 by this nation's founding fathers in the city of brotherly love—to draft a new constitution providing authentic liberty and justice for all. Although seldom even mentioned in mainstream accounts, this self-understood revolutionary event came at the high point of the sixties movement in the US and was arguably the most momentous event in the movement during this critical period in American history.

This essay seeks to develop an understanding of the hearts and minds of the diverse community drawn to the convention. By examining primary documents produced by the RPCC, I hope to shed light on the popular movement's aspirations. I seek to illustrate how the intelligence of popular movements sometimes outpaces even the most visionary statements of its leading individuals and organizations by comparing written statements of the RPCC with the original platform and program of the BPP drafted four long years earlier. Besides primary documents of the RPCC and accounts by a few historians and activists, I draw from my own personal experiences as a participant in the RPCC. For 30 years, I kept a copy of the original proposals generated by the workshops that formed when the large plenary session broke down into smaller working groups. Now in the possession of the Freedom Archives in Berkeley, these documents convey unambiguous statements of the movement's self-defined goals and provide an outline of a freer society. Although it has been practically forgotten by historians, the RPCC is a key to unlocking the mystery of the aspirations of the 1960s movement. The majority of my essay deals with the RPCC because so little has been written about it.[4] I hope this article encourages future work on the RPCC.

Many writers have examined the early history of the sixties, but far fewer look at the time when the movement spread beyond the upper middle-class constituencies and elite universities that gave rise to both the civil rights movement and student movement. Popular stereotypes of the sixties often end with Martin Luther King's assassination, yet by late 1969, the movement had become so massive and radical that its early proponents did not recognize (or sometimes even support) it. In 1970, when the movement reached its apex, working-class students, countercultural youth and the urban lumpenproletariat (unemployed street people and those who supported themselves through criminal endeavors) transformed its tactics and goals. Shortly before their murders, both Martin Luther King, Jr. and Malcolm X were coming to much the same radical conclusion as that shared by the participants at the RPCC: the entire world system needs to be revolutionized in order to realize liberty and justice for all.

Part of the problem involved with historical accounts of the 1960s concerns the profound character of the rupture of social tranquility and social cohesion that occurred in the USA. Consistently uncovered in Harris polls and Yankelovich surveys, the revolutionary aspirations of millions of people in the US in 1970 constitute a significant set of data for understanding how rapidly revolutionary upsurges can emerge—and how quickly they can be dissipated and even reversed. In 1970, immediately after the national student strike, polls found that more than one million students considered themselves revolutionaries.[5] The next year, a *New York Times* investigation found that 4 out of 10 college students (more than three million people) thought that a revolution was needed in the US.[6] While these are substantial numbers, they do not count millions more outside American universities in the ghettoes and barrios, the factories, offices and suburbs. For a brief historical moment, the movement in the US accomplished a decisive break with the established system. Unlike similar events in France in May 1968, whose discontinuity from the established society is common knowledge, the "break" in US history has been hidden. Neither revolutionary activists nor mainstream historians want to acknowledge the revolutionary stridency of that period, both preferring to promulgate more socially acceptable ideas like those of the young Martin Luther King, Jr. or the still-not-mature Malcolm X. Under these circumstances, it is understandable that the revolutionary upsurge of 1970 is quite difficult to recall thirty years later.

Elsewhere I have written that the popular imagination can best be comprehended in the actions and aspirations of millions of people during moments of crisis—general strikes, insurrections, episodes of the eros effect, and other forms of mass struggle.[7] The RPCC was one such episode, and even in apparent failure, the convention inaugurated many ideas that subsequently have become so significant that millions of people were actively involved in pursuing them. For revolutionary movements, the dialectic of defeat often allows aspects of their aspirations to be implemented by the very system they opposed.

The Revolutionary Peoples' Constitutional Convention

On Labor Day weekend, September 5-7, 1970, thousands of people, including sizeable contingents of students, feminists, gay people, Native Americans, Puerto Ricans, Chicanos and Asian-Americans, answered the Panthers' call for a Revolutionary Peoples' Constitutional Convention (RPCC) in Philadelphia. Despite massive police represion designed to scare people away from Philadelphia, as many as 15,000 people came.[8] From around the country, spontaneously assembled groups rented buses, drove cars and those that could afford it, took planes. In at least two cities, people reported that buses were suddenly canceled without explanation, compelling people to improvise rides. Twenty-two persons from East St. Louis in a three-car caravan were arrested and charged with firearms violations, and at least one New York Panther was arrested en route to Philadelphia.[9] Organizations and delegates from Florida and North Carolina made a notable impression, as did representatives from African liberation movements, Palestine, Germany, Colombia and Brazil.[10]

The week before people gathered in Philadelphia, police bloodily assaulted all three Panther offices in the city, arresting every member of the Party they could find. The Panthers had not accepted their fate without a gunfight, and three police were wounded. Afterward, the police forced captured Panther men to walk naked through the streets while being photographed by the press. Police Chief Rizzo gloated he had caught the "big, bad Black Panthers with their pants down."[11]

Publicized widely, these police attacks only steeled the courage amid fear created by intensified repression. Philadelphia Panther member Russell Shoats recounts that in the weeks before the RPCC that the Panther central office in Oakland made it clear to Philadelphia party members that even Huey Newton was "afraid to come to Philadelphia." Shoats remembers that they "went on to express their opinion that the racist Philadelphia police would feel comfortable in attempting to assassinate him during the planned Revolutionary People's Constitutional Convention Planning Session..."[12]

Rather than facing expected police assaults, we found hospitality in the homes of African-Americans. Churches were refuges, and streets alive with an erotic solidarity of a high order. Signs in storefronts read "WELCOME PANTHERS." Five flags flew outside the convention center representing the Panthers, the National Liberation Front of South Vietnam, Black nationalism (red, black and green), YIPPIES (green marijuana leaf on black flag), and Che Guevara. Evidently the Panthers had done a huge amount of planning for the event, as food was provided for many people. Russell Shoats recounts how a 15-ton refrigerated truck full of frozen meats was commandeered and unloaded on the same day as other Panther squads robbed a bank.

The Philadelphia Black community was incredibly in tune with the moment. After the police raids, Panther offices had been sealed, but people opened them back up on their own initiative. *The Black Panther* reported, "In North Philly, two rival gangs had made a truce...They emerged 200-300 strong and when 15 carloads of pigs drove up and asked them who gave them permission to open up the people's office, their reply was 'the people,' and the police had to eat mud rather than face the wrath of an angry armed people."[13]

An extraordinary alliance at the RPCC came together in open assemblies to discuss movement goals and future directions. Most remarkably of all, this diverse convention was able to write down their visions of a free society. History seldom cooperates by providing us with such clarity of participants' thinking in "spontaneously conscious"[14] crowds.

Inside Temple University's McGonigle Hall, a vibrant and festive atmosphere prevailed for plenary sessions. We had won. The police had been unable to stop us. A steady stream of people accumulated, the hall swelled to its capacity, and anticipation grew. Panther security people indicated speakers were about to begin. Suddenly, dozens of gay people entered the upper balcony, chanting and clapping rhythmically: "Gay, gay power to the gay, gay people! Power to the People! Black, Black power to the Black, Black people! Gay, gay power to the gay, gay people! Power to the People!" Everyone rose to their feet and joined in, repeating the refrain and using other appropriate adjectives: Red, Brown, Women, Youth and Student.

The first speaker was Michael Tabor a charismatic, young Party member who brilliantly held our attention for over two hours as he enumerated how the original US constitution excluded and oppressed "240,000 indentured servants, 800,000 black slaves, 300,000 Indians, and all women, to say nothing of the sexual minorities." Tabor reminded us that President Richard Nixon, fresh from invading Cambodia and daily bombing Vietnam, "made Adolf Hitler look like a peace candidate." Other speakers included Audrea Jones, leader of the Boston Panthers, and Panther attorney Charles Garry.

During the break in nearby streets, Muhammed Ali, an "ordinary" participant, shook hands, signed autographs and offered words of encouragement. (The heavyweight champion had been stripped of his title for his anti-war stance and would not win his case before the Supreme Court until the following year.) People talked with old friends or made new ones as they looked for a place to stay. All the while, hundreds discussed their coming task: to draft a new constitution for the US. Jubilation alongside criticism, but nowhere, fearful resignation.

As evening approached, electric expectations filled the hall as we waited for our first encounter with Huey P. Newton. Thousands more people waited outside hoping for space to become available for them. Only released from prison on August 9, Huey had just published an important essay supporting women's and gay liberation. He also had publicly offered to send troops to fight on the side of the Vietnamese against the US. Although many of us had demonstrated for his freedom and read his essays, he was a stranger to practically everyone, even for many Panthers. Huey was everyone's hero but as soon as he took the microphone, we were stunned to discover that he was not at all an eloquent speaker. His high-pitched, almost whiny voice digressed into abstract arguments that had little impact — except to disappoint us, a fact not lost on Newton himself.[15]

The next day, we broke down into topical workshops that could be selected from a menu prepared by a planning group that had met at Howard University a month earlier.[16] As *The Back Panther* reported, "If only for a few hours, representatives of all major constituencies of the revolutionary popular movement huddled together to brainstorm and discuss ideas for achieving our goals of a freer society. The form of the gatherings was slightly different than in 1787. Each workshop was led by Panther members, who also coordinated security contingents that insured a trouble-free working environment."

Panthers prevented the media from attending, fearing their presence would only make a circus of the proceedings. While many journalists complained about being barred, the space created by the absence of media was too valuable to sacrifice to publicity. Here was the movement's time to speak among ourselves. Seldom do groups communicate with such a combination of passion and reason. Person after person rose and spoke of heartfelt needs and desire, of pain and oppression. As if the roof had been taken off the ceiling, imaginations soared as we flew off to our new society. The synergistic effect compelled each of us to articulate our thoughts with eloquence and simplicity, and the "right on!" refrain that ended each person's contribution also signaled that the time had arrived for someone else to speak. An unidentified Panther later described how the even the children had not been boisterous: "The children were to be for the three days like adults, infected with a kind of mad sobriety." The same author promised: "There is going to be a revolution in America. It is going to begin in earnest in our time…To have believed in a second American revolution before Philadelphia was an act of historical and existential faith: not to believe in a new world after Philadelphia is a dereliction of the human spirit."[17]

In describing the workshops, she/he went on: "The pre-literate Black masses and some few saved post-literate students were going to, finally write the new constitution…The aristocratic students led by the women, and the street bloods, they were going to do the writing. So there were the first tentative meetings, led brilliantly by 'armed intellectuals' from the Panthers…In the schools and churches—the rational structures of the past—the subversive workshops of the future met to ventilate the private obsessions of the intellectual aristocrats and the mad hopes of the damned."[18]

As the time allotted for the workshops drew to an end, each group chose spokespersons entrusted to present our ideas to the entire plenary's second session. As is clear in the documents, differences of viewpoint were sometimes simply left intact rather than flattened out in an attempt to impose a Party line.[19] Under more "normal" circumstances involving such a diverse collection of people in working groups as large as 500 persons, screaming fights (or worse) might have been expected, yet these workshops generated documents that offer a compelling vision of a more just and free society than has ever existed. Alongside an International Bill of Rights that prohibited US aggression on other nations, mandates were approved for redistribution of the world's wealth, a ban on manufacture and use of genocidal weapons, as well as an end to a standing army and its replacement by "a system of people's militia, trained in guerrilla warfare, on a voluntary basis and consisting of both men and women." Police were to consist of "a rotating volunteer non-professional body coordinated by the Police Control Board from a (weekly) list of volunteers from each community section. The Police Control Board, its policies, as well as the police leadership, shall be chosen by direct popular majority vote of the community." The delegates called for an end to the draft; prohibition on spending more than 10% of the national budget for military and police—a provision that could be overridden by a majority vote in a national referendum—and proportional representation for minorities and women (two forms of more democracy missing from the constitution adopted in 1789).

Universities' resources were to be turned over to people's needs all over the world, not sold to military and corporate needs; billions of dollars of organized crime wealth were to be confiscated; there was to be free decentralized medical care; sharing of housework by men and women; encouragement of alternatives to the nuclear family; "the right to be gay, anytime, anyplace"; increased rights and respect for children; community control of schools; and student power, including freedom of dress, speech and assembly. Although there is one paragraph in which "man" and "he" is used, the very first report of the workshops contained a mandate always to replace the word "man" with "people" in order to "express solidarity with the self-determination of women and to do away with all remnants of male supremacy, once and for all." As summarized by the BPP a week later: "Taken as a whole, these reports provided the basis for one of the most progressive Constitutions in the history of humankind. All the people would control the means of production and social institutions. Black and third world people were guaranteed proportional representation in the administration of these institutions as were women. The right of national self-determination was guaranteed to all oppressed minorities. Sexual self-determination for women and homosexuals was affirmed...The present racist legal system would be replaced by a system of people's courts where one would be tried by a jury of one's peers. Jails would be replaced by community rehabilitation programs...Adequate housing, health care, and day care would be considered Constitutional Rights, not privileges. Mind expanding drugs would be legalized. These are just some of the provisions of the new Constitution."[20]

In the society at large: racism, patriarchal chauvinism and homophobia; at the RPCC: solidarity, liberation and celebration of difference. From this vantage point, the RPCC provides a glimpse of the break from "normal" business as usual, and of international system to replace the existing one of militarized nation-states and profit-hungry transnational corporations. As a global uprising swept the planet, the Panthers were best positioned as the most oppressed in what Che Guevara called "the belly of the beast" to embody global aspirations to transform the entire world system. These documents convey unambiguous statements of the movement's self-defined outline of a freer society. Although it has been practically forgotten by historians, the RPCC is a key to unlocking the mystery of the aspirations of the 1960s movement.

The Philadelphia constitution's International Bill of Rights was one indication of just how much patriotism was transcended. The popular movement's imagination expounded the contours of a new world—not simply a new nation. The twin aspirations of the global movement of 1968—internationalism and self-management—were embodied throughout the articulated vision. The phrase "self-management" may not have been used in the documents, but its American version, "community control," was used in reference to schools, police, women's control of their own bodies, and more autonomy for children, students and youth. In our attempt to create paradise, our immediate task was to mitigate repressive powers of those who wanted to preserve the status quo (police, racism, patriarchal authoritarianism, and the military). We sometimes compromised and agreed to go halfway to paradise, fully conscious that humans will never be absolutely free. If we continually jump halfway to paradise, never reaching it, we nonetheless approach it.

Some of the demands today appear outlandish, particularly those related to drugs. After calling for "eradication" of hard drugs "by any means necessary" and help for addicts, the workshop on Self-Determination of Street People came to the conclusion that: "We recognize that psychedelic drugs (acid, mescaline, grass) are important in developing the revolutionary consciousness of the people. However, after the revolutionary consciousness has been achieved, these drugs may become a burden. No revolutionary action should be attempted while under the influence of any drug. We urge these drugs be made legal. Or rather they should not be illegal, that is, there should be no law made against them."

The RPCC position on drugs displays graphically that more individual freedom was part of the aspirations of the Panther-led bloc, that this impetus, while appearing to some as only concerned with minorities, *actually formulated universal interests*. No one should discount or trivialize the importance of the drug issue. As a symbolic vehicle used for the imposition of class rule and cultural hegemony, it affects hundreds of thousands of people daily. One in three male prisoners in New York was serving a drug sentence in 1997; nationally, that figure was six of ten women; and in California, one in four male state prisoners (and four out of ten females).[21] The existing system's abysmal failure to wage an effective "war on drugs," its continual enrichment of organized crime syndicates while hundreds of thousands of users languish in jails, and the irrationality of legal drugs daily tranquilizing millions of children and adults, of alcohol and cigarettes' widespread glorification are scandalous dimensions of an irrational system. History's judgment may yet prove that RPCC policies are more sane and prudent than those now in place.[22] In two European venues apparently unaware of the RPCC, the Panther position on drugs essentially was copied: among Italian youth in the 1970s known as the Metropolitan Indians and in Christiania, a counter-cultural community in Copenhagen for over 50 years.[23]

After the RPCC, true to its call to eradicate hard drug dealers by any means necessary, Panthers went on the attack against heroin dealers, confiscating cash and flushing their stash after giving them plenty of public warnings. In one of the more daring actions undertaken by movement activists, H. Rap Brown was captured by police after he robbed an after-hours club frequently by big dealers—a hangout his team others sought to close. Ron Brazao, underground from a 1970 bust of the Panther Defense Committee in Cambridge, Massachusetts, was killed in a shoot-out with a dealer in Marin, California in 1972.

More than any other US organization in the latter half of the twentieth century, the BPP accelerated the revolutionary process. The dialectical synchronicity of popular movement and revolutionary party, the interplay between the two, their dependence on each other and mutual amplification, accelerated and reached its climax at the RPCC. Our gathering accomplished more in a weekend than history usually accomplishes in years or even decades. How much longer must we wait until we again find such space for visionary unity? The Philadelphia convention was the apex of the US popular insurgency. Nikhil Pal Singh eloquently understood the unique human geography that unfolded: "...enactment of a Constitutional Convention under the auspices of the Panthers and in celebration of 'radical minorities', excluded in the initial formation of the great document, was an astonishing attempt to is imagine alternative forms of kinship and community to the one organized around a conception of a unitary and universal, national subject."[24]

The CIA held a different view. Their report characterized the RPCC as a "chaotic and nonproductive effort...white radicals in attendance numbered about 40 percent..."[25] Not all participants share my optimistic portrayal. Some questioned whether a visible and spirited gay presence existed at the RPCC.[26] Alice Echols mentions a conference of the Lesbian Feminism Movement in Washington D.C. that produced a feminist caucus for the planned second RPCC. She felt that in Philadelphia, the BPP was suspicious of feminist activists because autonomous women's workshops (without the leadership of Panther women) were canceled more than once.[27] Ruth Rosen also complained that Huey broke his promise for an autonomous women's caucus to meet.[28] Women did have at least one female-only meeting, but about twenty lesbians left after they were unable to get the group to agree to their demands for women to have "complete control of our social system" and "destruction of the nuclear family." The split broke along the lines of Black women wanting to have a "nuclear" family, having suffered centuries of slavery when their families were torn asunder. They were fine with lesbians having a collective raising of children, but they wanted the right to keep their children to their blood family; they were leery of another "state" raising their kids in "day care."

That workshop's final report sharply contradicted existing society: "We recognize the right of all women to be free...We will fight for a socialist system that guarantees all, creative, non-exploitative life for all human beings...We encourage and support the continued growth of communal households and communal relationships and other alternatives to the patriarchal family...Every woman has the right to decide whether she will be homosexual, heterosexual or bisexual."[29]

Divisions also existed among African Americans. Most severely, the US organization had murdered Panther leaders Bunchy Carter and John Huggins in Los Angeles in 1969. Antagonisms between the two groups, although exacerbated by the FBI, reflected larger political differences. In Atlanta, on the same weekend that the RPCC convened in Philadelphia, the Congress of African People gathered in Atlanta, with 3,500 participants from a variety of civil rights, Black Power and cultural nationalist organizations. The Congress was born out of a series of conferences held in the US and Bermuda from 1966. Atlanta was designed to unite Black moderate forces and cultural nationalists—and to differentiate them from the radical multicultural alliance led by the Panthers. Present were Rev. Jesse Jackson, Coretta Scott King, Louis Farrakhan, Queen Mother Moore, Ken Msemaji and Julian Bond as well as representatives from many countries. The group restricted its participants to the third world. In one of the most important speeches, Imamu Baraka (Leroi Jones) warned against "White mythology" written by Marx and Lenin and chided the Panthers for asking us to get "involved with another group of White boys." Ultimately, the group went on to help spur African-American politicians to run for office. Baraka would later become a committed Leninist, but in 1970, he sought to distance African-American activists from white radicals.

At the grassroots level, unity and solidarity prevailed in 1970. The intelligence of popular movements sometimes outpaces even the most visionary organizations, an insight verified by comparing the reformist 1966 Panther program with the

Comparing the Black Panther Party's 1966 Program and 1970 RPCC Proposals

October 1966 Black Panther Party Platform (Black Nationalist phase of the BPP)	September 1970 Revolutionary People's Constitutional Convention (Revolutionary Internationalist phase of the popular movement)
Rights of Black People	International Bill of Rights
UN plebiscite to determine the destiny of the Black Community	USA not a nation; No genocidal weapons; end to NATO, SEATO
Black men exempt from military service	No standing army; No draft; People's militia; return of all US troops from around the world
End to robbery of the Black community	Abolish capitalism
Freedom for Black prisoners; New trials by peers	Freedom for all prisoners; Decentralized revolutionary tribunals
15 mentions of "man" in 10 points	Replace "men" with "people"; Encourage alternatives to nuclear family; Support for women's and gay liberation
40 acres and 2 mules	International reparations
Education teaching the "true nature of this decadent American society"	Community control of education; Proportional representation; National referenda

revolutionary vision produced at the RPCC in 1970. When held up against the RPCC documents, the program is timid, its vision limited. Nowhere in the program are gay people's rights, the liberation of women, and proportional representation of minorities and women.

The original plan was to have two RPCCs, the first to draft the new constitution followed by its subsequent ratification. After Philadelphia, groups worked feverishly to build a second convention scheduled for November 27-28 in Washington, D.C. On November 18, Newton gave a speech at Boston College and encouraged people to attend. He announced its theme as "Survival Through Service to the People" and promised to present "our total survival program."[30] In this path-breaking speech, he reformulated the Panthers' goal as "revolutionary intercommunalism." Rather than seizing national power, he maintained revolutionary forces should instead build up self-governing regional structures that could link together along horizontal lines. In his view, the global village created by the communications revolution as well as the international reach of US imperialism had created the preconditions for revolutionary intercommunalism.[31] According to Newton, capitalism long ago made nations obsolete and treated people everywhere as similar objects for exploitation: "We see very little difference in what happens to a community here in North America and what happens to a community in Vietnam. We see very little difference in what happens, even culturally, to a Chinese community in San Francisco and a Chinese community in Hong Kong. We see very little difference what happens to the Black community in Harlem in a Black community in South Africa, a Black community in Angola and one in Mozambique...What has actually happened, is that the non-state has been accomplished, but it is reactionary."[32]

Although the September convention had roared its approval of the program as a whole and thousands of people made their way to Washington, the gathering there never happened. Despite two months of effort, meeting space could not be secured. The FBI and local police agencies had pressured venues such as the University of Maryland and local armories not to allow Panthers to rent their spaces. Howard University insisted upon a $10,000 deposit, a sum the Panthers could not or would not pay. The CIA expected 20,000 to 25,000 people to attend—double the number in Philadelphia—and predicted even more whites because of sympathy among the "hippie community." When thousands of people arrived, there were simply no facilities available for them. A smattering of events transpired, including an outdoor concert by the Panthers' R&B band "The Lumpen." Newton finally spoke on November 29 to 600 people inside a packed church, while 2,000 more listened through speakers outside, and he promised to reconvene the convention in the near future.[33]

The Panthers Split

In the next 89 days, Newton had an unexpected change of heart and made a snap decision that building a "popular front" to write a new constitution was a mistake.[34] He changed the Party's orientation "back to the Black community" and endorsed electoral politics as the defining tactic of the Panthers. He later disclaimed any responsibility for the "crazy Constitutional Convention" and portrayed it as part of Eldridge Cleaver's misdirection of the party, even though the 1966 Panther program he had written with Bobby Seale pointed precisely toward such a convention. While Newton could not understand it, Cleaver's implementation of the Panther program was part of his desire to follow the leadership of Newton—not, as Huey subsequently

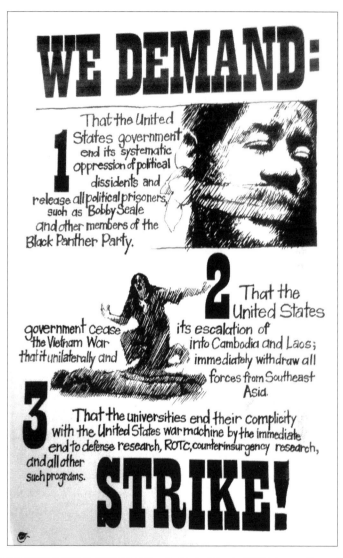

Poster from the 1970 national student strike, largest strike in US history with participation of some four million students and half a million faculty and staff

maintained—an attempt to overthrow him. Cleaver insisted the RPCC was "actually implementation of Point 10 of the Black Panther Party platform and program."[35] David Hilliard relates that Huey thought his original vision ran completely counter to "Eldridge's plan to create a national popular front with this crazy Constitutional Convention..."[36] At the time of both conventions, Cleaver was in Algeria where he opened the International Section of the Party on September 13, only days after the first RPCC. For a time, the BPP were afforded official recognition by the Algerian government and, in June 1970, they were given the previous embassy of Vietnam's NLF as their own. They made contact with the governments of Vietnam, North Korea, and China as well as liberation movements in Africa, Palestine and around the world.

Huey's erratic behavior precipitated a bitter and bloody internal feud that tore apart the Black Panther Party. Like a mad genius artist who destroys their canvasses, he ripped up the Party in fits of anger. During a televised international phone conversation with Cleaver on February 26, 1971—only 89 days after promising to reconvene the convention—he ridiculed and expelled Eldridge. No one knew it at the time, but with that phone call, the movement's high point had passed. In Philadelphia, the popular impetus represented millions of people, but when the split in the BPP turned into internecine war, public revolutionary engagement collapsed.

Dynamic tensions among various tendencies contained within the BPP proved unmanageable within their organizational form. Inside one vanguard party were many conflicting directions: formation of armed groups or consolidation of a legal political party; autonomy for African-Americans or leadership of an emergent rainbow; plebiscite on a Black nation or an International Bill of Rights. As long as the Party was tied to a vibrant popular movement, its various tendencies were able to coexist even though the FBI continually sent false letters to Panthers and employed other "dirty tricks" to exacerbate divisions between Huey and Eldridge. The Los Angeles bureau wrote a memo recommending that "each division which had individuals attend [the RPCC] write numerous letters to Cleaver criticizing Newton for his lack of leadership...[in order to] create dissension that later could be more fully exploited."[37]

Rather than continue to build the strident multicultural insurgency, Newton unilaterally undermined and blunted it. Without bothering to convene a central com-mittee meeting, he expelled key activists and forbade members from communicating with them. Insisting the Party go "back to the Black community," he confined the Party's public actions to maintenance of Oakland's survival programs and electoral politics. He closed down all chapters of the BPP and concentrated cadre in Oakland where he could personally supervise them. He claimed ownership of the Party, copyrighted the newspaper, and even beat up Bobby Seale to assert his autocratic control. He named himself Supreme Commander and became chief enforcer of party discipline, using a bullwhip to discipline members. In a manner reminiscent of how Stalin had treated Trotsky, every form of political deviation from Huey's new line was blamed on Cleaver. With these revisions underway, Newton secretly tried to control Oakland's drug trade and fell into drug addiction. He pistol-whipped his tailor and brutalized a young woman who called him "baby." With the Party split, the system destroyed the most radical advocates of revolution (George Jackson, the Attica inmates, the Black

Liberation Army) while reforming itself in order to prevent further popular mobilization. Attacked by his Party and feeling that exile as a "form of living death," Cleaver saw the revolutionary upsurge receding.[38] After a profound religious experience, he became a Christian and made his way back to the US.

As the movement disintegrated, the Philadelphia constitution was apparently tossed on the dustbin of history—or was it? The popular movement's vision continues to animate action. In the decades since the RPCC, millions of people have acted to implement various portions of the Philadelphia constitution. The day after the August 26, 1970 Women's General Strike, a lobbying campaign for an Equal Rights Amendment began on Capitol Hill. For years, advocates work tirelessly for it, garnering support of Congress in 1972 but falling three states short of the 38 needed by 1982. Despite opinion polls showing that more than two-thirds of the country favored it, the ERA never became law. In the 1980s, the disarmament movement sought a ban on the manufacture and use of genocidal weapons. Despite massive popularity, it too never became legally binding.

The most impressive actions in response to Philadelphia's RPCC were undertaken by the prisoners' movement that swept the United States in the months after the Philadelphia convention. From California to New York, imprisoned Americans like no other constituency were activated by the movement's call for justice. As inmates demanded decent, humane treatment, a wave of rebellions swept through the nation's prisons, reaching its high point at Attica State Prison in New York and San Quentin in California. By the end of September 1971, more than fifty persons had been killed in the bloody suppression of the wave of prison rebellions that rocked the nation. The majority of those killed were at Attica, where forty-two people died after Governor Nelson Rockefeller refused to negotiate with the inmate committee coordinating the revolt.

Many years later, RPCC ideas stimulated social movements, and they will undoubtedly do so again in the future. If just two RPCC provisions were enacted—proportional representation and a provision for national referenda—the current political structure would be far more representative of people's needs and desires. How can we call the US a "democracy" after elections with the system offering people an abysmal choice between singularly unpopular, self-serving candidates who agree to maintain corporate rule over as much of the world as possible? Real democracy demands the kinds of decentralized, self-managed forms of governance advocated by the RPCC.

If not for the split in the Party and the disintegration of the movement, where might the hegemonic bloc led by the Panthers have taken us? Barely out of its infancy, the revolutionary movement of 1970 was immature—unprepared to provide long-term responsible leadership capable of leading the whole society forward. Unable to reach the second stage of struggle—consolidation of the revolutionary impetus—it split into thousands of pieces. It would be an enormous mistake simply to blame Huey Newton for the movement's failure to sustain its revolutionary momentum. Indeed, he was a key contributor to the unfolding revolutionary process. Subjective and objective forces of revolution were simply not historically aligned in 1970.

To this day, the RPCC remains unexplored, a unique event that sparkles with insight from the hearts and minds of thousands of participants who represented millions more. At the beginning of the twenty-first century, the phenomenal pace of change accelerates, and shifting group identities, changing affiliations, atomization and detachment characterize our daily lives. Reactionary violence intensifies. In place of the Panthers, fragmentation and divisions make it problematic today for any group to provide universal vision. The RPCC was simultaneously the last of the great public gatherings of modernity and the first gathering of our multicultural future. In so being, it was the hinge around which an entire historical period turned.

NOTES

1   An earlier version appeared in *Liberation, Imagination and The Black Panther Party*, edited by Kathleen Cleaver and George Katsiaficas (New York: Routledge, 2001).

2   In *Bitter Grain, the Story of the Black Panther Party* (Los Angeles: Holloway House Publishing Co., 1980), author Michael Newton maintains that the event analyzed in this essay never took place. See p. 157.

3   I develop this concept in relation to the autonomous movement (or Autonomen) in Europe to indicate that seemingly spontaneous crowd behavior can have a great underlying intelligence. See *The Subversion of Politics: European Social Movements and the Decolonization of Everyday Life* (Atlantic Highlands, N.J.: Humanities Press, 1997) and *Oakland: 2006*, AK Press.

4   Checking a dozen of the most important histories of the sixties in the US, ten did not even mention the RPCC and the other two contained only brief references to it. To the best of my knowledge, this is the first attempt to deal with it even in an essay. Charles Jones, one of the pre-eminent historians of the BPP, points out that leaders' autobiographies and analyses of events are more common in Panther historiography than are rank-and-file accounts or longitudinal studies. The paucity of material about the RPCC indicates the extent to which it is a forgotten case even among movement events. See Jones, *Reconsidering Panther History: The Untold Story* in Charles E. Jones, editor, *The Black Panther Party Reconsidered* (Baltimore, Md: Black Classic Press, 1998) pp. 9-10.

5   See Joseph A. Califano, Jr., *The Student Revolution: A Global Confrontation* (New York: W.W. Norton, 1970) p. 64.

6   *The New York Times*, January 2, 1971.

7   *The Global Imagination of 1968* (Oakland: PM Press, 2019).).

8   Various estimates of the numbers exist, none of which claims to be definitive. David Hilliard says there were 15,000; Hilliard, 313. The Panther paper used numbers ranging from 12,000 to 15,000; *The Black Panther*, 9/19/70; 10/31/70, 7. Social scientist G. Louis Heath states that the plenary sessions on September 5 and 6 attracted 5,000 to 6,000 people (of whom 25 to 40 percent were white) but doesn't count thousands more who were outside and could not get in; *Off the Pigs! The History and Literature of the Black Panther Party*, G. Louis Heath, editor, (Metuchen, N.J.: Scarecrow Press, 1976) 186-7. The *New York Times* declared there were 6,000 people inside with another 2,000 outside (about half of whom were white); "Newton, At Panther Parley, Urges Socialist System," *The New York Times*, September 6, 1970, 40; Paul Delaney, "Panthers Weigh New Constitution," *The New York Times*, September 7, 1970, 13. The *Washington Post*, probably parroting the *Times*, later claimed 8,000. *Washington Post*, November 27, 1970, C10.

9   *The New York Times*, September 6, 1970, 40.

10   Kit Kim Holder, *The History of the Black Panther Party, 1966-1972*, doctoral dissertation (University of Massachusetts, 1990), 131.

11   Hilliard, 312.

12   Russell Shoats, unpublished memoir, sent to me by the author.

13   *The Black Panther*, 9/19/70, 11.

14   I develop this concept further in relation to the autonomous movement (or Autonomen) in Europe to indicate that seemingly spontaneous crowd behavior can have a great underlying intelligence. See *The Subversion of Politics: European Social Movements and the Decolonization of Everyday Life*.

15   Hilliard, 313.

16   Present at the planning meeting were representatives of welfare mothers, doctors, lawyers, journalists, students, tenant farmers, greasers from Chicago, Latin Americans, high school students, and gays, as well as concerned individuals. *The Black Panther*, 8/22/70; 8/29/70, 11.

17   "Not to Believe in a New World after Philadelphia is a Dereliction of the Human Spirit," unsigned article, *The Black Panther*, 9/26/70, 19.

18   Ibid., 20.

19   See point 2 of the workshop on the Family and the Rights of Children for one example.

20   "The People and the People Alone were the Motive Power in the Making of the History of the People's Revolutionary Constitutional Convention Plenary Session!" *The Black Panther*, Vol. V No. 11, September 12, 1970. 3.

21   Laurie Asseo, "Study Ties Drug War, Rise in Jailed Women," *Boston Globe*, November 18, 1999, A18; According to the FBI, there were 682,885 arrests for drugs in 1998, 88% for possession not for sale or manufacture, and since Clinton has been president, more than 3, 500,000 people have been arrested for drugs. Chris Bangert, "Marijuana: the hemp of the past and the 'drug' of the present," unpublished paper, Brewster, MA, 1999.

22   Enforced at a cost of billions of dollars per year and tens of thousands of perpetrators of victimless crimes in jail, the present drug policy includes decades of evidence of the CIA's involvement with both the heroin trade in Afghanistan and Southeast Asia and the cocaine trade in Central America—as well as existence of a Contra-connected crack pipeline to Watts (South Central Los Angeles) first reported in the pages of the *San Jose Mercury-News*. As a result of continual generation of mega-profits based on certain drugs' illegal status (witness the price of oregano or baking soda in any supermarket), control of the drug trade by the "government within the government" is a major source of funds for covert operations hidden from public and Congressional oversight. To understand these dynamics, one could begin with Leslie Cockburn, *Out of Control: The Story of the Reagan Administration's Secret War in Nicaragua, the Illegal Arms Pipeline, and the Contra Drug Connection* (New York: Atlantic Monthly Press, 1987). Also see Alfred McCoy, *The Politics of Heroin: CIA Complicity in the Global Drug Trade* (New York: Lawrence Hill, 1991).

23   For more information on these groups, see my book, *The Subversion of Politics*.

24   Nikhil Pal Singh, "The Black Panther Party and the 'Undeveloped Country' of the Left," in Charles Jones, 87. Richard Cambridge lent me the wonderful phrase preceding Singh's quotation.

25   CIA document C00018170, 5 October 1970, p. 1766/2662 at archive.org/stream/OperationCHAOS/CHAOS, accessed 9-21-2016

26   See Lois Hart, "Black Panthers Call a Revolutionary People's Constitutional Convention: A White Lesbian Responds," http://outhistory.org/oldwiki/images/d/do/V1_n5_p15-16.pdf accessed January 7, 2017.

27   Alice Echols, *Daring to Be Bad: Radical Feminism in America 1967-1975* (Minneapolis: University of Minnesota Press, 1989), 222.

28   Rosen, 133.

29   Echols appears not to have seen the final reports, which are an appendix to *Liberation, Imagination and the Black Panther Party* and also available on my website, eroseffect.com.

30   "Speech Delivered at Boston College: November 18, 1970" in *The Huey P. Newton Reader*, 161.

31   See "Intercommunalism: February 1971," in David Hilliard and Donald Weise (eds.), *The Huey P. Newton Reader* (New York: Seven Stories Press, 2002), 188. Anarchist Murray Bookchin's formulation of "libertarian municipalism" in the mid-1980s has much in common with Newton's conception of revolutionary intercommunalism.

32 Ibid., 170-171.

33 https://washingtonspark.wordpress.com/2012/11/25/black-panther-party-revolutionary-peoples-convention-november-1970/ accessed January 7, 2017.

34 Little is known of exactly what happened in the 89 days between Newton's speech in Washington and his televised split with Cleaver. Newton expelled Geronimo Pratt in December, followed by members of the New York Panthers who objected to that unilateral action.

35 See *The Black Panther*, June 13, 1970,14.

36 Hilliard, 308.

37 Hilliard, 317.

38 *Target Zero: Eldridge Cleaver, A Life in Writing*, Kathleen Cleaver, editor, (New York: Palgrave Macmillan, 2006), 264.

Global Insurgencies Since 1968[1]

WHETHER MURDEROUSLY repressed in the US or assimilated in France, movements of 1968 imploded and disappeared—or so it seemed. Vast mobilizations had momentarily posed threats to the system, challenging police powers, wars and racism, yet emergent dreams of freedom beyond patriarchy and capitalism remain unfulfilled. The vision of free societies governed through direct democracy, of a world without hunger or an arms race, without militarized nation-states and arbitrary authorities is unabashedly optimistic, and possibly unattainable. Yet even discussing such a possibility is a legacy of the global imagination that emerged half a century ago.

Imagination is generally regarded as residing in individual minds, yet I use it in reference to collective actions that embody dreams, aspirations and desires. Despite enormous cultural differences between France and the US, millions of people during uprisings in 1968 and 1970 shared aspirations for international solidarity and local self-management. In their everyday lives during trying times of heartfelt fears and burning desires, people acted according to very similar revolutionary norms and values.

Traditionally, revolutions are understood as changes in elites that control existing economic and political structures, but the global imagination of 1968 envisioned destruction of unjust power and creation of mechanisms for autonomous self-determination. Decentralization and self-government were on everyone's lips—whether "revolutionary intercommunalism" or "*autogestion*" (self-management). More than a struggle against inherited injustices and irrational structures, people did not want to take over militarized nation-states but to destroy them.

Obsolescence of the nation-state was not an idea invented out of thin air. It was presented by the actual development of history. Neither were nation-states originally "invented" by clever folks, nor inspired by fancy ideas. They emerged as products of humanity's transformation of ancient villages, city-states, kingdoms, and empires. As congealed forms of power that consolidated after centuries of European wars and economic changes, nation-states were then imposed by force upon the rest of the world.

Looking at contemporary forms of political congregation from 1968 to the present, we find the free assembly continually coming into being, not on anyone's orders or any organization's dictate, but from autonomously determined needs of human beings. That kind of governance has little to do with elections and representative "democracy" managed by professional politicians. In an interview in 1968, when asked what form of democracy he wanted, German activist and SDS member Klaus Meschkat responded, "A form of democracy that is not confined to the heads of states, but is accomplished in all arenas—namely a democracy that is really built from the bottom up. You could say, self-management of producers in all arenas. In the universities, students have seriously demanded democratization of the universities. I believe that such a democratization—including in the factories, the schools, and in all facilities where people work together—is long overdue."[2]

In its internal organization and vision of freedom, the movement strove for popular participation in all aspects of life, including decisions about war and peace, how to run factories and offices, what to teach in universities, as well as what are acceptable patterns of authority in everyday life. The New Left raised the issue of the goal-determination of the whole organization of society, a questioning which—then as now—lies outside established politics, "democratic" or authoritarian, to say nothing about academic theory.

Participatory democracy was central to the global movement's identity from the non-violent 1955 struggle to desegregate buses in Montgomery, Alabama to the armed 1980 Gwangju Uprising. Direct democratic norms spontaneously emerged among Polish workers, Copenhagen's communards in Christiania, San Francisco's Diggers, Yugoslav students, Amsterdam's Provos, and Berkeley's People's Park partisans. As in Gwangju, Asian uprisings contained parallel forms of deliberative democracy during uprisings in 1973 at Thammasat University in Thailand, and in 1990 at both Chiang Kai-shek Square in Taipei and Kathmandu's liberated Patan. Beginning in the late 1970s, Germany's autonomous movement used consensus in general assemblies to make key decisions and sustained itself over several generations of activism. As they developed through militant actions, the Autonomen transformed themselves from civil Luddism into a force targeting the whole system of capitalist patriarchy. The 1999 Seattle protests against the WTO were largely prepared by direct action networks based upon strict principles of consensual decision-making. In the anti-corporate globalization move-ment that grew by leaps and bounds after Seattle, social media lubricated proliferation of participatory ethics. The armed Zapatista uprising involves creating participatory democracy in the everyday life of thousands of people. Rather than trying to seize state power directly, they build counterinstitutions and strive to create a "new person." The Oaxaca Commune of 2006 practiced self-government through open assemblies. Chapters of Black Lives Matter are empowered to take independent initiatives and action, not dictates of a central authority. All of these developments highlight a globally interconnected movement. Given these trajectories, grassroots movements in the twenty-first century will continue to be structured according to a grammar of direct democracy, autonomous self-organization, and international solidarity.

Another dimension of 1968 that remains definitive is an enlarged constituency of revolution—a factor discerned on every continent. Significant participation of the lumpenproletariat among Gwangju's armed resistance fighters, mobilization of the new working class such as Seoul's "necktie brigade" in 1987, and committed protests of Nepalese medical professionals, lawyers, and journalists in 1990 provide empirical instances in Asia. Recent movements rapidly assimilated new technologies like fax machines, cell phones, the Internet, and social media. Magazines like *Adbusters* and *Crimethinc* reactivate New Left playfulness, humor, irony, and autonomous artistic expression as opposition tactics.

In the decades since 1968, most noticeable is the growth in size and deepening of vision of globally synchronized insurgencies.

Global Uprisings after 1968

After 1968, the global movement's capacity for synchronous international coordination has grown by leaps and bounds. Not simply a product of social media and technical innovations, internationally coordinated actions emanate from the accumulation of experiences by generations of popular insurgencies. Each wave builds upon victories and defeats of its predecessors. As history becomes increasingly endowed with direct action by self-conscious human beings, our collective intelligence becomes an ever-more powerful material force. We may regard global insurgencies involving millions of human beings acting in concert with each other as a living organism. Born in 1968 as "the whole world was watching," the infant's development has continued through subsequent uprisings, and has yet to reach maturity. Learning from previous episodes, recent global waves have focused on transformation of the world economic system, not simply on opposing its weapons, wars, debt crises, and ecological devastation. Today there are more people consciously opposed to international capitalism than ever before in history, a potential for action that has yet to be fully realized.

In 1968, no one understood the power of global mobilizations better than the leadership of Vietnam. In February 1972, four years after the Tet Offensive, they organized a worldwide peace offensive at an international conference in Versailles, France. Delegates of anti-war movements from more than eighty countries formulated an internationally coordinated action calendar set to begin around Easter in Vietnam, followed by a wave of demonstrations from East to West—from Moscow to Paris to New York and finally to San Diego, where US President Nixon was due to be nominated for reelection at the Republican National Convention.[3]

To my amazement, Vietnam's Easter Offensive involved, for the first time, tanks among the insurgents' arsenal. Vietnamese forces had disassembled them, carried them south, and then reassembled them without being spotted by the world's most advanced electronic battlefield. Half a world from Versailles, Vietnamese fighters timed deployment of smuggled tanks precisely for the date agreed upon for the start of the international offensive. They liberated the city of Quang Tri, and named it capital of their Provisional Revolutionary Government. The US response was to destroy the city. Scarcely a building's wall was left standing after Nixon employed more explosive power than that used on Hiroshima or Nagasaki in 1945.[4] Despite horrific brutality inflicted against its land and people, Vietnam prevailed, reunified itself, and today is increasingly prosperous. In 2001, Vo Nguyen Giap, military commander of Vietnamese forces who defeated both the French and Americans, summarized the reasons why the Vietnamese were able to win. The anti-war movement inside the United States was a prominent part of his list. For years, Vietnamese leaders cultivated the US movement until it grew into a force with which they were able to coordinate their battlefield tactics.

In 1972, the Vietnamese centrally orchestrated global actions, but no single organization has been responsible for more recent waves of "conscious spontaneity"— for five subsequent episodes of the international Eros effect.

1. The disarmament movement of the early 1980s

Beginning in the fall of 1981, Russian and American plans to install medium-range missiles in Europe meant that a nuclear war could have been fought without the Soviet Union or the US being damaged. A key event came on September 13, when US Secretary of State Alexander Haig visited Berlin. Amid a flurry of attacks on American personnel and bases in West Germany, over 7,000 riot police were needed to guard Haig from at least 50,000 demonstrators in West Berlin. In the ensuing turmoil, hundreds were arrested and over 150 police injured.[5] Less than a month later, on October 10, more than 250,000 people in Bonn marched against the missiles. Within two weeks, similar enormous marches occurred in Paris, London, Brussels, and Rome.

The disarmament movement then spread to the United States. In the spring of 1982, during Ground Zero Week, activists organized events in 150 cities and 500 towns, and the Union of Concerned Scientists sponsored teach-ins at 360 campuses drawing an estimated 350,000 observers.[6] On June 12, at least 800,000 people (some estimates were as high as one million) converged on New York City to express their support for a nuclear-free world. Nuclear freeze initiatives on the ballot in the fall of 1982 won in eight of nine states and in thirty-six of thirty-nine cities and counties. Besides more than 11 million votes (out of a total of 19 million) that the nuclear freeze received in these initiatives, it was approved in 321 city councils, 446 New England town meetings, 63 county councils, and 11 state legislatures.

Besides helping to spark electoral efforts, European street confrontations and mobilizations contributed to the end of the Cold War.

2. The wave of East Asian uprisings from 1986-1992

Leading up to the 1980s, East Asian dictatorships had been in power for decades and seemed unshakable, yet a wave of revolts soon transformed the region. In six years, eight dictatorships were overthrown in nine places in Asia, as uprisings exploded in the Philippines in 1986, South Korea in 1987, Myanmar in 1988, Tibet and China in 1989, Taiwan, Nepal and Bangladesh in 1990, and Thailand in 1992.[7] These insurgencies threw to the wind the common bias that Asians are happier with authoritarian governments than democracy.

After the 1980 Gwangju massacre, the movement suddenly blossomed in 1986, when a massive occupation of public space overthrew dictator Ferdinand Marcos in the Philippines. Overnight, "People Power" became activists' common global identity—cutting across religious, national, and economic divides. East Asia's string of uprisings from 1980 to 1998 had a huge political impact, overthrowing eight more entrenched regimes. South Korea's dictator Chun Doo-hwan was disgraced and compelled to grant direct presidential elections before being imprisoned; Taiwan's forty-year martial law regime was overturned; Burma's mobilized citizenry overthrew two dictators only to see their successors massacre thousands; Nepal's monarchy was made constitutional; military ruler Muhammad Ershad in Bangladesh was forced to step down and eventually sent to prison; Army Chief Suchinda Kraprayoon in Thailand was forced to vacate the office of prime minister; and Indonesia's longtime dictator Suharto was ousted after three decades in power.

These uprisings ushered in greater liberties and new opportunities for citizen participation—as well as for international capital. They also inspired Eastern Europeans to act.

3. Revolts against Soviet regimes in Eastern Europe

We can trace a direct line of key activists who kept alive the dream of the 1968 Prague Spring and helped spread it to many other countries, including Hungary, the U.S.S.R., Bulgaria, Romania, and Poland. Gorbachev himself was directly changed and inspired by Czech activists, who themselves remained engaged in the process of social transformation. If not for the Western European disarmament movement, Gorbachev and other members of the Soviet establishment would never have been prepared to loosen their grip on Eastern European buffer states—their insurance against a new German invasion. After massive protests against the possibility of nuclear war erupted on both sides of what was then called the Iron Curtain, neither buffer states nor short-range missiles were required to provide Soviet leaders with the assurances they needed. Millions of peace advocates taking to the streets helped convince Gorbachev that Western military intervention in Russia was out of the question.

Grassroots movements against Russian domination have a long history. By the 1980s, they had grown into forces nagging Gorbachev and Soviet leaders, but after Asian uprisings brought People Power onto the stage of history, movements in Eastern Europe gained encouragement and inspiration. Without anyone predicting their downfall, Eastern Europe's communist regimes in Hungary, Poland, East Germany, Czechoslovakia, Bulgaria, Yugoslavia, and Romania were all overthrown beginning in 1989. The Soviet Union could not remain aloof and it soon dissolved. The string of uprisings that swept away East Asian dictatorships and East European Soviet regimes in 1989 was "the continuation of 1968."[8]

Although poverty has increased and life expectancy decreased in these countries since the end of Soviet regimes, and despite massive outside interference leading up to the uprisings, people's self-determined will for freedom was the principal factor spurring the movements. Regime openness to change was also a factor. Sadly, this is not the case in the capitalist "democracies."

4. The alterglobalization wave
As the promised peace dividend at the end of the Cold War failed to materialize and global capitalism was strengthened, millions of people "spontaneously" chose to challenge giant corporations and their international institutions—the World Trade Organization, International Monetary Fund, and World Bank.

Without any central group deciding the focus of mobilizations, people themselves chose the global capitalist system as their target. The 1994 Zapatista Uprising was a huge inspiration. On November 30, 1999, Seattle protesters' victory in halting WTO meetings broke new ground when Teamsters and Turtles, workers and ecologists, Lesbian Avengers and Zapatista partisans all converged. The worldwide coordination of protests that day involved actions in dozens of other cities around the world.[9] Indymedia were born across the world.

For years thereafter, whenever elite summits took place, tens of thousands of protesters challenged their right to rule. The global movement reached a new level of synchronicity on February 15, 2003, when the US prepared to attack Iraq for the second time. With no central organization, as many as thirty million people around the world took to the streets on February 15, even though the war had yet to start.[10] People in eight hundred cities and sixty countries mobilized. From Damascus to Athens, Seoul to Sydney, and New York to Buenos Aires, millions constituted a global civil society that *The New York Times* named a "Second Superpower." In London 1.4 million took to the streets in the biggest demonstration in that city's two thousand years of history, and three million people appeared on the streets of Rome.[11]

5. The Arab Spring, Spanish Indignados, Greek anarchists, and Occupy Wall Street

In 2011, thousands of Spanish Indignados occupied major city squares and used direct democracy to fight back against the government's austerity programs. In more than a dozen countries, movements simultaneously appeared. Greek anarchists burned much of downtown Athens to protest their government's acceptance of German-imposed sanctions. After the suicide of vegetable vendor Mohamed Bouazizi, a chain reaction of uprisings spread from Tunisia to Egypt, and then to Yemen, Bahrain, Syria, and Libya. In 14 months, major protests took place in 14 countries in the region. Millions of people went into the streets. Their increasingly sophisticated use of social media (Facebook, Twitter, YouTube, SMS) and the cross-border speed with which the revolt spread offer a glimpse of People Power's potential in the twenty-first century. Disaster was the outcome in Syria, Libya and elsewhere as world powers and entrenched regimes obstinately waged war. In Egypt, divisions between Islamists and democrats abetted the military and its US enablers in installing an even worse dictator than Mubarak.

From humble beginnings in New York on September 17, 2011, Occupy Wall Street took control of public space in more than 1,000 cities. To illustrate the global inter-connection seemingly disparate events, American protesters and Egyptian veterans of Tahrir Square exchanged gifts of pizza deliveries.

These five global uprisings reveal patterns astonishingly similar to the global eruption of the Eros effect in 1968. Most recently, social media has facilitated synchronicity, but movements have been accumulating the capacity for international simultaneity since 1968. The global movement's mobilizations have changed from unconsciously synchronized to a form of "conscious spontaneity" as indicated in the chart below.

Each wave built from its predecessors' victories and defeats. International harmonization from people's intuitive identification with each other in all these cases is noteworthy.

We should expect that future global upsurges will surpass previous waves in cascading global resonance for two reasons: growing grassroots consciousness of the power of street protests and increasing global reach of the world system's impact on millions of people's everyday lives. If the past is any indication, future insurgencies will be increasingly marked by their sudden emergence and proliferation, and encounter the problem of sustainability apparent in Occupy Wall Street, which grew almost overnight but quickly dissipated.

Lessons for the Future

As Marx famously said, we do not make history under conditions we select, "but under circumstances existing already, given and transmitted from the past." It is no accident, therefore, that a decade after Huey P. Newton articulated his vision of "revolutionary intercommunalism," anarchist thinker Murray Bookchin arrived at a similar conclusion—although he named it "libertarian municipalism." Historical conditions have created the possibility of reduced governmental powers and increased power to the people. We already see emergent communal forms in the Gwangju Uprising, in Oaxaca's Commune, and seizures of Taksim and Tahrir Squares. No single vanguard party leads the way forward, but many vanguards, such as Zapatistas, Lesbian Avengers, Occupy Wall Streeters, Indignados, Greek anarchists and Tunisian pirates.

In the 1960s, the Provos, the Orange Free State, and Kabouters in Holland, the Situationists in France, Subversive Aktion in Germany, and the Diggers and Yippies in the United States were successful movement organizations modeled more on aesthetic avant garde groups than on Left parties. Seeking to transform the grammar of people's existence and to change the aesthetic form of life, Yippies threw money onto the floor of the New York Stock Exchange, a Dadaist action that not only succeeded in halting trading as brokers scurried for dollar bills but also brought wide publicity to young people's rejection of the rat race. By running a pig for US President in 1968, Yippies forever changed politicians' images, not only in the United States. As Stew Albert recalled, the Yippies bathed in the global counterculture of the 1960s: "We turned the streets and its objects into unbounded outdoor props for the creation of T.V. images.[12] The Yippies and Provos are but two examples of hundreds of playful episodes of autonomously organized resistance to the forces of seriousness and domination.[13]

Direct actions might be more appropriate vehicles than political parties for transformation of contemporary societies. During May 1968, a small group of older activists suddenly occupied the Sorbonne, creating a central meeting place for the movement that became a haven for dissident workers. The liberated Sorbonne became a direct democratic forum where people from different occupations and classes spoke freely. Soon millions of workers were on strike and France was on the brink of revolution. Exemplary actions by avant-garde groups can be powerful catalysts for instigating larger shifts and movements.

Militant street confrontations can be a crucible for psychic reworking of needs and desires, a living theater with enormous transformative value. After the 2001 Genoa protests against the G-8 (where 200,000 people gathered), one Black Bloc participant told me their experiences "changed me more in a few days than in the preceding years of meetings." Another person called it the "most important experience" of their life. If we accept that consumer culture is a form of cultural colonization, then the Black Bloc's destruction of McDonald's, Nike outlets, and banks are a form of decolonization —a freeing of space from corporate control and creation of autonomous zones not

Global Insurgencies After 1968

Insurgency	Years	Key events	Slogan	Organizations/Inspiration	Outcome
Disarmament Movement	1981-1982	Greenham Common occupation; militant anti-military protests	Peace	Women for Life on Earth; German Autonomen	Russian and US missiles not deployed; expected peace dividend vanishes
Asian Uprisings	1986-1992	Philippines uprising; Tiananmen Square	People Power	1980 Gwangju Uprising; Reform the Armed Forces	8 regimes overthrown in 6 years
Eastern European Regime Changes	1989-1991	Gorbachev announcement; Chernobyl	Peaceful Revolution	Solidarność; Leipzig Monday demonstrations	Eight Soviet regimes overthrown; increasing poverty
Alterglobalization Movements	1998-2003	1999 Seattle; Genoa 2001; Feb. 15, 2003	Another World is Possible	1994 Zapatista Uprising; Direct Action Network	WTO meetings halted and subsequent failure; elite summits confronted
Arab Spring, Occupy Wall Street, Indignados	2011-2012	Tunisian revolution; 14 countries in 14 months	Out With Them All; We are the 99%	Egyptian occupation of Tahrir Square; Spanish Indignados Greek anarchists	Conversation changed to include the 1%; Great Power military intervention and wars in Syria and Libya

controlled by the police. As Fanon long ago discovered, revolutionary force plays an essential role in decolonization movements.[14] The controlled militancy of the Black Bloc is not only a psychic reworking of individuals in the streets, it is also a moment of opposition to the system as a whole. By making concrete people's desires to be free, decades of deadening consumerism and debilitating comfort can be thrown off overnight.

All models inherited from the past need to be questioned today, including the Black Bloc as well as syndicalists' notion of the centrality of the working class. Proletarian dogmatism divides the 99%. The working class has been widely expanded with the enlarged reproduction of capital and the rise of enormous bureaucracies, the expansion of education, and the importance of information to economic development. The universities exist today at the center of production, and as such are critically important to capitalism—as well as to revolutionary movements. The precariat grows by leaps and bounds in the twenty-first century.

No one sector of the population has the capacity to transform society. Building a hegemonic block capable of transforming the entire society requires rethinking our past experiences. African-Americans played a vanguard role in the 1960s, but they alone were not enough. Latinos' 1960s activism was often unrecognized, and they were left out of subsequent commemorations decades later as well.[15] The 2006 Census recorded Latinos as 14.8% of population, more than African Americans. As Carlos Muñoz concluded after a lifetime of activism: "We are not islands unto ourselves. Latino/a liberation is not possible without making possible liberation of all people of all colors, including the millions of whites who are not part of the structure of power."[16] Native Americans, too, are often overlooked, although recent mobilizations at the Standing Rock Sioux reservation indicate their ability to act with unity and to catalyze larger forces. What has only recently been named "the 99%" has long been known as the *minjung* in South Korea. Everyone except the owners of the huge corporations that dominate the economy, the generals in the military and very few at the top united in *minjung* actions and overthrew an entrenched dictatorship.

The New Left in the United States began in a script dictated by reactions to genocide and injustices perpetrated by the system. In the midst of an escalating spiral of repression and resistance, both the Black and anti-war movements reached violent and spectacular culminations. But in 1970, when the movement transcended rebellion and went to the next level: Puerto Ricans ran Lincoln Hospital for the good of the community; students and faculty opened campuses for the needs of all; and in Philadelphia, a multicultural assembly of thousands wrote down their vision for a new society.

Karl Marx expected the dull discipline of factory life to help shape the emancipatory proletariat. We can observe today that the material conditions of consumer society, including its spectacles, like the Olympics and World Cup (despite the nationalist wrappings in which they are packaged), help craft an international identity of humanity. Around the world, people identify more closely with each other than ever before. Diffusion of uprisings via the Eros effect is one robust indication of such a universal identity, as is diffusion of tactical innovations across borders. People today

Detail of a mural on the side of one of the occupied houses in the Hafenstrasse, Hamburg, Germany, 1987.

continue to become increasingly intersectional in their identities, as formerly hard-line divisions of race, gender, and class blur and blend, revealing natural spectrums of identity that bridge formerly imposed and strictly enforced border lines — a signpost that we are awakening to the opportunity for global unity like never before.

While humanity, like Nature (and the Universe as a whole, according to modern physics), moves indelibly toward intermingling and interdependence, the patriarchal Establishment's impetus to isolate people into easily manageable segments of a societal machine continues to pervade ever-deepening aspects of life. The internalization of the imposed value system (which includes misogyny and body-shame, disciplinary "power-over" relationships with oneself, believing one is separate from Nature, the global epidemic of racism, depression and suicide) is one of the weapons used against us, so each person self-maintains inner prisons that perpetuate cycles of domination and colonization. Decolonization and healing of each individual's body, psyche, and spirit are more crucial than ever before and are steps toward the creation of liberated spaces, families, communities, and beyond. Another legacy of the global imagination of 1968 is the subsequent reemergence of healing arts and indigenous wisdom traditions that have everywhere been persecuted in attempt to annihilate the natural intelligence and birthright of every human to be connected, healthy, and empowered.

That major new upheavals will occur is certain; their outcomes remain unclear. New explosions could very well precipitate massive right-wing responses. If there is any chance of the aesthetic transformation of the established world system, such a possibility does not rest on any individual or organization. The self-activity of popular movements, the spontaneous emergence of an escalating spiral of actions, strikes, sit-ins, and insurrectionary councils (the Eros effect), cannot be brought into existence by conspiracies or acts of will. Neither can these forms of struggle be predicted in advance of their appearance, resting as they do upon the accumulation of political knowledge of our species' history.

NOTES

1   First presented at the Global Studies Association conference at UC Berkeley on June 16, 2017.

2   Klaus Meschkat, *Konfrontationen: Streitschriften und Analysen 1958 bis 2010* (Hannover: Offizen, 2010) 210 (my translation).

3   So terrified did Nixon become of approaching protests in San Diego that he sought to deport John Lennon (who had agreed to play there with the Grateful Dead and others) and moved the convention to Miami.

4   I consistently use conservative estimates since I have no intention to appear to be inflating the scope of events in question. At the anti-H demonstration, for example, it was estimated by some that at least 80,000 demonstrators were involved, probably a more accurate number than the police estimate of 50,000. German sources include the *Frankfurter Allgemeine* and *Die Tageszeitung*.

5   *Guardian*, April 28, 1982, p. 5 and November 10, 1982, 7

6   See *Asia's Unknown Uprisings* (Oakland: PM Press, 2011).

7   Giovanni Arrighi, Terence K. Hopkins, and Immanuel Wallerstein, "1989: The Continuation of 1968," in *After the Fall: 1989 and the Future of Freedom*, ed. George Katsiaficas (New York: Routledge, 2001), 35.

8   See Mark Laskey, "The Globalization of Resistance," in *Confronting Capitalism: Dispatches from a Global Movement*, eds. Eddie Yuen, Daniel Burton-Rose and George Katsiaficas (New York: Soft Skull Press, 2004).

9   See Barbara Sauermann, ed., *2/15: The Day the World Said NO to War* (Oakland: AK Press, 2003).

10   David Harvey, *Rebel Cities* (London: Verso, 2013) 116. Harvey's valuable contribution does not seem to comprehend the synchronicity of global protest waves, focused as he is on urban dynamics.

11   Interview, Stew Albert, Portland, Oregon, December 3, 1999.

12   Benjamin Shepherd, *Play, Creativity, and Social Movements: If I Can't Dance, It's Not My Revolution* (New York: Routledge, 2011).

13   Following Marcuse, we must always distinguish between the system's violence that kills tens of thousands daily and the movement's militancy. See *Counterrevolution and Revolt*, 53-55.

14   See Carlos Muñoz Jr., *Youth, Identity, Power: The Chicano Movement* (London: Verso Books, 1989; new edition published in 2007),14-16.

15   Ibid., 233.

Talk at Zuccotti Park[1]

HERE IN THE CHURCH they call Wall Street, money is worshipped as bankers drink the earth's blood and feast on her flesh. War machines of epic proportions are financed – and sent out to kill, maim, and destroy millions of people from Korea to Vietnam to Iraq. Every day that bankers gather, human lives are bought and sold in the name of stocks, bonds, derivatives, and futures. They steal our children's and grandchildren's futures as they profit from their clever machinations.

22 years ago on Earth Day, hundreds of us tried to shut down Wall Street. We were met with overwhelming police force and compelled to withdraw. The next year, we tried again, but once more, our numbers were too small. Now in 2011, the time has come when we've been able (at least temporarily) to overwhelm the forces of order – in fact, police – like the rest of us – have been hurt by the greed of bankers and stockbrokers.

What has changed today? Today there is a global mobilization against the system of death. From the streets of London and Athens, from Tunis to Cairo, people are rising up all over the world. That is what is different today – the global uprising has intensified.

I was at Woodstock; I was in the streets in the 1960s. I have been in the streets ever since. Today, we are in the streets together all over the world. We are not just against a war or any particular government. We are against the global system of corporate rule enforced by murderous wars. No one told us to take to the streets. Everywhere people decided for themselves.

The media seek our leaders in vain. We have no leaders. We are the 99%; we need no 1% to represent us! We, the people of the world, declare: Humanity will no longer tolerate bankers' greed and billionaires' rule. We will no longer sit by while life is a cheap commodity daily bought and sold so they can profit.

They say we have come to destroy; I say we are here to stop destruction. I say we are here to build a new world, a world in which people come before profits.

They say we are dirty; I say they are the ones up to their ears in filth; they are the ones who have polluted the planet, killed off thousands of species and decimated millions of human beings

They say we must leave; I say their time is up. Don't count our days – count theirs.

An Occupy Wall Street demonstrator is arrested by New York City police officers on Nov. 17, 2011. Photo: Mike Segar / Reuters

They say Wall Street is theirs. I say we built the wealth around us. The blood, sweat and tears of generations of working people created this wealth. Bankers and billionaires claim it as theirs. The profits from African slavery, from Chinese laborers building the railroads, from teenage girls like my grandmother toiling in the textile mills of New England built this place. We the people have built this country and created the wealth which billionaires have stolen.

[Call and Response] WHO BUILT WALL STREET? WE BUILT WALL STREET! WHO OWNS WALL STREET? WE OWN WALL STREET! WHOSE STREET? OUR STREET!

They say they will take care of us – they give us violent movies and plastic food.

They say we have all the freedom we want. I say, where is our freedom to live on a planet where we can freely breathe the air? Where is our freedom to live with world peace? Where is our freedom to live as equals? Where is our freedom for everyone to have enough to eat? Where is our freedom for everyone to have a place to live? Where is our freedom to live in safe and loving communities? Where is our freedom to think about our lives in terms other than jobs and money? Where is our freedom to take part in decisions that directly affect us?

Bloodied protester after police attack on Zuccotti Park, November 17, 2011.
Photo: Andrew Burton/Getty Images

I want to talk a moment about the crisis in Greece. For generations, people there struggled under foreign occupation, against Nazi invasion, against poverty. They won the right to retire at 55, to live well and to spend time with their families.

Now the banks and governments of the world are ordering them to work many more years, to spend less time at home and more in factories and offices. WHY? So banks and corporations can make larger profits.

When the prime minister of Greece announced a plan to hold a referendum, for people to vote on whether they would accept the bankers' deal, world leaders practically beat him up in public. According to the BBC of 11/11/11, the proposal for a referendum sparked a "financial and political crisis that threatened to engulf the euro zone."

Is democracy, real democracy, so threatening? Yes, it is! That is why we want to have a direct say in decisions that affect our lives. We will no longer let representatives elected by television and corporate contributions make decisions for us.

We can no longer leave major decisions up to representatives. Even the best of them betrays democracy. Look at Obama. In the first two and a half years he has been in office, Wall Street made billions more than in all the years of Bush II.

The system is the problem. The solution is real democracy, power to the people!

They know the stakes. That is why they are systematically cutting education, laying off tens of thousands of teachers. By dumbing down society, they believe they will leave us unable to see their tricks. They hope to leave us blind. Governments have attacked the BBC, and Canadian Broadcasting; corporations have turned CNN into entertainment news. They think they can rule through our ignorance, but guess what? We are the 99% and we will not be denied!

The time has come when we will no longer stomach their greed, when we can no longer allow a system based upon billionaires' stealing our future. We are sickened by the atrocities of war and daily starvation. More than 30,000 children perish from unnecessary causes every day. That amounts to more annually than the number of Jews, Communists and gays killed by the Nazis in their entire rule!

We will no longer be good Germans while they destroy the earth and compel us to live lives of their making. By occupying Wall Street, we not only stand here together, but we stand together for all time. WE OCCUPY HISTORY.

Historical antecedents to our actions can be found not only in our attempts 22 years ago to shut down Wall Street on Earth Day. Inspiration for the current global upsurge – from the Arab Spring to the Occupy movement – can be found in waves of movements in 1968, when a global series of uprisings resonated in relation to each other, a phenomenon I call the eros effect.

Instances of the spread of movements across borders, involving a process of mutual amplification and synergy, such as the present moment, are significant precursors for future mobilizations. We may not win a final victory today but step-by-step we prepare for that day!

By acting today, we enrich and enlarge this growing global insurgency against the system. Each time we act we build for the next phase in ever-larger waves. One day we will wash clean this bankers' church where billionaires worship greed and sanctify murder. What we are doing today is not the end, but neither is it the beginning. We will be free!

NOTES

1   Given at Zuccotti Park, New York, November 17, 2011.Originally published in *Socialism and Democracy* #59, July 2012: 19-25.

Global Significance of the April 19 Revolution[1]

On the way home from school,
Bullets flew through the air
And blood covered the streets.
The lonely discarded book bag
Was as heavy as it could be.
I know, yes, we all know
Even if Mom and Dad say nothing
Why our brothers and sisters were bleeding.
—ELEMENTARY SCHOOL PUPIL, APRIL, 1960

"The evil influence of political power has swallowed up the people's
right of fair elections, which constitutes a minimum requirement
of democracy. The knavish railings of ignorant despotism have
trampled down all remaining hopes of freedom of speech, assembly,
association, and thought. With an overpowering joy and happiness,
we are now lighting up the torch of freedom. Behold! We are proud
to toll freedom's bell which will shatter the stillness of the Dark Age."
—SOUTH KOREAN STUDENT DECLARATION, APRIL 19, 1960

WHEN PRUNED, some varieties of trees wither and die. Others grow back stronger than ever. The same may be true of peoples. In the twentieth century, Koreans responded to the severity of Japanese colonization and the devastation of the US war by rebuilding with reinvigorated strength. The cunning dialectic of history meant that the Korean War's extermination of old social structures nearly wiped out the *yangban* aristocracy and prepared the grounds for the emergence of the *minjung*—the new subject-object of Korea's history. Comprised of the vast majority of people—excluding very rich landlords and industrialists, former Japanese collaborators, elite military men and police officials—*minjung* became the name for the cross-class social force that overthrew decades of US-backed dictatorships and shaped southern Korea into an egalitarian and prosperous society. The first *minjung* victory came with the overthrow of the Syngman Rhee regime, a globally significant event. First, some background.

Rebuilding Korea After the War

In both North and South Korea, governments drew upon their impressive human resources, especially the civil society produced by 5,000 years of culture, to reconstruct quickly and efficiently after the devastation of one of the world's deadliest conflicts. In three short years, five million lives had been extinguished.[2] US bombs and artillery had destroyed nearly every major city, including every large building in northern Korea.

Despite being reduced to rubble, Korea's recovery made it the envy of many Third World countries wishing to emulate its rise from rags to riches. One of the world's poorest countries in 1953, Korea grew at "miraculous" rates for three decades. Although the North today lags far behind, in 1980, the two Korea's were roughly equivalent economically. South Korea continued its fabulous development from one of the world's poorest countries to one of its wealthiest. Today it is an OECD member with the world's 11th largest economy (in 2015) and a substantial high-tech sector. Her modern infrastructure, efficient public transportation, and safe social spaces make the US and much of Europe seem archaic. Gross National Product (GNP) is more than 100 times what it was in the 1950s—having increased from $200/person to more than $20,000 in 2008 (before falling back slightly during the financial crisis that began that year). As a sign of how the country has grown, the average male today is fully 5 inches taller than his 1961 counterpart.

Although it now seems unlikely, the North may even have outpaced the South in economic growth until 1978. At the time, many people maintained that it was superior in people's satisfaction with government and economy as well.[3] Che Guevara visited North Korea in the mid-1960s and described it as a model for what Cuba should become. Australian journalist Wilfred Burchett and British economist Joan Robinson both admired the North for its progress. Land reform was thoroughgoing and comprehensive, and millions of families still own their own land. Although it retains substantial technological sophistication, a number of factors combined to impoverish the country: decades of confrontation with the US and the ROK in the aftermath of an armistice—not a peace treaty—at the end of the war in 1953; systematic US economic blockade of material goods and financial services; collapse of Pyongyang's main trading partner, the USSR; poor decisions made by high leaders; and devastating droughts and floods. Korea's division into two states—named the "division system" by Paik Nak-chung—enervates the both nations' dynamism and eats away at their souls. In both North and South, the existence of an "enemy" regime claiming the right to rule the entire peninsula means limited political freedom and enormous sacrifices. Precious resources are diverted into unnecessary military expenditures. In both Pyongyang and Seoul, paranoia, hatred, and fear run wild, and an elusive sense of national security poisons government decisions.

During the Cold War, as in West Berlin and Taiwan, massive US aid was distributed to build South Korea into a model for the "superiority" of American capitalism (as opposed to communism). In Korea, US benefactors maintained elite rule by promoting former Japanese collaborators into high positions of power in the American imperial order. The result was a harshly regulated system that strictly compelled millions of people to decades of backbreaking toil in exchange for meager rewards. Aided by the US, the South Korean economy grew at astonishing rates, with GNP increasing an average of 9% or better from the 1960s into the mid-1990s. Millions of laborers paid for economic progress through a world record-setting industrial accident rate, a six or even seven-day workweek, and a centralized decision-making apparatus that restricted political inputs to a few men's ideas.

In this context, Syngman Rhee thrived, able to convince his supporters in the US to grant him enormous sums of money and considerable leeway as the "frontline" of their Cold War. In 1953, foreign assistance was well over 14% of GNP (reaching 22.9% in 1957). Throughout all of Rhee's tenure as President, foreign aid was a substantial portion of the total government budget.[4] Between 1953 and 1963, the ROK was the beneficiary of what Alice Amsden called a "unique" amount of foreign aid as the US sustained three-fourths of South Korea's total investment.[5] By the end of the 1950s, five-sixths of all economic inputs were from direct US grants. Dependence on America meant that in 1961, more than half of all consumer goods were provided by US aid.[6] Even though the US annually provided some $100/capita to the country, corruption was rampant, and thousands of people scavenged daily meals in garbage dumps. Extreme poverty compelled many others to work in dangerous and dirty jobs. US Army bases nightly brought in truckloads of young Korean women to service the soldiers.

While Rhee relied on the US for his base of support, behind American largesse and military might stood the ROK armed forces—at 600,000 men, the country's most powerful institution. Rhee had ceded sovereign control of the military to the US, but it didn't deter his machinations in power. Rhee increasingly ruled with an iron fist, and his murderous grip on power turned thousands of patriotic citizens into victims of persecution. Running on a platform of peaceful reunification of Korea, moderate politician Cho Pong-am received two million votes in the 1956 election as the candidate of the Progressive Party. Subsequently accused of being a North Korean spy, Cho was arrested in 1958 and executed in 1959.

Rhee and his team of advisors directed industry to produce for the domestic market in line with their policy of import-substitution. Using the model of Japanese *zaibatsu*, they organized family-owned conglomerates (like Hyundai, Daewoo, and Samsung) at the core of the country's economy, a legacy still central to South Korea's industrial and financial organization. As economic development between 1948 and

1960 demanded more off-line workers, the number of colleges in Korea doubled (from 31 to 62), and the number of college students nearly trebled (from 24,000 to 97,819), with a great proportion of students concentrated in Seoul. Although Korea's GNP was less than one-tenth of England's, it had more college students per capita, and Seoul was "one of the largest educational centers in the world."[7] The country's secondary schools experienced a similar surge in growth. In August 1959, an autonomous labor federation formed—the Korea Trade Union Council—which explicitly opposed the yellow FKTU's ties to government. The new democratic union signed up more than 160,000 workers in its first year.[8]

4.19: Students Overthrow Syngman Rhee

Rhee's disdain for ordinary Koreans finally became his undoing. In elections on March 15, 1960, Rhee and his cronies shamelessly stuffed ballot boxes or stole them from neighborhoods known to be opposition strongholds. When the official vote tally was announced, Rhee claimed an overwhelming mandate for himself and for his notoriously corrupt vice-presidential candidate, Lee Ki-bung. Weeks before citizens went to the polls, many people suspected that the results had already been decided. In Daegu on February 28, high schools students had gone into the streets to warn of Rhee's plot to extend his rule, and 120 people had been arrested. As soon as the election results were announced on the evening of March 15, a contingent of 10,000 students led a huge march in Masan, which converged on city hall and demanded fresh elections. Police immediately attacked, killing 8 students and wounding 123 more. As he always did, Rhee called the protests "communist inspired." Before the situation spiraled out of control, US commanding General Carter Magruder approved Rhee's request to send elite Korean marines to quiet the citizenry. Undeterred by the army, similar outbursts occurred in Pohang, Daejon, Suwon, Osan, and Jeonju. Organized groups of professors, journalists, and lawyers made public statements in support of protesting students.

On April 11, a fisherman discovered the bloated body of 16-year-old Kim Ju-yol in the sea near Masan. The young teenager from Namwon, a freshman at a Masan commercial high school, had been hit in the eye by a tear gas canister. Police claimed he was a communist, a charge "proven" by papers linking him to North Korea found in his pockets (which many people believed had been planted). Both the murder and the cover-up detonated a new explosion of protests. Immediately, 40,000 protesters gathered to view Kim's corpse, and by evening, an estimated 140,000 people had arrived.[9] As people refused to remain quiet, once again police resorted to force and killed many demonstrators. Sporadic mobilizations by high school students in several provinces refused to let the Rhee regime continue its unreasonable use of violence to impose its will.

In his arrogance, Rhee continued to believe unbridled force would convince Koreans to submit. On April 18, gangsters in Seoul attacked a protest by Korea University students near Dongdaemun. Using chains and metal rods, members of the Anti-Communist Youth Corps mercilessly beat unarmed students. Police witnessed the beating of students but did nothing to stop it. The chief of presidential security had summoned the goons to stop the protests.[10] In response to the attack, students from seven Seoul universities called for an all-out mobilization the next day. On April 19, thousands of students took to the streets of Seoul. By the time they approached the presidential palace, their ranks had swelled to as many as 100,000 people.[11] For the first time, students found massive support for their demonstrations among the general public. During the march, some students chanted, "Let us destroy communism by getting our democracy right!"[12] Here was an early indication of what would become the global New Left's opposition to dictatorships of both the communist and capitalist variety, of a gut-oriented intuition of freedom that cared little for the ideology of governments that unnecessarily limited it.[13]

At the presidential palace, the massive crowd demanded to see Rhee. They were answered when palace guards opened fire, killing at least 20 people in the first volley. Remarkably, students fought back, refusing to be intimidated by clubs and guns. They regrouped and spontaneously formed small action teams that destroyed the headquarters building of Rhee's Liberal Party as well as that of the Anticommunist Youth League, the editorial offices of the government newspaper, and five police substations.[14] Protesters burned houses belonging to Rhee's high-ranking subordinates, wrecked City Hall, and attacked dozens of other buildings linked to Rhee and his party.

Throughout the country, thousands of high school students mobilized, especially in Incheon, Jeonju, Mokpo, and Daegu. In Gwangju on April 19, high school students demanding new elections surged downtown. Organizers sent runners to visit every school in the city, and as soon as the initial protests occurred, the number of people swelled to 15,000—1,500 of whom were from Chosun High School.[15] Police and firemen fired water laced with red dye but failed to disperse demonstrators. Unpaved roads provided plenty of rocks for ammunition to fight back. Throughout the night, battles continued as protesters controlled the streets. In Busan, protesters set fire to many government buildings.

Before the violence ended, gunfire on "Bloody Tuesday" had claimed dozens of lives.[16] In Seoul alone, more than 100 people were killed and over 1,000 wounded. Ultimately, martial law was declared, the army was called out, and a 10 p.m. curfew was strictly enforced. Remarkably, the army did not open fire. General Song Yo-chan ordered his troops not to shoot, and soldiers and students reportedly shouted to each other, "We are brothers!"

The next day college students again massively mobilized. For seven consecutive days, there were major demonstrations in Seoul. On April 24, as the entire country appeared to reject the "honesty" of the elections, Vice-President elect Lee Ki-bung publicly declared he would not accept office. He and his family subsequently committed suicide. On April 25, some 258 university professors gathered at Seoul National University and issued a message proclaiming that, "Student Demonstrations are the Expression of Justice!" They marched through the city to demand Rhee's resignation as well as those of the nation's Chief Justice and speaker of the National Assembly. By the time they arrived at the National Assembly, more than 100,000 people were with them, and people listened intently as professors announced a 15-point declaration. This event was significant for many reasons, not least because it marked the first time in Korean history that professors as a group had entered the struggle against tyranny. The spontaneous gathering of so many people was unprecedented in a society where dictatorships had ruled for so long. Higher education in Korea had expanded, but there were fewer than 100,000 college students in the entire country and scarcely more than a quarter million in high schools, numbers that fail to account for central role of universities and high schools in overthrowing the government.[17] Positioned centrally in the cities and afforded great respect in the world's most Confucian society, students and teachers detonated a widespread social explosion.

People took full advantage of their newly found freedom to act—space created by the sacrifice of so many lives. After the gathering at the National Assembly, some 50,000 protesters attacked Vice-President Lee Ki-bung's house. Placing his elaborate furnishings on the street to be photographed, people proceeded to burn them before demolishing the house.[18] Their message was clear: not only must Rhee go, so must his entire administration. Evidently, the massive outpouring of anti-government sentiment and the capacity of people to act despite deadly police violence convinced the US to support Rhee's departure. A note delivered to the ROK embassy in Washington made clear his American handlers thought it was time for him to go. Rhee would never have been able to become President without US backing, nor was he able to remain in power without American support. On Friday, April 26, the US ambassador and General Magruder personally paid Rhee a visit to insure that he would to step down. They offered him the same means of transportation back to the US that had been provided him in 1945 to bring him to Korea: a US military aircraft. Shortly after the American officials had left, Rhee announced his resignation and boarded a US military plane bound for Hawaii.

Immediately, joyful gatherings suddenly cropped up everywhere. Thousands of arrested students were released, and police withdrew from public view. Students now

Jubilation when the army came over to the revolution.

directed traffic on city streets and took over many police stations. All over the country, as they swept the cities clean of the debris left behind from their hard-won victory, young people proudly stepped into positions of authority amid public acclaim. With the army in the streets, raucous celebrations transpired—spontaneous and joyful expressions of hope for the future of democracy. The success of the uprising in winning power surprised everyone—most of all those who had been at the center of organizing it.

Decades of pent-up grievances were suddenly possible to discuss in public. As one observer described it: "The April revolution was a giant social revolt…The students… touched off a general revolt in society. The people revolted against the government. The young revolted against the old. In many schools, students revolted against their teachers. In some government ministries, junior civil servants revolted against senior civil servants. In a more serious vein, some eight lieutenant colonels revolted against some generals, requesting that the army be cleared of corrupt elements."[19]

When the dead were identified and totaled, they numbered 186.[20] At least 46 of those people were high school students (7th to 12th grades), and the vast majority of those killed were less than 30 years old. An additional 6,000 people had been injured.

Age of People Killed in the April Uprising, 1960

Age	Number
15 or younger	11
15-19	92
20-24	49
25-29	11
30 or over	17
Unknown	6
TOTAL	186

Source: So Baek O (editor), *Uriga koroon kil* (*The Path of Our Life*) (Seoul: 1962) p. 341 from Han, "Student Activism," p. 159.

Evidently, a new generation had moved to the center of Korean political life. In 1960, more than half of all South Koreans were 19 years old or younger. In a highly literate society, youth's newly found powers derived from more than their numbers: Confucian ethics accorded students great respect as well as a felt need among ordinary citizens to protect them. Concentrated on campuses with room to reflect amid the idealism of youth, students' passionate involvement in politics would soon sweep the world in the global revolt of 1968.

The 1960 victory won by Korean students inspired others around the world. Newspapers reported that protesting students in Turkey bowed their heads to show respect to their Korean counterparts. US activist Tom Hayden, one of the main authors of the Port Huron Statement, the founding document of Students for a Democratic Society (SDS), remembered his feelings when he first heard the news from Seoul: "I was exhilarated when I saw young people our age overthrow the dictator Syngman Rhee. Through that movement, I learned the history of the Cold War for the first time. Those events challenged our naïve belief that our parents were fighting for a free world. I can tell you that movement helped inspire SNCC [the Student Nonviolent Coordinating Committee] and the black movement in the South. Two days after Syngman Rhee's forced resignation, SDS held its first meeting."[21]

Japanese colonialism and the Korean War had destroyed much of the traditional Left. The 419 Movement was spontaneously democratic and anti-dictatorial. Korean students clearly expressed political affinity with the global New Left when they articulated their aspirations by chanting, "Democracy in Politics, Equality in Economy." The professors who led the April 25 demonstration were also harbingers of new social forces that would appear globally in struggles during the 1960s. Dubbed the "new working class" by Serge Mallet, proletarianized professionals and white-collar employees increasingly played a significant role in social movements. As an especially privileged sector, professors were easily co-opted by being handed plum positions and held in high status.[22] Significantly, farmers, industrial workers, and rural dwellers were marginal to the national movement that overthrew Rhee. Indications of the new social landscape constructed after the Korean War's devastation also included the increased capacity of ordinary people to organize themselves without central control, to rise up against entrenched power and overthrow it. The absence of entrenched opposition leadership may have facilitated the movement's success. As Sungjoo Han understood:

> "…the demonstrating students and masses did not have an organized leadership of their own. Although leaders of the Democratic Party later claimed that they were largely responsible for touching off the protest movements, their actual leadership within the demonstrating masses was not present. Ironically, this absence of clearly definable leadership may have contributed to the early abdication of Syngman Rhee."[23]

Outside his coterie of pro-American Koreans, Rhee had no real base of support. When the time came to rally around him, no one did, not even the US—which repeatedly sacrifices discredited regimes (Trujillo, Diem, and Pinochet) to install new governments that continue to defend American interests while dissipating revolutionary upsurges.

Social Movements in the Second Republic

On July 29, 1960, a few scant months after the student revolution, elections swept the Democratic Party into the leadership of the Second Republic. Emboldened by their newfound power, students grew increasingly visionary and militant. Student power was so strong, they even organized talks aimed at reunification with North Korean students at Panmunjom. Alongside demands like lower tuition and a cultural break with their elders, students continued to lead the entire society.

The uprising's success led to an upsurge of movements among many different sectors of the population and ushered in a vibrant new realm of possibilities. After April 19, students and ordinary citizens were energized as never before. Decades later, activist Kim Gun-tae explained that, "Since 1960, street protests became a tradition in Korea politics."[24] Street mobilizations remain to this day significant vehicles of political participation in South Korea. In the first year after Rhee was sent home to the US, some 2,000 demonstrations involved around a million persons. The military would later release an estimate that an average of 3,900 people took to Seoul's streets every day. Many protests demanded stiffer penalties for ex-Rhee officials, reunification of the country, and a declaration of permanent neutrality.[25]

Hundreds of labor disputes suddenly occurred, involving 340,000 workers. Wage increases of 15% to 50% were won, and 315 new unions created, including among teachers, bank employees, and journalists.[26] On June 14, 1960, about 400 Samsung workers went on a hunger strike, demanding the reinstatement of 152 fired colleagues, an end to an illegal lockout by Samsung, and for the company to respect existing law.[27] On July 4, police were called in to evict the sit-in, and the struggle ended without success. To this day, Samsung still has no union. The country's unemployment rate stood at 28%, a major problem for 51,000 demobilized soldiers and tens of thousands of college students who finished their studies at the end of 1960.

Buoyed by their newly found powers, students organized themselves into a force that sought to alter Korea's division into two states. The Student Federation for National Unification and left-wing trade unions together demanded immediate reunification. Simultaneously, a coalition of 17 parties and organizations campaigned against the US-Korea economic accord. Seeking to initiate direct discussions with their counterparts in North Korea aimed at reunifying the country, students set a date for a joint meeting, and a large rally in Seoul called on the government to support the talks. On October 8, 1960, after many defendants charged with the April shootings were found not guilty in the absence of a special law, students who had been wounded during the uprising occupied the empty National Assembly building.[28]

Led by the Democratic Party after the July 29 general elections, the new Chang Myon government had immediately instituted freedom of the press. The second republic's bicameral legislature functioned with greatly reduced presidential powers. Under the new regime, hundreds of police officials who had remained since the days of Japanese occupation were fired, and police chiefs who had ordered their men to open fire of unarmed protesters were punished. Nonetheless, most of Rhee's mid-level officials remained, and Chang showed little interest in qualitatively changing the institutions. Although he initiated an investigation of the massacre on Jeju, Chang closely consulted the US, especially CIA station chief Peer de Silva, on nearly all major decisions.[29] At the same time as protesters continued to call for even more extensive punishment of politicians and police authorities responsible for the use of violence against the movement, the new government came under increasing pressure to clamp down.

People continued to struggle for democracy. On November 28, sixty members of the Student Christian Federation were arrested in the Christian Broadcast System building. When a new repressive law was proposed, a significant all night protest remained in the streets on March 22, 1961. Uprisings are crucibles that temper activists, hardening them to lead the next phase of struggles. The 1960 revolution transformed Christians from ardent supporters of the regime—as they had been under Rhee—to some of the most important opponents of dictatorship. As one Christian publication put it, "The April 19th Student Revolution was the moment of repentance for the Korean Church."[30] The National Council of Churches was even more explicit: "The church finally opened its eyes to see what was going on, and opened windows to see the dawn of a new day...The nation has achieved a revolution, fought against tyranny...The Christian papers which were so eloquent until the eve of the revolution have suddenly turned into silence."[31]

Students' euphoric belief in their autonomous power after they had overthrown Rhee led them to intensify their initiative to reunify the country. They proposed a joint North-South conference that would create a confederation whose highest body would be composed of an equal number of representatives from North and South, an idea personally considered by Kim Il-sung. For Koreans, with tens of thousands of families divided by the nation's partition, reunification was a heaven-sent prospect, but not for the US, whose next war against communism, this time in Vietnam, was just beginning.

Four days before the scheduled conference in Panmunjom, a small coterie of US-backed officers, with leading roles played by Park Chung-hee and other former members of the Japanese army, seized control of the government.[32] As the coup d'état unfolded at midnight on May 16, 1961, the army moved into cities with force. At 3:30 a.m., Chung Myon telephoned Magruder for US troops to put down the coup, but the US refused the government's request. The next day, although the US retained operational control of South Korea's military, Park moved two full divisions into Seoul without Magruder's formal approval. Defenders of the US maintain there is no known evidence of prior US knowledge of the coup, but recently released CIA documents indicate that the United States had advance knowledge of Park Chung-hee's coup d'état.[33] Moreover, James Hausman (leader of the US campaign to suppress the Yeosun Insurrection in 1948 and self-described "father of the South Korean Army") claimed to have had advance knowledge.[34] Professor Carlos Muñoz of UC Berkeley, who worked in the Intelligence (G2) section of the Korean Military Advisory Group (KMAG) in 1961, also told me he had advance knowledge of the coup. Twenty years after the coup, Hausman was honored by US military commander General John Wickham with a "Meritorious Civilian Service Award." The citation carried the following words: "Through his close personal relationship with President Park, he was able to persuade the military junta to take actions which eased the apprehensions of US officials, and his comprehensive understanding of the background and aspirations of newly emerged military leadership enabled him to convince US officials at a national level that under this leadership, the Republic of Korea would move forward in a manner that would enhance the United States position in Asia."[35] Remembering that Hausman had personally intervened with Rhee to save Park's life in 1948, we can only guess how much Park was indebted to him in 1961.

The day after the coup, a "revolutionary committee" of 30 generals and colonels pledged to return power to civilians. But in their first acts, coup leaders arrested 2,000 political leaders, including Chang Myon. They quickly purged more than 13,000 government officials and armed forces officers, and closed 49 of Seoul's 64 newspapers.[36] Cracking down on freewheeling urban youth culture, they used stiff penalties, corporeal punishment, haircuts, and imprisonment to impose cultural conformity. The day after Park's coup, the investigators of the 1948 Jeju massacre were arrested. The dictatorship clamped down on all investigations of past atrocities, so any public hint of the Jeju massacre would have to wait until 1978 when Hyun Ki-Young published his short story, "Aunt Suni."[37] Only in 1999 would the US slaughter of hundreds of unarmed refugees at No Gun Ri in 1950 first be reported. Nearly half a century would pass before dozens of such massacres would become publicly known.

Looking Back at the April 19 Revolution: Its Continuing Impact

Korean culture continually returns to yin and yang, to the dialectical unity of opposites. In its early history, three consecutive dynasties lasted nearly half a millennium each, yet in the twentieth century, Korea has an unmatched and unique history of grassroots social movements, uprisings and social upheavals.

Indigenous Korean political developments in the first half of the twentieth century were stunted by Japanese colonialism, after which the Korean War uprooted and destroyed long-standing social relationships. The modern culture that emerged from colonialism and war contains one of the world's most robustly civil societies, a resource that makes possible political transformations with a minimum of bloodshed. The April 19 revolution created a lasting legacy. It bequeathed to Koreans a means of expressing the people's will through massive and militant protests that subsequently helped to make possible the 1980 Gwangju People's Uprising, the 1987 June Uprising and workers' rebellion, the 1997 strike against neoliberalism, and the 2008 candlelight protests against a lopsided American beef treaty. Most recently, massive protests against the Park Gun-hye presidency led to her impeachment by the National Assembly.

By preserving essential documents and artifacts from the 1960 revolution, this archive will help to ensure that future generations will be able to look back upon the social conditions, popular ideas and emotions that produced one of the world's first examples of what is today called People Power. The important new ground broken by the April 19 revolution is significant not only for Koreans but for all the peoples of the world.

In the twenty-first century, social media make possible unprecedented opportunities for citizens whose voices have often gone unheard to make public their needs and desires. No one should overestimate the world-historical possibilities opened by procedures for translating grassroots aspirations into political change without military force. For far too long, humanity has suffered murder, torture and abuse at the hands of those who would maintain unjust power. For generations to come, this archive will help insure that Korea's April 19 revolution will remain a shining beacon of people's enduring need for freedom.

NOTES

1   Originally presented in the South Korean National Assembly building, Seoul, December 2016.

2   Dong-Choon Kim, *Der Korea-Krieg und die Gesellschaft* (Munster: Wesphalisches Dampfboot, 2000) estimates 1.3 million South Korean soldiers and civilians killed, 2.5 million North Koreans, an additional 650,000 refugees from the North who were killed in the South, and in addition, Chinese and American troops.

3   Published CIA data reported that until 1978, North Korea was ahead of South Korea in GDP per capita.

4   *History of Korean Finance for 40 Years* (Seoul: KDI, 1991) p. 157.

5   Alice H. Amsden, *Asia's Next Giant: South Korea and Later Industrialization* (New York: Oxford University Press, 1989) p.43; Lars Lindstrom, *Accumulation, Regulation, and Political Struggles: Manufacturing Workers in South Korea* (Stockholm: Stockholm Studies in Politics, 1993) p. 37.

6   Christian Institute for the Study of Justice and Development, *Lost Victory: An Overview of the Korean People's Struggle for Democracy in 1987* (Seoul: Minjungsa, 1988) p. 13.

7   Gregory Henderson, *Korea: Politics of the Vortex* (Cambridge: Harvard University Press, 1968) p. 170.

8   Sunhyuk Kim, *The Politics of Democratization in Korea: The Role of Civil Society* (Pittsburgh: University of Pittsburgh Press, 2000) p. 34.

9   Interview with Paik Han-gi, Masan, October 29, 2009.

10 Sungjoo Han, *The Failure of Democracy in South Korea* (Berkeley: UC Press, 1974) p. 29; Henderson, p. 175.

11 Ingeborg Göthel, *Geschichte Südkoreas* (Berlin: Deutscher Verlag der Wissenschaften, 1988) p. 73, and Mi Park, *Democracy and Social Change: A History of South Korean Student Movements, 1980-2000* (Bern: Peter Lang, 2008) p. 65.

12 Namhee Lee, *The Making of Minjung: Democracy and the Politics of Representation in South Korea* (Ithaca: Cornell University Press, 2007) p. 106.

13 See my book, *The Imagination of the New Left: A Global Analysis of 1968* (Boston: South End Press, 1987), especially Chapter 2.

14 Ingeborg Göthel, p. 73.

15 Interview with Kim Ye-Hyan, 4.19 Institute, Seoul, December 13, 2001.

16 Sungjoo Han, "Student Activism: A Comparison Between the 1960 Uprising and the 1971 Protest Movement," in Chong Lim Kim (ed.), *Political Participation in Korea: Democracy, Mobilization, and Stability* (Santa Barbara: Clio Books, 1980) p. 145.

17 Kang Man-gil, *A History of Contemporary Korea* (Kent, UK: Global Oriental, 2005) p. 318.

18 Mi Park, p. 65.

19 H.B. Lee, *Korea: Time, Change, and Administration* (Hawaii: East-West Center, 1968) p. 119, as quoted in Alice H. Amsden, *Asia's Next Giant: South Korea and Later Industrialization* (New York: Oxford University Press, 1989) p.42.

20   See Sungjoo Han, "Student Activism" p. 159; Interview with Kim Ye-Hyan, 419 Institute, Seoul, December 13, 2001. Other reports provide a variety of figures: Lee Chae-Jin reports 115 killed and 730 injured p. 43; Wickham claims 142 students were killed, p. 231; Gleysteen asserts that when students marched on Rhee's residence to protest the rigged elections, some 200 were killed by his guards, p. 9; Ingeborg Göthel reports 183 dead and 6,259 wounded, *Geschichte Südkoreas*, p. 76; finally a church source tells us 185 students or citizens were killed. See *Lost Victory*, p. 14.

21   Tom Hayden made these remarks in Gwangju during a speech at the International Conference Commemorating the 30th Anniversary of the Gwangju Uprising in May 2010.

22   Recent evidence indicates the possibility of collaboration between protesting professors and the US Embassy.

23   Han, *The Failure of Democracy in South Korea*, p. 32.

24   Interview with Kim Gun-tae, Seoul, August 2, 2008.

25   Wonmo Dong, "University Students in South Korean Politics: Patterns of Radicalization in the 1980's," *Journal of International Affairs*, Vol. 40 No. 2 (Winter 1987) p. 234; Henderson, p. 179.

26   Koo, p. 135; Han, *The Failure of Democracy in South Korea*, pp. 178-193; Ingeborg Göthel counted 485 disputes with 340,000 participants. See p. 77.

27   Dae-oup Chang, editor, *Labor in Globalising Asian Corporations: A Portrait of Struggle* (Hong Kong: Asia Monitor Resource Center, 2006) p. 11.

28   Kang Man-gil, p. 202. Also see Martin Hart-Landsberg, *The Rush to Development: Economic Change and Political Struggle in South Korea* (New York: Monthly Review Press, 1993) p. 135.

29   Cumings, *Korea's Place in the Sun*, p. 344.

30   *Democratization Movement and the Christian Church in Korea during the 1970s* (Seoul: 1985) p. 23.

31   *Korean Church: History and Activities* (Seoul: National Council of Churches in Korea, 1990) p. 32.

32   Cumings, 1-175.

33   In 2010, I filed a Freedom of Information Act request for documents related to the coup (as well as to Park's 1979 assassination). On August 19, 2016, the CIA released documents that were only partially redacted. Unredacted portions clearly indicate advance US knowledge of both the coup and assassination. Researcher An Chi Yong's web site also contains such information: http://andocu.tistory.com/

34   Cumings, *Korea's Place in the Sun*, p. 349.

35   Harvard University Yenching Institute, Hausman archive, Box 7, p. 3 of the citation.

36   Cumings, *Korea's Place in the Sun*, p. 351.

37   Hyun Ki-Young, *Aunt Suni* (Seoul: Kak Press, 2008) translated by Song Jong Do.

Remembering the Kwangju Uprising[*1]

ARCHIMEDES ONCE declared, "Give me a fixed point and I can move the earth." Historically speaking, the Kwangju people's uprising of 1980 is such a fixed point. It was the pivot around which dictatorship was transformed into democracy in South Korea. Twenty years afterwards, its energy resonates strongly across the world. Among other things, its history provides both a glimpse of the free society of the future and a sober and realistic assessment of the role of the US government and its allies in Asia.

The most important dimensions of the Kwangju uprising are its affirmation of human dignity and prefiguration of a free society. Kwangju has a meaning in Korean history that can only be compared to that of the Paris Commune in French history, and of the battleship Potemkin in Russian history. Like the Paris Commune, the people of Kwangju spontaneously rose up and governed themselves until they were brutally suppressed by indigenous military forces abetted by an outside power. And like the battleship Potemkin, the people of Kwangju have repeatedly signaled the advent of revolution in Korea—from the 1894 Tonghak rebellion and the 1929 student revolt to the 1980 uprising.

Forged in the sacrifices of thousands, the mythical power of the Kwangju people's uprising was tempered in the first five years after 1980, when the dictatorship tried to cover up its massacre of as many as 2000 people. Even after the Kwangju Commune had been ruthlessly crushed, the news of the uprising was so subversive that the military burned an unknown number of corpses, dumped others into unmarked graves, and destroyed its own records. To prevent word of the uprising from being spoken publicly, thousands of people were arrested, and hundreds tortured as the military tried to suppress even a whisper of its murders.[2] In 1985, thousands of copies of the first book about the Kwangju uprising, Lee Jae-eui's classic history (translated into English as *Kwangju Diary: Beyond Death, Beyond the Darkness of the Age*[3]), were confiscated and its publisher and suspected author arrested. Korean civil society is so strong that when the truth about the military's brutal killing of so many of its own citizens and subsequent suppression of the facts finally became known, the government quickly fell. As Lee Jae-eui put it: "The reason why the Korean people could overcome that

---

*In 2000, when the Korean government instituted new rules for Romanization, Kwangju became Gwangju.

terrible violence so quickly in 1987 was because of Kwangju's resistance."[4] President Chun Doo Hwan and his military government may have won the battle of May 1980, but the democracy movement won the war—seven long years later when the Minjung movement ousted the military dictatorship.

Like the Paris Commune and the battleship Potemkin, Kwangju's historical significance is international, not simply Korean (or French or Russian). Its meaning and lessons apply equally well to East and West, North and South. The 1980 people's uprising, like these earlier symbols of revolution, has already had worldwide repercussions. As a symbol of struggle, Kwangju has inspired others to act. As an example of ordinary people taking power into their own hands, it was (and is) a precursor of events to follow. In 1996, activist Sanjeewa Liyanage of Hong Kong expressed this dimension of the uprising when he wrote:

> The "power of people" is so strong that it just cannot be destroyed by violent suppressive means. Such power, from the people, spreads a spirit that will last for generations. Kwangju is a city full of that "people power." What happened in 1980, in Kwangju, was not just an isolated incident. It has brought new light and hope to many people who are still suffering from brutally oppressive regimes and military-led governments…the strength and will of people of Kwangju to carry on their agitative actions was very impressive…Today many look up to them, paying tribute to that they have achieved…I was inspired by their courage and spirit. Kwangju remains a unique sign that symbolizes a people's power that cannot be suppressed. That sign is a flame of hope for many others…[5]

In this paper, I seek to understand the power of the people's uprising of 1980 in three dimensions:

- the capacity for self-government
- the organic solidarity of the participants
- the international significance of the uprising

The Capacity for Self-Government

As monumental as the courage and bravery of the people in Kwangju were, their capacity for self-government is the defining hallmark of their revolt. In my view, it is the single most remarkable aspect of the uprising. The capacity for self-organization that emerged spontaneously, first in the heat of the battle and later in the governing of the city and the final resistance when the military counterattacked, is mind expanding. In the latter part of the twentieth century, high rates of literacy, the mass media, and universal education (which in Korea includes military training for every man) have forged a capacity in millions of people to govern themselves far more wisely than the tiny elites all too often ensconced in powerful positions. We can observe this spontaneous capacity for self-government in the events of the uprising.

On May 15, 1980, one million people participated in a student demonstration in Seoul, a huge outpouring of sentiment against the dictatorship. While many people believed the time to overthrow the dictatorship had come, student leaders, flush with their success and under pressure from liberal politicians, decided to suspend actions scheduled for the 17th and 18th in the hopes that the government might end martial law. Instead the military clamped down, sending thousands of combat troops to all the large cities, especially to Kwangju. On May 14, students there at Chonnam National University had broken through the riot police cordon enveloping their campus. When they reached the city, many citizens supported their demonstration for democracy. On May 16, when the rest of South Korea was quiet, students from nine universities in Kwangju rallied at Province Hall Square, renamed it "Democracy Square," and then marched through the city in a torchlight procession. The next night, military intelligence personnel and police raided homes of activists across the city, arresting the leadership of the movement. Those leaders not picked up went into hiding. Already at least 26 of the movement's national leaders (including Kim Dae Jung) had been rounded up. According to one observer: "The head of the movement was paralyzed."[6] Another wrote that the "leading body of the students' movement was in a state of paralysis."[7] Nonetheless the very next morning, students spontaneously organized themselves— first by the hundreds and then by the thousands—to march in protest of the occupation of their city by police and freshly arrived units of the army.

With US approval, the government had released from the front lines of the DMZ some of its most seasoned paratroopers, the same army units that had crushed movements in Pusan and Masan a year earlier. Once these troops reached Kwangju, they terrorized the population in unimaginable ways. In the first confrontations on the morning of May 18, heads of defenseless students were broken by specially designed clubs. As demonstrators scrambled for safety and regrouped to counterattack, 45 riot police were suddenly surrounded and captured by demonstrators at Sansu-tong Junction on May 18. For a time, people debated what to do with their captives. They soon decided to release them, and immediately after they were set free, the paratroopers viciously attacked: "A cluster of troops attacked each student individually. They would crack his head, stomp on his back, and kick him in the face. When the soldiers were done, he looked like a pile of clothes in meat sauce."[8] Bodies were piled into trucks, where soldiers continued to beat and kick them. By night the paratroopers had set up camp at several universities. As students continued to fight back, soldiers used bayonets on them and arrested dozens more people, many of whom were stripped naked and further brutalized. One young child who witnessed these events asked her parents when *their* army was coming. Another child, having been taught political values at a tender age, screamed that Communists had taken over the army. One soldier brandished his bayonet at captured students and screamed at them, "This is the bayonet I used to cut 40 VC women's breasts [in Vietnam]!" The entire population was in shock from the paratroopers' overreaction. The paratroopers were so out of control that they even stabbed to death the director of information of the police station who tried to get them to stop brutalizing people.[9] Despite severe beatings and hundreds of arrests, students continually regrouped and tenaciously fought back.

As the city mobilized the next day, the number of students among the protesters was dwarfed by people from all walks of life.[10] This spontaneous generation of a peoples' movement transcended traditional divisions between town and gown, one of the first indications of the generalization of the revolt. When working people began to participate, the paratroopers once again resorted to callous brutality—killing and maiming people whom they happened to encounter in the streets. Even cab drivers and bus drivers seeking to aid wounded and bleeding people were stabbed, beaten and sometimes killed. Some policemen secretly tried to release captives, and they, too, were bayoneted.[11] People fought back with stones, bats, knives, pipes, iron bars and hammers against 18,000 riot police and over 3000 paratroopers. Although many people were killed, the city refused to be quieted.

On May 20, a newspaper called the *Militants' Bulletin* was published for the first time, providing accurate news—unlike the official media. Tens of thousands of people gathered on Kumnam Avenue and sang, "Our wish is national reunification." They were dispersed by paratroopers' clubs. At 5:50pm, as the brutality and resistance continued, a crowd of 5000 surged over a police barricade. When the paratroopers drove them back, they reassembled and sat-in on a road. They then selected representatives to try and split the police from the army.[12] In the evening, the march swelled to over 200,000 people (some say 300,000) in a city with a population of 700,000. The massive crowd unified workers, farmers, students and people from all walks of life. The procession on Kumnam Avenue, the downtown shopping area, was led by nine buses and over 200 taxis. Once again, the paratroopers viciously attacked, and this time, the whole city fought back. During the night, cars, jeeps, taxis, and other vehicles were set on fire and pushed into the military's forces. Although the Army attacked repeatedly, the evening ended in a stalemate at Democracy Square. At the train station, many demonstrators were killed, and at Province Hall, the paratroopers opened fire on the crowd with M-16s, killing many more.

The censored media had failed to report killings that occurred right under their noses. Instead, false reports of vandalism and minor police response were the news that they fabricated. The brutality of the army was still unmentioned. After that night's news again failed to report accurately the situation, thousands of people surrounded the MBC media building. Soon the management of the station and the soldiers guarding it retreated, and the crowd surged inside. Unable to get the broadcast facility working, people torched the building. The crowd targeted buildings quite intelligently:

> At 1:00 in the morning, citizens went in flocks to the Tax Office, broke its furniture and set fire to it. The reason was that taxes which should be used for people's lives and welfare had been used for the army and the production of the arms to kill and beat people. It was a very unusual case to set fire to the broadcasting stations and tax office while protecting the police station and other public buildings.[13]

Besides the Tax Office and two media buildings, the Labor Supervision Office, Province Hall car depot and 16 police boxes were burned down. The final battle at the train station around 4 a.m. was intense. Soldiers again used M-16s against the crowd, killing many in the front ranks. Others climbed over the bodies to carry the fight to the army. With incredible fortitude, the people prevailed, and the army beat a hasty retreat.

At 9 a.m. the next morning, more than 100,000 people gathered again on Kumnam Avenue. A small group shouted that some people should go to Asia Motors (a military contractor) and seize vehicles. A few dozen people went off, bringing back only seven (the exact number of rebels who knew how to drive). As they shuttled more drivers back and forth, soon 350 vehicles, including three armored personnel carriers, were in the hands of the people. Driving these expropriated vehicles around the city, the demonstrators rallied the populace and also went to neighboring villages to spread the revolt. Some trucks brought bread and drinks from the Coca-Cola factory to the main demonstration. Negotiators were selected and sent to the military. Suddenly gunshots pierced the already thick atmosphere, ending hope for a peaceful settlement. For ten minutes, the army indiscriminately fired, and in the carnage, dozens were killed and over 500 wounded.

The people quickly responded. Less than two hours after the shootings, the first police station was raided for arms.[14] More people formed action teams and raided police and national guard armories, and assembled at two central points. Apparently the long-held tradition, so valued in Korea, of never rising with arms against a Korean government was suddenly transcended by thousands of people. With assistance from coal miners from Hwasun, demonstrators obtained large quantities of dynamite and detonators.[15]

Seven busloads of women textile workers drove to Naju, where they captured hundreds of rifles and ammunition and brought them back to Kwangju. Similar arms seizures occurred in Changsong, Yonggwang and Tamyang counties.[16]

The movement quickly spread to Hwasun, Naju, Hampyung, Youngkwang, Kangjin, Mooan, Haenam, Mokpo—in all to at least 16 other parts of southwest Korea.[17] The rapid proliferation of the revolt is another indication of people's capacity for self-government and autonomous initiative. Hoping to bring the uprising to Chunju and Seoul, some demonstrators set out but were repulsed by troops blocking the expressway, roads, and railroads. In Mokpo, birthplace of Kim Dae Jung, 100,000 people marched to protest the arrest of their favorite son, and there were five consecutive days of rallies for a democratic constitution.[18] In Chonju, people took over city hall. In Jeonji and Iri, police were reported to have joined the demonstration.[19] Helicopter gunships wiped out units of armed demonstrators from Hwasun and Yonggwang counties trying to reach Kwangju.[20] If the military had not so tightly controlled the media and restricted travel, the revolt may well have turned into a nationwide uprising, as some people hoped. The Sabuk miners' revolt, Pu-Ma Incident and hundreds of other struggles indicated that conditions were ripe for action in many quarters.[21]

Assembling at Kwangju Park and Yu-tong Junction, combat cells and leadership formed. Machine guns were brought to bear on Province Hall (where the military had its command post). By 5:30, the army retreated; by 8 p.m. the people controlled the city. Cheering echoed everywhere. Although their World War 2 weapons were far inferior to those of the army, people's bravery and sacrifices proved more powerful than the technical superiority of the army.

For five days, the citizens held the city. Spontaneously formed citizens' councils organized all essential services, including defense of the city, and they simultaneously negotiated with the military for more coffins, release of the thousands of prisoners (some of whom were already being viciously tortured),[22] as well as for a peaceful end to the conflict. Rubbish from the fighting was quickly cleared away without anyone being told to do so. At the same time, the armed resistance was organized in earnest. At Kwangju Park, 78 vehicles lined up, were painted with numbers and assigned to patrol specific parts of the city to guard against the coming counterattack. An operations office of the Citizens' Army (CA) was established and issued passports for access to their headquarters, safe conduct passes for vehicles and coupons for gasoline. An investigations bureau was formed to ferret out military agents, but it appears that it was itself heavily infiltrated.

The emergence of organization appears to have happened quite naturally. The process was obvious to everyone. Even the government at one point publicly referred to the uprising as "community self-rule." At about 10:30 a.m. on May 22 a group of eight evangelical pastors met to appraise the situation. One of them was Arnold Peterson, a Baptist missionary who happened to be in Kwangju. He later remembered the pastors' appraisal:

> The consensus of their feeling is summed up in the phrase "This cannot be." It was unheard of that the citizens of a city should rise up and throw off their government with no conscious planning and leadership.[23]

There may have been no leadership in place when the uprising began, but the crucible of the fighting produced many resolute enemies of the military. Others only feared the army all the more because of their brutality. Soon two groups, sometimes referred to as councils,[24] formed in liberated Kwangju: a Citizens' Settlement Committee (CSC) and a Student Action Committee (SAC). The CSC, or May 18th General Citizens Settlement Committee, as it was formally known, consisted of about 20 people: priests, clergymen, lawyers, professors and politicians. Led by Ch'oe Han-yong, a respected anti-Japanese activist, they formed hours before the SAC (also on the 22nd) and almost immediately began negotiating with the martial law authorities. They attempted to find as peaceful as possible a solution to the uprising.

Unlike the CSC, the tempestuous origins of the SAC involved many people who had not previously been introduced to each other. Testifying years later about his personal experiences in the uprising, Professor Song Ki-sook recounted these events. He and Professor Myeong Lo-geun were approached at a rally at the fountain on May 22, the same day Peterson was attending his pastoral meeting. Myeong was asked to gather activists and create a headquarters to "lead an effort to cope with the situation."[25] People were concerned that the past histories of members of the CSC indicated that they were not going to lead the struggle but to sell it out. Song Ki-sook was against taking any action, but he went along with Myeong. Holding a bullhorn given to him by a student, Myeong began to speak: "Please choose five representatives among Chonnam National University and Chosson University students respectively." He continued:

> Though paratroopers are now driven out, the citizens' army is bewildered and in the middle of confusion with no headquarters. A citizens' settlement committee has already formed and went to Sangmudae with the settlement conditions, but it cannot control the citizens' army. This whole thing was started by students and they should take a lead in straightening things out. Let's go into the provincial government building and organize a student settlement committee.

With that, Professor Myeong led the crowd to the front gate of Province Hall, where the citizens' army, wearing backwards the protective helmets taken from the riot police, kept guard in a tense atmosphere. The 10 student representatives were allowed to enter the building, and were escorted into the administrative office, where "complete chaos" transpired.[26]

Many of the militants inside refused at first to even discuss a student settlement committee—preferring to "fight until death" for democracy and dignity. Patiently Professor Song prevailed and a political arm of the students, the SAC, was formed, and it soon took care of funerals, alternative media, vehicle control and weapons collection and distribution, while the CSC negotiated with the military. Sometimes the two councils issued joint statements, but they also worked at cross purposes. On May 24, for example, when more than 100,000 people assembled for that day's rally, the CSC scuttled the loudspeakers. Amplification equipment was finally brought in from elsewhere, but members of the CSC kept unplugging it. Despite pouring rain, people stayed, and an electrician hooked the sound system up to a car battery. Afterwards, the SAC convened an emotional meeting. There was much debate, and a small majority favored turning in all their weapons. The minority, however, refused to consent to such a surrender. As the night wore on, moderates resigned from the group, leaving the minority in charge. Workers and activists were then added to its leadership, and its name was changed to the Citizen-Student Action Committee (CSAC).

This transformation of the SAC into the CSAC reflected the leading role now played by the working class. Although students had sparked the uprising, they were unable to remain the leading force. I have already mentioned the Hwasun coal miners and women textile workers. There are numerous other examples of working-class leadership to which one can point. Peterson reported that on the 21st, "In a conversation I had with Pastor Chang, he was careful to emphasize that the ones who seized guns were not students. Instead they were young jobless and working men."[27] Lee reports that while many citizens surrendered their firearms to the Citizen Settlement Committee on May 22, "Workers and members of the underclass, however, would not abandon their guns."[28] These militants hoped to spark a nationwide uprising to overthrow the dictatorship—and they were willing to die trying to restore democracy in one fell swoop. They demanded qualitative changes in Korean politics— not only the lifting of martial law, release of all prisoners, and a caretaker government, but the resignation of Chun Doo Hwan[29] and full democratization. The struggle for student autonomy had spontaneously metamorphosized into a struggle for social autonomy and democracy.

As should now be clear, the SAC served as the nucleus of an increasingly dedicated constellation of people whose resolute courage and clear vision guided the peoples' uprising. Of all the remarkable individuals who starred in the battle of Kwangju, no one shone brighter than Yun Sang-won. During the huge rally on May 21 (with over 200,000 people), Yun personally led one of the assaults on arms depots, and he was also involved in the group that took control of three armored personnel carriers and 350 other vehicles at Asia Motors Company. In the intense atmosphere of military snipers firing on public areas, endless meetings, daily mass rallies, and occasional skirmishes, Yun emerged as the "only one who had a strategic view."[30] He believed that by creating "pockets of resistance," thereby helping "to make the price higher" for the dictatorship, the uprising would raise the stakes, in effect telling the regime: "if you do not have the guts to kill more people, you surrender. And if you do have enough guts, then you prove yourself barbarians."[31] They also hoped other rebellions would break out.

Along with a small number of others, some of whom were members of groups like Wildfire (a night school for workers), Clown (an activist theatrical troupe), and the National Democratic Workers' League, Chun and Yun published a daily newspaper, the *Militants' Bulletin*, which they used to stiffen and inspire the armed resistance. They successfully outmaneuvered the mayor and more conservative members of the council. Making an alliance with Park Nam Son, the emergent leader of the armed fighters, Yun appears to have been the energy center as a spectrum of militant individuals merged together and devoted themselves to a single focus—continuing armed resistance. Significantly, many of the members of this more militant group had previously participated in a study group about the Paris Commune with poet Kim Nam-zu.[32]

Refusing to place his name at the titular head of the council, he approved the appointment of a chairman and vice-chairman. Named the "spokesman" for the council, he also coordinated public relations, planning and supply. The P.R. division organized four working clusters of people: one to drive vehicles with loudspeakers through the streets to make announcements; another publishing the daily *Militants' Bulletin* and other materials; a third to raise funds and encourage people to donate blood; and finally a group that organized the daily rallies. They also coordinated a rapid response unit and made sure the outposts were supplied.

On the night of May 26, families of soldiers stationed near Kwangju, informed the resistance fighters that the military was going to move in the next morning. Yun was among the hundreds of people who fought to the death. In the final battle, on May 27, a tank column led the assault to retake the city, and dozens more people—including Yun Sang-won—were killed.

As significant as the role of Yun Sang-won was, he and his small organization were unable to control the popular movement. In the dialectic of spontaneity and organization, it was clearly the popular movement's impulses that held sway in Kwangju. Many of the militants who fought the army used their own initiative rather than following the suggestions of the Citizens' Army. On May 22, for example, Bag Naepoong refused to head to Youngsan-Po as the CA thought he should. Instead he went to Hwasun train station with four others, where they were able to procure arms for themselves and return to Kwangju.[33] This particular case of individual initiative ended well, yet the lack of strategic organization cost the communards dearly. The *Militants' Bulletin* called for people to "occupy the KBS [television station] to let our reality be known to the whole country through broadcasting."[34] During the fighting, however, the crowd torched the place. If people had listened to Yun's group, would they have been able to broadcast news of the uprising to the rest of the country? Would a nationwide uprising have then occurred? Clearly, strategic leadership both in Kwangju and the nation was needed, particularly for the militants to have succeeded in overthrowing the government.[35] In hindsight, of course, this weakness of the movement is easily visible, but options were limited in the heat of battle. The main feeling in Kwangju was one of solidarity, and it is to this dimension of the Commune that I now turn.

Organic Solidarity

"The city was no longer under government control. The people of Kwangju were building a commune, but the price for the new system was their blood. The morning of May 21 saw a new sight on the street corners. Meals had been prepared for demonstrators and were prepared on every street, at all the busy intersections. Women stopped the appropriated vehicles to offer food to the occupants. Street and market vendors, some of the main eyewitnesses to the government's brutality, organized food distribution. Meanwhile the rich parts of town emptied out…Hundreds of housewives fed the demonstrators on Kumnam Avenue. Nobody drank…This unity fed the fighting spirit of all the rebels."[36]

After the military had been driven out of the city on May 21, hundreds of fighters in the citizens' army patrolled the city. Joy and relief were shared by everyone. The fighting was over and the city was free. Markets and stores were open for business, and food, water and electricity were available as normally. No banks were looted, and normal crimes like robbery, rape or theft hardly occurred—if at all. Foreigners freely walked the streets. Indeed, Peterson reported that his car, flying an American flag and with a large sign reading "Foreigners' Car," was cheered by people in the streets.[37]

Coffins, gasoline and cigarettes were in short supply. While the CSC attempted to procure more coffins from the army, gasoline was rationed by the CSC, and cigarettes were shared by people with their newly found comrades in arms, happy to be alive. For some people, sharing cigarettes symbolized an important part of the communal experience.[38] Storeowners who still had cigarettes often sold—or gave away—one pack at a time (to be fair to everyone). Blood had been in short supply at the hospital, but as soon as the need became known, people flooded in to donate it, including barmaids and prostitutes, who at one point publicly insisted that they, too, be permitted to donate. At many of the rallies, thousands of dollars for the settlement committees was quickly raised through donations. All these examples are indications of how remarkably the whole city came together. Many eyewitnesses commented on the new feeling of solidarity among the populace:

> …during the whole period of the uprising, Kwangju City coped with the crisis through humanitarian cooperation. Kwangju citizens shared possessions with each other, and being dependent on each other, they encouraged each other in their isolated situation. They shared food with those who were in need of it, donated blood to the wounded, and willingly helped anyone who was in need…In spite of the complete absence of an official peace and order system, the Kwangju citizens maintained peace and order perfectly. Though so many firearms were in the hands of citizens, no incident took place due to it. Even financial agencies or jeweler's shops in which crimes are apt to happen in ordinary times were free from any criminal act.[39]

A professor at a Kwangju university who remained anonymous for his own safety wrote:

> The citizens, who used to buy up everything in sight no matter what the price, shared their daily necessities. Merchants who used to be impatient and charge high mark-ups didn't raise prices at all. Citizens participated, offering tobacco, pajamas, food, and drink…No infamous crime which might have been expected was committed, no robbery of money from defenseless banks was undertaken by the armed citizens. They did not harm any of the resident aliens in Kwangju.[40]

Indeed, the Japanese Catholic Association for Peace and Justice wrote a statement on June 6, 1980 in which they verified these observations:

The ones who didn't join in, who didn't witness the firmly united citizens, can't understand this feeling of liberation. They could have seen the tears on the faces of the young men, who devoted themselves to defend democracy. Their chests were splattered with blood. They shouted the slogans with bloody bands around their heads, until their throats got sore. Our beloved neighbors, young and innocent children, and even housekeepers were now joining the parading cars…People who couldn't get on the cars brought rice wrapped in seaweed and drinks…They wanted to give eggs, bread, cokes, milk, and juices to the demonstrators. Stuffing all the food into a box, an old man was not able to lift it up. I lifted it up and put it into a car that I just stopped. I could read the resolution to struggle to the death on their faces. Housekeepers who couldn't prepare food brought buckets of water, offered it to them to drink and cleaned up their faces. Some citizens ran along with the vehicles…It was a struggle of blood and love to share lives with others: a man who tapped a participant's back to cheer, a pharmacist who brought out medicines and drinks, and the crowd who did their best, clapping and cheering.[41]

In June 1980, the Roman Catholic priests of Kwangju Archdiocese reiterated these same themes:

While the army cut off communication with the outside and no necessities or food were provided, no one made undue profits by buying things up or being indisposed to sell things. Without knowing when the situation was going to end, people shared their food with each other. As the number of patients who got shot increased and blood was needed, the number of citizens who donated blood skyrocketed…Kwangju citizens swept the scattered stone, glass and fragments of tear gas canisters, doctors and nurses moved patients from the city while risking getting shot; bus and taxi drivers protected young people without thinking about their own lives; juvenile vagrants and abandoned children were more virtuous than ever before…[42]

How do we explain this sudden solidarity, this emergence of a new form of bonding between people? How do we understand the suspension of normal values like competitive business practices and individual ownership of consumer goods and their replacement with cooperation and collectivity?

For days, citizens voluntarily cleaned the streets, cooked rice, served free meals in the marketplace, and kept constant guard against the expected counterattack. Everyone contributed to and found their place in liberated Kwangju. Spontaneously a new division of labor emerged. The citizens' army, many of whom had stayed up all night, nonetheless were models of responsibility. People dubbed the new militia the "Citizens' Army" or "our allies" (as opposed to the army, "our enemy.") They protected the people and the people, in turn, took care of them. Without any indoctrination and none of the military madness that elicits monstrous behavior in armies around the world, the men and women of the CA behaved in an exemplary fashion. Unafraid to impose a new type of order based on the needs of the populace, they disarmed all middle school and high school students, an action for which the *Militants' Bulletin* took responsibility.[43] When the final assault was imminent, Yun Sang-won personally insisted that the high schoolers among the militants return home so they could survive and continue the struggle. After many protests and with tears in their eyes, the younger militants departed.

The CA served the people, and the popular will was directly formulated at daily rallies around the fountain at Prrovince Hall Square. Renamed "Democracy Square" on May 16, the space was holy even before the liberation of the city. A poem written that day by the Congregation for the Democratization of Chonnam Province began with these inspired lines:

The sky of the south was beautiful
There was no angel blowing a trumpet.
Nor colorful butterflies scattering flowers around.
Still the sky of the south was beautiful.

The day when the fountain stopped scattering colorful water,
The day when the artificial flower withered,
I came to you and you came one step closer to me.

The day when the pepper fog and tear gas stopped.
People came from the Mujin plain.
All democratic citizens: intellectuals, laborers, farmers.

People gathered in front of the fountain of the provincial capital.
People tried to touch the fountain.
Sitting on the lawn, hugging each other
Exchanging smiles with each other

There is no song as beautiful as this,
The song we sang all together.[44]

The ability to assemble peacefully by the thousands was a right won through the blood of too many friends and neighbors. Instinctively, the people of Kwangju recognized the square as their spiritual home, and they assembled there every day by the tens of thousands. The daily rallies became the setting for a new kind of direct democracy where everyone had a say. Of the five rallies that occurred during the time the city was liberated, huge crowds attended each. The first massive rally was a spontaneously organized gathering to celebrate the defeat of the military the day after the army retreated. The next day, (May 23) at the First Citywide Rally for Democracy, the crowd swelled to 150,000. It ended with the people singing "Our Wish is National Unification." On May 24, over 100,000 people assembled; there were 50,000 on May 25 (where the resignation of the Settlement Committee was demanded); and 30,000 at the end of the final rally on May 26. At this last gathering, the demand for a new government of national salvation emerged. The final act of the people that day was to sing once again "Our Wish is National Unification."

Even though the rallies were huge, many people were able to express heartfelt needs. As Lee Jae-eui described it:

> The fountain was now the center of unity. All walks and classes of people spoke—women street vendors, elementary school teachers, followers of different religions, housewives, college students, high school students and farmers. Their angry speeches created a common consciousness, a manifestation of the tremendous energy of the uprising. They had melded together, forging a strong sense of solidarity throughout the uprising. For the moment, the city was one.[45]

Alongside the unity of the city, regional loyalties—long the cause of division and strife in Korea—became less important than the struggle for democracy. On May 21, the Jeonnam *Newsletter of Democracy* proclaimed: Let us actively participate in the struggle for democracy, remembering that what we want is not to blur our goal under the spell of regional animosity, nor do we want indiscriminate destruction but autonomous action based on the democratic spirit.[46] The suspension of regionalism is another indication of the universal appeal of the revolt—an appeal not confined to Cholla or even to Korea. I now turn to the uprising's international implications.

International Revolts After the Kwangju Uprising

In 1985, East Asian dictatorships, in power for decades, seemed unshakable. Both Kim Dae Jung and Benigno Aquino, popular leaders of vast democratic strata, were in exile in the US where they got acquainted. Although brutally repressed, the Korean

Gwangju citizens expelled the military and governed themselves through direct democracy in May 1980. Photo: The May 18 Memorial Foundation

movement continued the struggle to overthrow the dictatorship. After the massacre of May 27, 1980, it took two years for the families of the victims to meet, and five years passed before the first book about the uprising appeared. On May 17, 1985, coordinated protests at 80 colleges and universities involved some 38,000 students who called for the truth about the killings to be made public. A week later, 73 Seoul students occupied the US Information Service building for three days in an attempt to compel an apology from the US government for its role. On August 15, as protests continued, Hong Ki Il burned himself to death on Kwangju's main street because of the government's failure to reveal the truth.

After decades in which democracy was repressed throughout East Asia, a wave of revolts and uprisings transformed the region. In 18 days of February 1986 in the Philippines, the walk-out of 30 computer operators counting the votes in an election sparked a sudden end to the Marcos dictatorship. The confrontation was won by hundreds of thousands of people who refused to leave the streets. The Philippine people-power revolution in turn inspired the slowly rebuilding movement in South Korea.[47] Less than a month after the outbreak of the people-power revolution, the Cardinal and his Bishops in Seoul began talking about the people of South Korea having learned a lesson. Within a year, the military dictatorship was overthrown.

The glorious victory of the Minjung movement centers around a massive outpouring of popular protest beginning on June 10, 1987. For more than ten days, hundreds of thousands of people mobilized in the streets demanding direct presidential elections. When Kwangju native Yi Han Yol was killed in a student protest near Yonsei University, more than one million people gathered to bury him. As in the Philippines, massive occupation of public space compelled the military to relent—in this case by agreeing to hold direct elections for president. In July and August, thousands of strikes involving millions of workers broke out. Although major concessions had been granted by the government, the struggle continued.

All through Asia, people's movements for democracy and human rights appeared: an end to martial law was won in Taiwan; in Myanmar (Burma) a popular movement exploded in March 1988, when students and ethnic minorities took to the streets of Rangoon (much as had happened in Kwangju). Despite horrific repression, the movement compelled President Ne Win to step down after 26 years of rule. In August, five days of new student-led protests forced his replacement to resign. A general strike committee representing workers, writers, monks and students coordinated the nationwide movement for multiparty democracy, but the military shot down thousands more people—bringing to 10,000 the number of people it killed that year. Arresting thousands more, including over 100 elected representatives, the Burmese military government continues to use an iron fist to remain in power.

The next year, student activists in China activated a broad public cry for democracy, only to be shot down at Tiananmen Square and hunted for years afterward.[48] Even within the halls of communism, however, as the chain reaction of revolts against military dictatorships continued, a member of the Politburo of Vietnam, General Tran Do, publicly asked for multi-party democracy in Vietnam in 1989, an unprecedented event. The next country to experience an explosion was Thailand, when 20 days of hunger strike by a leading opposition politician brought hundreds of thousands of people into the streets in May 1992. Dozens were killed when the military suppressed street demonstrations, and because of this brutality, General Suchinda Krapayoon was forced to step down.[49] In 1998 in Indonesia, students called for a "people-power revolution" and were able to overthrow Suharto. Interviews conducted by an American correspondent at the universities in Indonesia determined that the people-power slogan was adopted from the Philippines, as was the tactical innovation of the occupation of public space. Students successfully surged into the parliament building and were able to compel a resolution of the conflict only by the withdrawal of Sukarno.

The relationship of these revolts to each other is an understudied dimension of these movements. Elsewhere I have developed the concept of the eros effect to explain the rapid spread of revolutionary aspirations and actions.[50] By the eros effect, I mean events like the spontaneous chain reaction of uprisings and the massive occupation of public space—both of which are examples of the sudden entry into history of millions of ordinary people who act in a unified fashion, intuitively believing that they can change the direction of their society. In moments of the eros effect, universal interests become generalized at the same time as the dominant values of society (national chauvinism, hierarchy, domination, regionalism, possessiveness, etc.) are negated. This is what I referred to as the organic solidarity of participants in the Kwangju Commune. The eros effect is not simply an act of mind, nor can it simply be willed by the "conscious element" (or revolutionary party). Rather it involves popular revolutionary movements emerging as forces in their own right as thousands of ordinary people take history into their own hands.[51]

By developing the concept of the eros effect, I seek to rescue the revolutionary value of spontaneous actions of millions of ordinary people from the scorn of theorists. I also seek to stimulate a reevaluation of the unconscious and emotions, to overturn their portrayal as being linked to reaction rather than to revolution. My notion of the eros effect seeks to bring emotions into the realm of positive revolutionary resources whose mobilization can result in significant social transformation. As Marcuse said, nature is an ally in the revolutionary process, referring not only to external nature, to nature out there in the world, but to internal nature, to human nature. Humans have an instinctual need for freedom—something that we grasp intuitively, and it was this instinctual need that was sublimated into a collective phenomenon during the Kwangju uprising.

Is the eros effect an analytical construction or a tactic for a better world? It is certainly the former. The sudden emergence of people massively occupying public space; the spread of the revolt from one city to another and throughout the countryside; the intuitive identification with each other of hundreds of thousands of people and their simultaneous belief in the power of their actions; the suspension of normal values like regionalism, competitive business practices, criminal behavior, and acquisitiveness: these are dimensions of the eros effect in Kwangju. After World Way 2, the sudden and unexpected appearance of massive contestation of power has become a significant tactic in the arsenal of popular movements.

Future Prospects

If the eros effect can be activated, I see at least two possibilities for how this dynamic can be crafted in practical situations. When the Zapatistas used the internet to call for demonstrations against neoliberalism during the summer of 1999—and activists in several cities responded, including in London which experienced its largest riot in at least a decade—clearly they were seeking internationally synchronized popular uprisings. For this method to succeed, the group(s) initiating the call must be a socially legitimate leadership in the hearts of many people and must wisely wield hegemonic power. Most significantly, the spark lit by organized forces of the movement must land in flammable territory. Besides the Zapatistas, Kwangju might increasingly play such an international role. Like the Battleship Potemkin, Kwangju's actions might again signal the time for uprising—and not only in Korea. In 1972, the Vietnamese revolution meticulously prepared an internationally synchronized offensive. After convening a Paris conference to coordinate the action calendars of anti-war movements in over 80 countries, the Vietnamese launched a military offensive in April 1972, during which they declared the existence of a Provisional Revolutionary Government.

Secondly, confrontations with the principal instruments of global corporate domination (the IMF and World Bank meetings in Berlin in 1988, Clinton's recent visit to Athens, anti-WTO protests in Seattle in 1999 and the more recent protests against the IMF and World Bank in Washington DC) help to create a global dynamic of escalating confrontation that spreads throughout the world like a wave in a stadium. Abetted by global institutions of capital (the IMF, World Bank and WTO), local ruling classes— both in East Asia and in the USA—use force when persuasion fails to maintain the regime of corporate exploitation and cultural hegemony. When people confront such dictatorial tendencies in one country, they intuitively mobilize movements, creating a global dynamic of solidarity and struggle.

Globalization as we know it has been built on the backs of the world's working poor. The concentration of greater quantities of capital is based on the increasing misery of hundreds of millions of people at the periphery of the world system. As the global tendencies of the world system intensify in their impact on millions of peoples' everyday lives, internationally coordinated opposition is more and more a necessity. For the eros effect to be activated, thousands and then millions of people who comprise civil society need to act—to negate their existing daily routines and break free of ingrained patterns. This process is not simply enacted by the will power of a small group—although it may be sparked by one. Like falling in love, enacting the eros effect is a complex process. It appears that leaderless situations often produce the eros effect. If the eros effect were continually activated, we would have passed from the realm of what Marx called prehistory, to the realm of real human history in which human beings for the first time are able to determine for themselves the type of society in which they wish to live.

To catch a glimpse of such a society we need to look no further than the Kwangju People's Uprising, for during the brutal reality of May 1980 Korean workers and students briefly tasted freedom. The example set by the people of Kwangju in their spontaneous capacity for self-government and the organic solidarity of the population may well be their most important legacy. Alongside these indications of the unrealized potential of human beings today, there were concrete gains—the overthrow of the military dictatorship and the inspiration of other democratic movements—and specific lessons taught through the blood and sacrifices of so many—the need for strategic organization and the centrality of working people to fundamental change. Today, twenty years later, the uprising continues to provide all of us with a palpable feeling for the dignity of human beings and the necessity of intensifying the struggle for liberation.

NOTES

1   This article is a revised version of a speech delivered at the Global Symposium on the 20th Anniversary of the Kwangju Uprising, "Democracy and Human Rights in the New Millennium," Chonnam National University, Kwangju Korea, May 15-17, 2000. I wish to acknowledge the help and support of Ngo Vinh Long, Yoon Soo Jong, Victor Wallis, Greg DeLaurier, Soh Yujin and the staff of the May 18 Institute at Chonnam National University. Also published in *Socialism and Democracy* Vol. 14 No.1 (Spring-Summer 2000). Although the Western media did carry reports at the time, the Kwangju Commune and the massacres were never fully analyzed, nor have most non-Koreans even heard about it. US complicity in the massacre is embodied in the man who is today our United Nations ambassador—Richard Holbrooke. Although he has claimed that "the Americans didn't know what was going on," Holbrooke was the leader of the US team that approved the release of the South Korean troops from the DMZ to crush the Kwangju uprising. In the midst of negotiations for a peaceful settlement in Kwangju, the citizens' councils asked the US to mediate: Holbrooke and Co. refused. Rather he promised the Korean government that the "US would not publicly contest" their version of whatever events transpired. After hundreds had been killed, Holbrooke stepped up US economic and diplomatic ties to the new military government, and he personally profited by serving as a key adviser to Hyundai in the 1980s. Apparently Holbrooke's complicity in hundreds of murders earned him a promotion to UN ambassador.

2   Lee Jae-eui, *Kwangju Diary: Beyond Death, Beyond the Darkness of the Age* (UCLA Asian Pacific Monograph Series, 1999). This is the single best source in English and I highly recommend it. It can be ordered from Mr. Leslie Evans, 11372B Bunche Hall, UCLA, Los Angeles, CA 90095-1487).

3   Other English language sources I have relied on in my research include a collection of foreign journalists' accounts, *Kwangju in the Eyes of the World* (Kwangju Citizens' Solidarity, 1997). The above quote is from an article by Bradley Martin, p. 94. Also helpful was *The May 18 Kwangju Democratic Uprising* (The 5.18 History Compilation Committee of Kwangju City, 1999). Arnold A. Peterson's essay, "5:18 The Kwangju Incident" is contained in a Korean language book. Last but not least, I have benefited greatly from the May 18 Institute's recent translation of documents and personal testimonies (hereafter referred to in my footnotes as *Documents*). These are available in digital format. In some cases, I have tried to make the translations flow more easily.

4   Sanjeewa Liyanage, "Kwangju, The Flame of People's Power," International Youth Net, Volume 1, 1996, p. 29.

5   Lee Jae-eui, p. 41.

6   *The May 18th*...p. 121.

7   Lee, p. 46.

8   *Documents*, p. 79.

9   *The May 18th*, p. 127.

10   *Documents*, p. 113.

11   Lee, p. 64.

12   *The May 18th*, p. 138.

13   The firing began at 1:00 sharp on the afternoon of the 21st, and at 2:30, weapons and ammunition was commandeered from the Sampo Branch office of Naju police station, and police boxes at Youngkwang, Keumsung, and Suan. The first groups of armed protesters began firing back at 2:20. Arnold Peterson relates that "At about 2:00 p.m. some of the citizens captured the military arsenal in the town of Hwa Soon, just south of Kwangju. From that time on many of the citizen fighters carried guns." Peterson, p. 44.

14   *The May 18th*, p. 143.

15   Lee, p. 77.

16   *The May 18* Kwangju Democratic Uprising, p. 164; *Documents*, p. 72.

17   *Documents*, p. 105.

18   *Documents*, p. 61.

19   Lee, p. 137.

20   In *Documents*, p. 132, the number 719 was used to count the number of struggles.

21   *Documents*, p. 43.

22   Peterson, p. 49.

23   See Cummings, "Introduction" to Lee.

24   This incident is described in *Documents*, pp. 9-10.

25   Lee (p. 107) says there were 15 representatives.

26   Peterson, p. 44.

27   Lee, p. 107.

28   Fighters' Bulletin No. 5, May 23, *Documents*, p. 71.

29   Chun Yong Ho quoted in Kwangju in the Eyes of the World, p. 88.

30   Park Song Hyon summarized Yun's strategy in Kwangju in the Eyes of the World, p. 88.

31   Interview with Chun Yon Ho, November 29, 1999.

32   *Documents*, p. 31.

33   *Documents*, p. 68.

34   See Lee's analysis as well as the insightful criticisms written two years after the uprising by the Kwangju Citizens' Movement for Democracy, p. 133 *Documents*. In my view, such organization needs to be decentralized for many reasons, chief among them being the ease with which centralized organizations are decapitated. For more discussion, see chapter 5 of The Imagination of the New Left.

35   Lee, p. 72.

36   Peterson, p. 47.

37   See Documents, pp. 11-12.

38   *The May 18th*, pp. 174-5.

39   *Documents*, p. 113.

40   *Documents*, p. 119.

41   *Documents*, p. 127.

42   Fighters' Bulletin, *Documents*, p. 71.

43   *Documents*, p. 58.

44   Lee p. 105.

45   *Documents and Testimonies*, p. 67.

46   "Lee Jae-eui, "The Seventeen Years of Struggle to Bring the Truth of the Kwangju Massacre to Light," in *Kwangju in the Eyes of the World*, p. 143.

47   Although the government claims far fewer, it appears some 700 people were killed. See Bruce Cummings, "Introduction," in Lee.

48   The Thai Interior Ministry claims 44 dead, 38 disappeared, 11 disabled and over 500 wounded. Human rights activists have noted that hundreds were killed or disappeared. No Thai government has ever been held responsible for massacres of pro-democracy demonstrators in 1973, 1976 or 1992.

49   See *The Imagination of the New Left: A Global Analysis of 1968* (Seoul: E-who Press, 1999) and *The Subversion of Politics: European Autonomous Social Movements and the Decolonization of Everyday Life* (Seoul: E-who, forthcoming).

50   With the psychic energy and swings in emotions of crowds, a mixture of sentiments simultaneously co-exist. While many sacrificed their lives, the survivors have many opportunities to quit. What Marcuse called a "psychic Thermidor," an internally conditioned process of self-defeating behavior within revolutionary movements, may have been operative in Kwangju. Do we see this in the release of the 45 riot police captured in May 18 at Sansu-tong Junction? Almost certainly the paratroopers' rampage after the release of the police would not have happened, but would the hostages have made good bargaining chips to free some of the prisoners being tortured? Other indications of a psychic Thermidor can be found. On May 23, thousands of carbines, M-16's and pistols were abandoned. That same night Kim Ch'ang-gil and some SAC members permitted an explosives expert, in reality a military agent, to remove all the detonators from the arsenal of dynamite, rendering it all useless. Would the military have moved in so brutally if they had known they might have lost some tanks?

Comparing the Paris Commune and the Gwangju Uprising[1]

IN THE PAST two centuries, two events in world history stand out as unique beacons of the spontaneous ability of hundreds of thousands of ordinary people to govern themselves: the Paris Commune of 1871 and the Gwangju People's Uprising of 1980. In both cities, an unarmed citizenry, in opposition to their own governments, effectively gained control of urban space despite the presence of well-armed military forces seeking to reestablish "law and order"; hundreds of thousands of people created popular organs of political power that effectively and efficiently replaced traditional forms of government; crime rates plummeted during the period of liberation; and people felt previously unexperienced forms of kinship with each other.

The Paris Commune arose in 1871 as the victorious Prussians moved to seize the capital of France at the end of the Franco-Prussian War. The French government's capitulation and mollification of the Prussians angered Parisians, and on March 18, the National Guard of Paris seized control of the city in a relatively bloodless coup d'etat. Despite the government's attacking them, the Communards held out for 70 days against French troops armed and aided by their Prussian conquerors. They established a functioning government that coordinated defense and met the daily needs of Parisians. Twice elections were held, and the delegates chosen sought to govern the liberated city in a robustly democratic manner. Finally, on May 27 overwhelming military force crushed the uprising and thousands were killed in a "Bloody Week" of urban warfare.

Over a century later, the Gwangju People's Uprising occurred at a time when the firepower of militaries was multiplied by several orders of magnitude. There was no conquering foreign army advancing on the city, but the citizenry rebelled nonetheless against their own government's military dictatorship (which was aided and abetted by the USA). After horrendous barbarity was inflicted on the people of Gwangju by elite paratrooper units, thousands of people bravely fought the military and drove them out of the city. They held their liberated space for 6 days, a far shorter period than the Paris Commune. Inside liberated Gwangju, daily citizens' assemblies gave voice to years-old frustrations and pent-up aspirations of ordinary people. Local citizens' groups maintained order and created a new type of government—one of, by and for the people. Coincidentally, on May 27—the same day that the Paris Commune was crushed 109 years earlier—the Gwangju Commune was also overwhelmed by military force.

There are remarkable ways in which the two events converge. Within these liberated territories, a number of similar dynamics arose:

1. spontaneous emergence of popular organs of democratic decision-making
2. emergence of armed resistance from below
3. attenuation of criminal behavior in the cities
4. existence of genuine solidarity and cooperation among the citizenry
5. suspension of hierarchies of class, power and status
6. appearance of internal divisions among the participants

The most important historical legacy of these uprisings is their affirmation of human dignity and prefiguration of a free society. Like the Paris Commune, the people of Gwangju spontaneously rose up against insuperable forces. Both uprisings were produced by the accumulation of grievances against injustice and precipitated by extreme events. In order to contain the uprisings and prevent them from spreading, the established governments isolated both cities. Cut off from the provinces, the Paris Commune nevertheless found many supporters, and similar communal experiments erupted in many cites, from Marseilles to Tours. In Paris, Communards flew balloons filled with letters to the provinces to try to spread the revolt,[2] and circulars for farmers were dropped successfully.[3] In Gwangju, the revolt spread to at least 16 neighboring sections of South Cholla province. Many people were killed attempting to break out of the military cordon around Gwangju to spread the revolt, and dozens more died trying to get into Gwangju to help in its defense.

In both cities, traitors to the uprisings and people who supported the government (including spies and saboteurs sent inside the communes to disrupt and destroy them) were quite numerous. In Gwangju, government agents took the detonators from the basement of Province Hall, thereby rendering useless the dynamite brought there by Hwasun coal miners. During the Paris Commune, the decision by a small group of Communards to leave their post guarding one of the forts overlooking the city led to the loss of a most strategic position—one the reactionary forces soon used to bombard the city with artillery. Paris was "full" of internal enemies, and there were riots at Vendome Place and the Bourse, instigated by "loyal" citizens in constant contact with Versailles. In Gwangju, the "poison needle incident" is but the most famous incident in a series of internal problems.

In both 1871 and 1980, after the halcyon days of liberation were bloodily brought to an end, brutal repression was the order of the day. Estimates of the number of people executed in the aftermath of Commune reach to 30,000, a number that does not include thousands more who were summarily deported to distant Pacific holdings of the French Empire.[4] In Korea, hundreds of people simply disappeared. Although the official count of the dead hovers around 200, most people believe that as many as 2000 died in the uprising. Afterwards, there were seven long years of attempts to suppress the truth and to repress any democratic impulses. The Gwangju uprising continued in new forms, and ultimately led to the overthrow of the military dictatorship.[5]

The liberated realities of the Communes in Paris and Gwangju contradict the widely propagated myth that human beings are essentially evil and therefore require strong governments to maintain order and justice. Rather, the behavior of the citizens during these moments of liberation revealed an innate capacity for self-government and cooperation. It was the forces of the government, not the ungoverned people that acted with great brutality and injustice. Reading this description of the brutality of government, it is difficult to tell whether it occurred in Paris or Gwangju:

> "You shall perish, whatever you do! If you are taken with arms in your hands, death! If you beg for mercy, death! Whichever way you turn, right, left, back forward up down, death! You are not merely outside the law, you are outside humanity. Neither age nor sex shall save you and yours. You shall die, but first you shall taste the agony of your wife, your sister, your mother, your sons and daughters, even those in the cradle! Before your eyes the wounded man shall be taken out of the ambulance and hacked with bayonets or knocked down with the butt end of a rifle. He shall be dragged living by his broken leg or bleeding arm and flung like a suffering, groaning bundle of refuse into the gutter. Death! Death! Death!"[6]

After the uprisings, years of repression fueled renewed struggles. In France as in Gwangju, police harassed funerals for years, refusing to allow the somber burial of anyone publicly associated with the movement. In France this practice continued as late as 1887,[7] and in South Korea until at least 1987. Even after the Gwangju Commune had been ruthlessly crushed, the news of the uprising was so subversive that the military burned an unknown number of corpses, dumped others into unmarked graves, and destroyed its own records. To prevent word of the uprising from being spoken publicly, thousands of people were arrested, and hundreds tortured as the military tried to suppress even a whisper of its murders.

Both uprisings took place after many years of economic growth. Although repressive, the Yushin system of Park Chung-hee galvanized great gains in the Korean economy in the 1970s, albeit at the price of superexploitation of the working class through long workweeks, low wages and systematic suppression of people's basic rights. In France, output had expanded during the Second Empire of Louis Napoleon. Between 1853 and 1869, agriculture grew from an output of 64 to 114, industry from 51 to 78; building from 51 to 105; and exports from 25 to 66. [8] Between 1860 and 1870, national income rose from 15,200 million Francs to 18,800, and real wages increased from 60 to 72 from 1852 to 1869. [9] Cholla Do in 1980 and Paris in 1871 were undergoing similar transitions from agriculture to industry, a trend resulting in great migration from the countryside to the cities. The 1872 census put the number of industrial workers in France at 44% of the workforce, but there were probably no more than 15 factories that employed more than 100 workers each, and an additional hundred factories employed between 20 and 50 workers. [10] Similarly, Gwangju in 1980 was the site of many small factories, a feature typical of the transition to higher forms of industrialization.

Differences Between the Two Uprisings

Differences between these two historic events are quite apparent. As previously mentioned, the Paris Commune lasted from the insurrection of March 18 to the final suppression on May 27—some 70 days. The Gwangju People's Uprising held liberated Gwangju for only 6 days—May 21-27. For political events, however, time is not a key variable—at least not as we ordinarily measure it. If one doubts the veracity of this observation, think only of the impact and significance of one day— September 11, 2001—in the overnight political transformation of world consciousness and political reality.

A more significant difference is that in Gwangju, no preexisting armed force like the Parisian National Guard led the assault on power. Rather a spontaneous process of resistance to the brutality of the paratroopers threw forward men and women who rose to the occasion. Many had little or no previous political experience. Some had little or no formal education. All emerged in the concrete context of unfolding historical events. Liberated Gwangju was organized without the contrivance of governments or planning by political parties.

The capacity for self-organization that emerged spontaneously in Gwangju, first in the heat of the battle and later in the governing of the city and the final resistance when the military counterattacked, is mind expanding. In the latter part of the twentieth century, high rates of literacy, the mass media, and universal education (which in South Korea includes military training for every man) have forged a capacity in millions of people to govern themselves far more wisely than military dictatorships or tiny elites all too often ensconced in powerful positions. We can observe this spontaneous capacity for self-government (as well as the deadly absurdity of elite rule) in the events of the Gwangju uprising. Not only was there no preexisting organization to stage a coup d'etat, but known leaders of the movement were either arrested or in hiding when the uprising began. On the night of May 17, military intelligence personnel and police raided homes of activists across the city, arresting the leadership of the movement. Almost all of those not picked up went into hiding. Already at least 26 of the movement's national leaders (including Kim Dae Jung) had been rounded up. According to one observer: "The head of the movement was paralyzed."[11] Another wrote that the "leading body of the students' movement was in a state of paralysis."[12]

Nonetheless the very next morning, students spontaneously organized themselves —first by the hundreds and then by the thousands—to march in protest of the occupation of their city by police and freshly arrived units of the army. As the city mobilized the next day, people from all walks of life dwarfed the number of students among the protesters.[13] The spontaneous generation of a peoples' movement transcended traditional divisions between town and gown, one of the first indications of the generalization of the revolt. On May 20, this capacity for self-government was present in the streets. Tens of thousands of people gathered on Kumnam Avenue and sang, "Our wish is national reunification." Paratroopers' clubs dispersed them. At 5:50 p.m., as the brutality and resistance continued, a crowd of 5000 surged over a police barricade. When the paratroopers drove them back, they reassembled and sat-in on a road. They then *selected representatives* to try and split the police from the army.[14]

After driving the military out of the city, citizens voluntarily cleaned the streets, cooked rice, served free meals in the marketplace, and kept constant guard against the expected counterattack. Everyone contributed to and found their place in liberated Gwangju. Spontaneously a new division of labor emerged. The fighters of the Citizens' Army, many of whom had stayed up all night, nonetheless were models of responsibility. People dubbed the new militia the "Citizens' Army" or "our allies" (as opposed to the army, "our enemy.") Without any indoctrination and none of the military madness that elicits monstrous behavior in armies around the world, the men and women of the Citizens' Army behaved in an exemplary fashion. They protected the people and the people, in turn, took care of them. Unafraid to impose a new type of order based on the needs of the populace, they disarmed middle-school and high-school students,[15] and ordered government workers to return to their jobs. When the final assault was imminent, Yoon Sang-won personally insisted that the women and high schoolers among the militants return home so they could survive and continue the struggle. After many protests and with tears in their eyes, they departed.

In the heat of the moment, a structure evolved that was more democratic than previous administrations of the city. The uprising was such a clear embodiment of freedom that nearly everyone who witnessed it grasped intuitively its liberatory impulse. Years later, dispassionate scholars, including some with conservative backgrounds, could only praise the uprising's resonance with aspirations of Gwangju's citizens. As in Paris, military and police sometimes sided with the insurgents. General Chung Oong bravely refused to order the killing of innocents. The police chief in Gwangju, cognizant of the death sentences meted out to police officers who ordered the deadly shootings on April 19, 1960, also refused to participate in the slaughter. Many individual policemen helped wounded citizens and cooperated with the new civil authority once Gwangju had been liberated.

While Korean military and police personnel acted individually, during the Paris Commune, whole unites went over to the side of the Commune (or remained faithful to the government). During the war against Prussia, the French government on August 11, 1870 had organized 200 new National Guard battalions from the poorer classes to fight alongside the 60 battalions already drawn from the propertied classes. When the newly elected National Assembly of February 8, 1871 voted for France to surrender to Prussia, the people hated it, and the National Guard became the sole source of national pride. With the support of at least 215 of the existing 260 National Guard battalions, their leaders carried out a relatively bloodless coup d'etat on March 18. The Central Committee of the National Guard, composed of 3 representatives from each of the 20 arrondissements (neighborhoods) of Paris, effectively became the new government.

Military units, which sided with the Commune, were at times undisciplined. According to one observer: "The artillery battalions were in effect more completely a law unto themselves, having their own arrondissement committees, which refused to merge with the main National Guard Central Committee."[16] Confusion and poly-centric authority patterns marked the Paris Commune. On March 1, "the guiding personalities of the Paris International still had no definite political program."[17] On March 26, 287,00 men voted in fresh elections (after the National Guard's coup), and 90 members of the Commune were selected—but they included 15 government supporters and 9 citizens against the government but also against the March 18 "insurrection."[18] The next day, 200,000 people attended the announcement of the results and installation of the new government at the Hotel de Ville (City Hall). Unlike the free flowing gatherings at Democracy Square in Gwangju when everyone had a voice, the crowd in Paris watched as their representatives were sworn in, after they left. The new government created nine commissions to manage Paris, the most socialist being for Labor and Exchange. The government was not the only power to

In the midst of battle on May 20, 1980, when the military seemed to have the upper hand, autonomously organized bus and taxi drivers led the people of Gwangju in a massive counter-attack that won control of the city. Photo: Hwong Chong-gun/The May 18 Memorial Foundation.

be reckoned with however. In the analysis of one observer, "The Republican Central Committee acted as a shadow government."[19] In addition, the National Guard also gave orders to its units. Sometimes, military commanders received three sets of conflicting orders! Elected leaders' orders were often reversed by one of the other groups claiming authority—the Central Committee of the National Guard or the Republican arrondissement associations. Even though the Paris Commune had elections, the elected government was practically powerless, rivaled in military affairs by the Central Committee of the National Guard and diminished in political power by the arrondissement associations. Tragically, the elected government was also mired in personal antagonisms among its members and depleted by elected representatives who refused to serve or resigned. Most significantly, it was weakened internally by those loyal to the old government, the bitter enemy of the Commune.

Despite the presence of as many as 3000 Blanquists in 1871,[20] and even though the Commune had its disposal something like 60,000 men, 200,000 muskets, 1200 cannon, five forts and enough munitions for years,[21] decisive action was difficult. No attempt was even made to seize the Bank of France.[22] In the first week of April, more than 200 priests had been arrested,[23] but mainly through popular initiative. Louise Michel tells us that 15,000 people stood up to clash with the army during the Bloody Week,[24] but when the Versailles army first broke into the city on May 21, there were large crowds listening to a concert in the Tuileries Gardens.[25] Even more indicative of the lack of discipline and unity in Paris was a poster of the Central Committee of the National Guard: "Death for Looting, Death for Stealing"[26] In liberated Gwangju, by contrast, incidents of looting or stealing were practically nonexistent.

The Paris Commune's Role in the Gwangju Uprising

In a series of interviews, Lee Jae-eui, author of the definitive narrative history of the Gwangju Uprising,[27] offered penetrating analysis of the differences and similarities between the Paris Commune and Gwangju People's Uprising.[28] "During the Paris Commune, they had enough time to organize elections and set up an administrative structure. But in Gwangju, there was not the time for the leadership to get authority from the people." Lee continued: "In response to the situation. I suppose it's very similar. Even though there were so many differences—ideological, historical, social, cultural—human beings respond to protect their dignity and existence."

In my interview with Yoon Hang-bong, we discussed the Paris Commune at some length.[29] Yoon felt the Paris Commune and the Gwangju Uprising were not similar because the Paris Commune was more "systematic and ideological." In his view, Gwangju was more "voluntary." "People's level of democracy was very low here," he said. "They believed US ships were coming to help them, showing they had no understanding of international political dynamics." Yoon felt that the workers of the Paris Commune had a high consciousness but that in Gwangju the workers were not educated. The Gwangju Uprising was "moral"—stores and banks were not robbed. "If they had some conception of class consciousness, they would have redistributed these goods and funds to the poor." When I interjected that the Bank of France had also been left alone during the Paris Commune—indeed guarded by the Communards— we decided to continue the discussion at greater length another time.

According to Kim Sang-gil, the Paris Commune and Gwangju Uprising were similar in their community spirit, in the ways people "lived and struggled together" under difficult circumstances. Like the Paris Commune, there were many calls for an uprising before the actual event transpired. Kim recalled how he, Kim Nam-ju and Park Sung-moo called for an uprising in 1972. They secretly threw leaflets at from the administration and law school buildings at CNU on December 8, after which they repeated their action at Gwangju Ilgo and the girls' High School.[30] He also mentioned other calls for an uprising long before 1980.

Not only were the Paris Commune and Gwangju People's Uprising similar events,

With the city surrounded by the army, Gwangju citizens banded together in a loving community.
Woodblock print by Hong Sung Dam.

but the conscious memory of the Paris Commune played a role in the events of 1980 Gwangju. Of the 29 interviews I conducted in 2001 with participants in the Uprising, many persons indicated that they had been part of study groups that for a time focused on the Paris Commune before the Gwangju Uprising. Moreover, one person remembered that Yoon Sang-won had attended a 1976 speech given by poet Kim Nam-ju at Nokdu bookstore in which Kim Nam–ju discussed the Paris Commune.[31] During the uprising, Yoon Sang-won spoke publicly at least once about the Paris Commune in his discussions with other leading members of the Uprising.[32]

A history major in his undergraduate years at Chonnam National University, Lee Yang-hyun read about the Paris Commune in the 1970s. From his readings, he recalled that "3 to 4-year-old kids threw rocks at the French Army." Though he thought that was an exaggeration, he observed his own 3-year-old son throw rocks at the police during the Gwangju Uprising.[33] During high school, Lee and his classmate Chang Sang-Yon (also a prominent participant) were part of a book club that focused for a time on the Paris Commune. Kim Jong-bae reported that Chang Sang-yong, Yoon Gang-ok, Kim Yong-chol, Yoon Sang-won, and Park Ho-son were all members of a Paris Commune study group prior to the uprising.[34] Yoon Gang-ok described the group as "loose-knit"—meaning anyone could join—and recalled the key role of Professor Lee Young–hee. Kim Hyo-sok read about the Paris Commune during one of the meetings of his "good book club" at the YWCA.[35] Organized by Yoon Young-kyu and Song Gi-suk, these clubs attracted a wide following. According to Yoon Young-kyu, at least 18 readers' clubs were organized in Gwangju in the late 1970s. Bringing together high schoolers, college students and professors, these groups included "opinion leaders" and leaders of illegal organizations. Many books were available about the Paris Commune, all illegal and many of poor quality printing.[36]

Chong Sang-yong remembered reading about the Paris Commune before the uprisings in a group called Kwang Rang (Gwangju Young Men), which had been created after the overthrow of Syngman Rhee on 4.19.61.[37] As he recalled, in 1966 the texts were read in Japanese by older college colleagues who then presented summaries in a group of about 20 people—several from each grade level. These people then, in turn, discussed the subject with their own colleagues, a structure that facilitated learning by a large number of people. Kim Sang-yoon remembered a study group in 1978 that focused on the Paris Commune. "At most 5 people would study together. Each member would then form another group on almost the same topic. Kim Nam-ju got a Japanese book about the Paris Commune."[38] While Lee Chun-hee read intensively about the Paris Commune after the uprising, she recalled that during the uprising, leading people talked about the Paris Commune at the YWCA, along with the significance of the Argentinean-born revolutionary Che Guevara.[39]

These direct connections between the Paris Commune and the Gwangju Uprising illustrate how the legacy of uprisings, whether in Paris or Gwangju, is to empower other humans to struggle against oppression. Even when an uprising is brutality suppressed—as in both cases here under consideration—their being experienced publicly creates new desires and new needs, new fears and new hopes in the hearts and minds of participants and all those standing in the path of the ripples of history being made.

Conclusion

The sudden emergence of hundreds of thousands of people occupying public space, the spread of the revolt from one city to another and throughout the countryside, the intuitive identification with each other of hundreds of thousands of people and their simultaneous belief in the power of their actions, the suspension of normal values like regionalism, competitive business practices, criminal behavior, and acquisitiveness are dimensions of the "eros effect" in both the Paris Commune and the Gwangju Uprising.[40] After World War 2, the sudden and unexpected contestation of power has become a significant tactic in the arsenal of popular movements. Popular uprisings remain a powerful weapon of social transformation.

As an example of ordinary people taking power into their own hands, the Gwangju Uprising and Paris Commune were (and are) the precursors of a truly free society. To catch a glimpse of such a society we need to look no further than liberated Paris or Gwangju during the People's Uprising. Despite the brutality of the states, people briefly tasted freedom. The example set by citizens of Paris and Gwangju in their spontaneous capacity for self-government and organic solidarity may well be their most important legacy. Alongside these indications of the unrealized potential of human beings today, there were concrete gains in Gwangju—the overthrow of the military dictatorship and the inspiration of other democratic movements—and specific lessons taught through the blood and sacrifices of so many. Today, the uprisings continue to provide all of us with a palpable feeling for the dignity of human beings and the necessity of intensifying the struggle for liberation.

NOTES

1   An earlier version appeared in *New Political Science* 25, no. 2 (June 2003), pp. 261–70.

2   Louise Michel, *The Red Virgin: Memoirs of Louise Michel* (Tuscaloosa: University of Alabama Press, 1981), p. 65.

3   Eugene Schulkind, ed., *The Paris Commune of 1871: The View from the Left* (New York: Grove Press, 1974), p. 152.

4   Roger L. Williams estimates between 17,000 and 20,000 were killed, "many of whom had been given no quarter but simply butchered." p. 151. See Williams, *The French Revolution of 1870-1871* (New York: W.W. Norton, 1969). In addition, of the 46,835 cases heard in trials from 1871 to 1875, 24,000 were acquitted. Of the nearly 13,000 convictions, 110 were sentenced to death—of which 26 were actually executed (p. 152). Louise Michel (pp. 67 and 168) put the number at 35,000 killed. Patrick Hutton (p. 96) estimates 25,000 were executed at the wall after the suppression of the Commune. See Hutton, *The Cult of the Revolutionary Tradition: The Blanquists in French Politics, 1864-1893* (Berkeley: University of California Press, 1981), p. 96.

5   See Na Kahn-chae, "A New Perspective on the Gwangju People's Resistance Struggle: 1980–1997," *New Political Science* 23, no. 4 (2001), pp. 477–91.

6   Quoted in Peter Kropotkin, "The Commune of Paris," which first appeared in English as *Freedom Pamphlets* No. 2 (London: W. Reeves, 1895).

7   Hutton, p. 127.

8   Alain Plessis, *The Rise and Fall of the Second Empire 1852-1871* (Cambridge University Press, 1987), p. 69. (This index was calculated in constant Francs with 1890 = 100.)

9   Plessis, p. 115.

10   Stewart Edwards, *The Paris Commune, 1871* (Chicago: Quadrangle Books, 1973), p. 15.

11   Translated into English as Lee Jae-eui, *Gwangju Diary: Beyond Death, Beyond the Darkness of the Age* (Los Angeles: UCLA Asian Pacific Monograph Series, 1999), p. 41.

12   *The May 18 Kwangju Democratic Uprising* (The 5.18 History Compilation Committee of Kwangju City, 1999), p. 121.

13   *The May 18*, p. 127.

14   Lee, p. 64.

15   Fighters' Bulletin, *Documents*, p. 71.

16   Edwards, p. 32.

17   Schulkind, p. 294.

18   Plessis, p. 171 estimates the number of voters at 230,000 out of 470,000 who were registered.

19   Williams, pp. 90, 122, 130.

20   Hutton, p. 30.

21   Lissagaray, *History of the Commune of 1871* (New York: Monthly Review Press, 1967), p. 183.

22   Williams, p. 138.

23   Hutton, pp. 81–82.

24   Michel, p. 67.

25   Edwards, p. 40.

26   Schulkind, p. 136.

27   Lee.

28   Lee Jae-eui, interview March 17, 2001.

29   Interview with Yoon Hang-bong, October 29, 2001.

30   Interview with Kim Sang-gil, November 7, 2001.

31   Interview with Kim Sang-gil, November 7, 2001.

32   Interview with Lee Yang-hyun, June 22, 2001.

33   Interview with Lee Yang-hyun, June 22, 2001.

34   Interview with Kim Jong-bae, November 27, 2001.

35   Interview with Kim Hyo-sok, November 6, 2001.

36   Interview with Yoon Young-kyu, April 10, 2001.

37   Interview with Chong Sang-yong, October 17, 2001.

38   Interview with Kim Sang-yoon, April 15, 2001.

39   Interview with Lee Chun-hee, December 21, 2001.

40   See *The Imagination of the New Left: A Global Analysis of 1968* (Seoul: E-who Press, 1999) and *The Subversion of Politics: European Autonomous Social Movements and the Decolonization of Everyday Life* (Seoul: E-who, 2000) for discussion of what I call the "eros effect."

Germany's Autonomous Movement[1]

WITHIN POPULAR MOBIILIZATIONS in Europe, whether those of the peace movement, the contestation of nuclear power plants at Brokdorf, or the prolonged attempt to stop the Startbahn West runway in Frankfurt, radicals provided the militant cutting edge to struggles. By the mid-1980s, they consolidated themselves and served as an organizing base separate from single-issue campaigns and locally defined groups. They built urban bases in Berlin, Hamburg, Amsterdam, and Copenhagen. After the high point of autonomous "dual power" of the squatters in Kreuzberg in 1983, activists moved on to other projects and campaigns. By 1984, all the squatted houses in Germany had been legalized, and the antinuclear power and weapons insurgencies were momentarily quiet, but the Autonomen (radical clusters of activists galvanized in the crucible of years of militant struggles) helped create a "renaissance" of resistance.

Their most significant victory occurred at Wackersdorf, Bavaria, the site of a nuclear reprocessing facility being built with the capacity to provide Germany with bomb-grade plutonium. Twice in 1985–86, Autonomen initiated the occupation of the construction site.[2] Demonstrations of between forty thousand and eighty thousand persons were pulled together with regularity, often despite police bans on such gatherings.[3] On December 12, 870 persons were arrested when the first *Hüttendorf* was cleared out, and on January 7, another 700 people were taken into custody at a nearby encampment.[4] Impressed with the sincerity and determination of the Autonomen, Bavarian farmers and middle-class people became involved in the protracted campaign to prevent Wackersdorf from ever opening. Every weekend for months, thousands of people gathered at the site, and when confrontations occurred, autonomous groups received support from the local population. As one unsympathetic observer put it: "Stunned Germans watched unprecedented scenes on their TV screens as old ladies led masked Autonomen away to hide them from the police, and farmers wielded shovels and pitchforks against police."[5] The response of the authorities was to forbid public events (even the performance of Haydn's *Creation* in June 1987) and private meetings (as when antinuclear groups were prevented from having a national meeting in Regensburg at the end of November 1986). Nonetheless, the movement continued its mobilizations and militant actions, eventually winning closure of Wackersdorf (although the government claimed that it was for technical reasons).

As exemplified at Wackersdorf, autonomous movements synthesized a new militance—neither armed guerrilla actions nor passive civil disobedience. Their conscious spontaneity provided an alternative to party membership that facilitated activism and provided a new means of impacting political developments. Besides Wackersdorf, Autonomen also played a critical role in a victorious campaign against a national census that would have authorized half a million bureaucrats to pry into the private lives of West Germans.[6] During the same time that the Common Market unified European planning and production, autonomous movements resisted world economic developments that impacted cities and regions without taking local needs into account. Opposition to gentrification and capital-intensive building projects, exemplified in the struggles against Startbahn West and Wackersdorf, is part of the defense of localized life—worlds being destroyed by the giant governments and global corporations.

Despite conservative interpretations of autonomy as meaning isolation from the rest of the world—or worse, autonomy at the expense of others, as in the case of Serbia—the type of autonomy practiced by the transnational Autonomen was in harmony with the downtrodden. In solidarity with the "wretched of the earth," they acted according to ethical and moral imperatives of international solidarity. In June 1987, the day before Ronald Reagan paid his second presidential visit to Berlin, more than fifty thousand people went into the streets to protest, and ten thousand riot police mobilized to protect him.[7] The next day, in order to prevent a disruption of Reagan's speech, the city fathers and their US military governors issued an order banning three scheduled demonstrations. To make sure that their will prevailed, they sealed off the Autonomen stronghold in the Kreuzberg neighborhood of Berlin, claiming that "technical difficulties" caused the subways there to stop running. Promised replacement buses never appeared, and anyone trying to leave Kreuzberg was stopped at one of nine checkpoints ringing the neighborhood. Despite all these precautions, when a spontaneous demonstration erupted in the middle of the city, the police quickly surrounded it and held over five hundred people in a "kettle" (an encirclement of police) for over five hours. Several of these measures violated existing laws, causing a legal crisis of no small proportions. But the shooting deaths of two policemen at Startbahn West on November 2, 1987, soon overshadowed the government's abuse of power in Berlin.

In September 1988, the autonomous movement moved to the next level of confrontation against the world system. Using the international conventions of the World Bank and the International Monetary Fund (IMF) to dramatize the contradiction between internationalization from the top and the destruction of autonomy at the grassroots, they were the motor force behind a broad mobilization on Berlin.

While the Greens met to discuss alternatives to the existing world financial system and dozens of other groups organized events, the Autonomen declined to cooperate with reformists vis-à-vis the IMF.[8] *Der Spiegel* quoted one radical as saying: "A death machine can only be combated."[9]

Acting on their understanding of the imperialist role of the IMF, the Autonomen mobilized thousands of militants from across Germany as well as from England, Italy, Holland, Denmark, Austria, and the United States. When eighty thousand protesters arrived to demonstrate against the conventions of these globally decisive organizations, thousands of bankers were compelled to cut short their meetings and leave Berlin a day earlier than they had planned. During the convention's first four days, the twelve thousand police and and four thousand private bodyguards were able to maintain order only by banning demonstrations and viciously attacking hastily assembled groups of protesters. As members of the international press corps and local residents were brutalized by roaming police snatch squads, public sympathy for the Autonomen grew. On their side, the Autonomen enforced a strict ban on alcohol at movement bars. In preparation for their confrontations, they tried to drive heroin users and dealers out of Kreuzberg in a campaign dubbed "Fists Against Needles." Most importantly, rather than inviting riots into their neighborhood, they took great pains to make sure that street fights would happen in the fashionable sections of Berlin, indicating that the movement had built a base area that it was now protecting from police invasion.

The importance of social movements in the new epoch we have entered since the demise of Soviet Communism, far from being determined by an ability to wield national power, will be more a function of a capacity to limit the powers of nation-states and to create free spaces in which self-determined decisions can be made autonomously and implemented directly. At best, the existing system offers a facade of popular input into state agencies or allows space for cooperative groups to function within a larger context of obedience to the state and market profitability. Although it provides unprecedented consumer wealth for a majority of people in the advanced capitalist societies, the world system is founded upon unprecedented misery for tens of millions of people at its periphery—as well as an increasingly marginalized strata in its core. Powerful nation-states and mammoth transnational corporations are essentially products of the modern world—that is, the epoch between the industrial revolution and World War II. As the behemoth powers of governments and corporations expanded, popular control over significant decisions of life were eroded. Privacy continues to be invaded, family life destroyed, job security made nonexistent, environmental conditions degraded, water made unfit to drink, and air made poisonous to our health. In short, the conditions of life are being destroyed at the same time as previously independent realms of everyday life are increasingly subsumed by the commodity form and criteria of profitability. This "colonization of the life-world" shifts the sites for the contestation of power by social movements from politics to everyday life.

In contrast to the centralized decisions and hierarchical authority structures of modern institutions, autonomous social movements involve people directly in decisions affecting their everyday lives. They seek to expand democracy and to help individuals break free of political structures and behavior patterns imposed from the outside. Rather than pursue careers and create patriarchal families, participants in autonomous movements live in groups to negate the isolation of individuals imposed by consumerism. They seek to decolonize everyday life. The base of the autonomous movement in dozens of squatted and formerly squatted houses reflects a break with the established norms of middle-class propriety in their everyday lives: communes instead of traditional families; movement restaurants and bars where the "scene" can have its own space, as opposed to the commercialized world of mass culture; an international community defined by its radical actions, in contrast to the patriotic spectacles so beloved in Europe.

In this context, the Autonomen represent a paradigm shift in politics that began with the New Left but has become increasingly well defined. Unlike other movements of the twentieth century that have been preoccupied with seizing national power they seek to dissolve it. Their subversion of politics means a complete reorientation of our understanding of the role of nation-states and individual obedience to their laws. In place of massive systems of representative democracy and majority rule, they live according to principles of direct democracy and self-government. They do not seek to create mammoth structures of power, nor are they interested in participating in existing ones. Although their numbers are small, their actions often have a significance beyond what quantitative analysis would indicate. Autonomous movements have been called "postpolitical" because of their lack of regard for elections and political parties. I prefer to think of these movements as subverting politics, as transforming public participation into something completely different from what is normally understood as political.

The Meaning of Autonomy

Clearly, autonomy has a variety of meanings. Western philosophy since Kant has used the term to refer to the independence of individual subjectivity, but as I use the term, autonomy refers mainly to collective relationships, not individual ones. In my analysis of social movements, several meanings of autonomy emerge: first and most saliently, the independence of social movements from political parties and trade unions. Thus, movements for regional or national autonomy are not autonomous movements in the sense in which I use the term if they are aligned with established political parties. The Irish independence movement, for example, struggles for Ireland's autonomy from Great Britain, but I do not consider it to be an autonomous movement, because it is controlled by hierarchically organized parties and traditional conceptions of politics. Separatist movements of all kinds abound today, but few, if any, are autonomous movements. National and regional autonomy has long been a central issue for movements in peripheral areas of the world system. In the current period, the demand for autonomy is present within movements in Kurdistan, India, the Basque country, and many parts of the former Soviet Union. Subcomandante Marcos of the Zapatistas in Chiapas, Mexico, presented the major demands of the peasants as "food, health, education, autonomy, and peace."[10] In Brazil, the United Black Movement, founded in 1978 when blacks gathered to protest the murder by the police of a black man accused of stealing an apple, considers political autonomy for blacks to be one of its main goals. Aspirations for greater regional autonomy for Native Americans in Chiapas or Afro-Brazilians in Bahia, although not precisely the same type of autonomy as is present in European movements, nonetheless demonstrate the formal similarity of these emergent movements. They all call for "Power to the People" and decentralization of decision making concentrated in nation-states.

In Italy in the 1970s, thousands of factory workers participated in Autonomia, and the meaning of autonomy extracted from their experiences was sometimes defined exclusively in workerist terms. According to Johannes Agnoli, the concept of autonomy in northern Italy had two dimensions: class struggle made itself autonomous of the circulation of capital; and the class struggle was not led by traditional organizations of the Left (Communists and their trade unions).[11] Although widely propagated, workerist definitions of autonomy are but one of its many forms, even in reference to the movement in Italy. Italian and German autonomous women's movement were vital to subsequent formations, because of feminists' innovative internal procedures as well as their capacity to act separately from men in accordance with their own autonomously defined needs and aspirations. These autonomous feminist movements set an example of a "politics of the first person," as opposed to traditional notions of revolutionaries leading the nation or the working-class. Within these movements, moreover, individuals did not take orders from higher-ups but voluntarily acted according to their own will (thereby preserving the original Kantian kernel of autonomy within an enlarged meaning and collective context). Many feminist groups operated according to self-managed consensus, making decisions independently of central leaders and implementing them according to their own self-discipline. This organizational model remains vitally important to the definition of autonomous movements.

A final meaning of autonomy emerged in the course of prolonged popular struggles against nuclear power in Germany in the mid-1970s. Activist groups began referring to themselves as autonomous to establish distance from party-oriented Marxist-Leninist groups within the antinuclear movement that denied the value of spontaneous forms of militant resistance. As radical clusters also appeared within the peace movement and the counterculture and among squatters, they merged into a multifaceted formation that eventually became known as the Autonomen. By creatively synthesizing direct-democratic forms of decision-making and militant popular resistance, the Autonomen embody what I call "conscious spontaneity."

The Autonomen do not subscribe to the belief that there is one overriding truth or one true form of autonomy. There are, nonetheless, a number of principles that provide coherence: they see their ideas as a revolutionary alternative to both authoritarian socialism (Soviet-style societies) and "pseudodemocratic capitalism." Unlike Communists, they do not believe in the need for one true revolutionary party or revolutionary sector of society. They believe in diversity and continuing differentiation. Nowhere written down, this principle emerges in the actions of thousands of people in their everyday lives. They believe in self-management and the need for individuals and groups to take responsibility for their own actions. Although these notions may be contradicted in the actions of some, they materialize in the enduring patterns of movement activity. The Autonomen seek to change governments as well as everyday life, to overthrow capitalism and patriarchy.[12]

Viewed from the perspective of how they constitute a determinate negation of the structural imperatives of the world system, the Autonomen should be understood as verification of my prognosis that the cultural-political character of the New Left would continue to define the long-term form of antisystemic movements.[13] As autonomous movements find adherents in places such as Prague, Athens, Lyon (France), Moscow, San Francisco, and New York, it becomes increasingly apparent that, though often invisible to the mainstream, they define the phenomenal form of contemporary radical activism.

The Autonomen: an Invisible Movement

Relative to the voluminous literature on France and England in print in the United States, few books exist about Germany, and those in print deal mainly with the Nazi past, the rise and fall of Communism, or the neo-Nazis of today. It is no wonder that prejudice against Germans is not uncommon among Americans. So long as Germans are characterized as orderly and obedient, we Americans feel secure in our superior democratic values and cultural pluralism. After all, the Allies liberated the German people from their Nazi overlords, we Americans gave them their first democratic constitution, and we also financed the postwar reconstruction that made possible their current prosperity.

To the extent that Americans are aware of progressive Germans, it is generally the Greens. Taking advantage of the proportional representation rule governing German elections,[14] the Greens (and more recently, the Left Party) quickly established a presence within local and national governments and became the third largest party in Germany in the mid-1990s. In 1983, they got over two million votes in the federal election. When they took their seats in parliament, their long hair and casual attire signaled a larger change in German society and politics. On both sides of the Atlantic, mainstream analysts worried about the "threat" constituted by German pacifism to the Cold War. Due to the media's focus on them, it was commonly assumed that the Greens created and led Germany's progressives.

One of my purposes is to dispel that myth. Often considered by outsiders to be identical with Left radicalism in Germany, the Greens are but the most prominent organization to emerge from a broad-based and diverse social movement. Since there is so little information in the United States concerning the Autonomen, the assumption is often made that this invisible movement is irrelevant or even nonexistent.[15] Long before the Green Party was founded in 1979, an autonomous women's movement had waged a militant campaign for the decriminalization of abortion and created dozens of women's centers. Other extraparliamentary direct-action movements arose and challenged the conservative spell that had gripped German national politics from Hitler to the *Berufsverbot* (government decrees in the 1970s that effectively stifled dissent by civil servants). Grassroots groups (*Bürgerinitiativen*) first thawed the frozen political terrain when they began a process of publicly challenging unpopular policies such as the construction of nuclear power plants, the expansion of the gigantic airport in Frankfurt, and the continuing housing shortage.[16] As local communities organized to protect their surroundings from encroachments by the industrial-political behemoth, their initiatives slowly gathered supporters seeking greater democratic input into significant social decisions. The country's heavy reliance on nuclear fission as a source of energy became a key issue. Confrontations against nuclear power projects posed the need for a parliamentary presence within the system that could articulate the aspirations of the emergent antinuclear movement, whose popular support was clearly greater than anyone had anticipated. As the Greens began to run for office, radicals squatted in hundreds of abandoned houses in the inner cities and used them as a base from which to radicalize the peace, ecology, and feminist movements.

The Green Party was formed to fulfill needs dramatized by these extraparliamentary impulses—to clean up Germany's environment; to make its governing structure more democratic; and to break the hold of the patriarchal, small-town mentality that encroached upon women's freedom, denied gays the right to be themselves, and crippled the capacity of young people to live according to their own ideas. In the crucible of years of struggles, direct-action movements galvanized the radical Autonomen. Employing militant confrontational tactics against the police in the 1980s, the Autonomen played a major role in defeating the government's plans for a nuclear reprocessing plant at Wackersdorf in Bavaria that would have provided Germany with bomb-grade plutonium. Their noncooperation campaign caused the government to cancel a national census, and they helped undermine Berlin's bid to host the Olympics in 2000. These victories of autonomous movements are arguably more important than any gains won through the parliamentary system in the same period.

At first glance, the different levels of political action on which direct-action movements and political parties operate appear to complement each other. Within the German movement, however, the contradiction between building domains autonomous from the government and participating in parliamentary activity within it animates a complex political discourse all but unknown in the United States. On the surface, since the movements and the parties all appear to seek similar goals, it appears that they differ only in their tactics. The divergence between these two wings of the German movement is actually much greater than that, encompassing organizational forms as well as differences of strategy (building self-governing centers of dual power versus transforming the society from within parliament). Although militant actions and electoral activity often provide reciprocal benefits to each other, they can also generate bitter conflicts.

For many Autonomen, the Greens are not the movement in the government but the government in the movement. They are that part of the establishment that has penetrated the radical opposition, another mechanism used by the state to extend and legitimate its authority. As such, the Greens represent the latest example of co-opted movement groups following in the historical footsteps of the Social Democratic party (with whom the Greens have formed state and local coalition governments). For some readers, it may be disconcerting to read that the Greens are on the fringe of a radical egalitarian movement, but it would be less than honest for me to present them in any other manner.

To many Greens, the Autonomen are guilty of "blind actionism" (and worse); they substitute "the struggle for their goal instead of liberation." The Autonomen are "violent anarchists" who throw tomatoes and eggs at high government officials rather than engage them in rational debate. They are often linked to guerrilla groups such as the RAF, a group that has kidnapped and killed some of the country's leading bankers, industrialists, and political leaders.

I see these approaches (within and outside the system) as complementary. They require each other for their continual elaboration and historical impact. From my perspective, the Autonomen exist in a political terrain lying between the reformism of the Greens and the adventurism of the German guerrillas. Most Autonomen would vehemently disagree with my characterization of the Greens as even a part of the movement. They perceive the Greens as more of a threat to the movement's vitality than any other established political force, because the Greens are able to gain access to so many movement activities, blunt their radical potential, and even aid the police in isolating the movement. During preparations for a planned demonstration against the Brokdorf nuclear power plant in 1986, for example, many of the more than fifty thousand people going to protest refused to submit to mandatory police inspections of their automobile caravans before they went on the autobahns. Green organizers, however, agreed to allow their vehicles to be searched for helmets and other materials that might be used to confront the massed police defenders at Brokdorf. Naturally, the police simply waved the Greens through their checkpoints and then bloodily dispersed the remaining protesters before they could even assemble (as occurred in Berlin). Near Hamburg, hundreds of people were brutally attacked while stopped in their cars. Many of those injured in the police attack blamed the Greens' cooperation with the police for effectively identifying those who refused to submit to the searches.

A less severe example of the Greens' distance from the Autonomen came in September 1988, when the Autonomen prepared demonstrations against the international conventions of the World Bank and the International Monetary Fund in Berlin. Thousands of militant demonstrators tried to stop the top finance ministers of 150 countries and over ten thousand world bankers from planning their future exploits (since the protestors blamed them for poverty and starvation at the periphery of the world economy). For their part, the Green Party and its affiliates attempted to defuse the planned confrontation by calling for a convention of their own to discuss the possibility of an "alternative world banking system." Unlike the Greens, the radical Autonomen would have little to do with banks—alternative or not—or any kind of system. The type of world they seek to create and to live in is as far removed as possible from money, centralization, government, and ownership in all their forms.

The autonomous framework of action constitutes a promising realm of politics that is not generally considered by analysts of social movements and activists outside Europe. Contained within the history of autonomous movements are many of their most salient points of departure from other types of politics:

1. The tension between working within the system and working entirely in opposition to it, and the, relative advantages and liabilities of each approach.

2. The importance of establishing alternative humane lifestyles right now, not only challenging power at the collective political level.
3. The formulation of a universal species interest and the transcendence of exclusive identities that delimit the aspirations and vision of groups.
4. The psychological disposition and Nazi heritage of the German people and the potential for these to affect radical social movements.

The first three are certainly enduring questions, and the fourth can also be understood in a more general form: how can we prevent decentralized popular movements from attracting and incorporating hateful elements, particularly those drawn from ethnic chauvinism?

The Autonomous Women's Movement

As the APO and the popular upsurge of the 1960s faded, feminism in Germany went from the margins of a student revolt to become an enduring movement that affected German society far more profoundly than any postwar social movement. In 1988, twenty years after the appearance of militant feminism, Alice Schwarzer, one of the autonomous women's movement's most important spokespersons, declared, "We feminists have made a cultural revolution! The only real one since 1945."[17] Although her optimism may have been exaggerated, her point was not incorrect.

The direct impact of feminism was clear enough in the newfound political power enjoyed by women, as well as in new opportunities in other domains previously reserved for men. Most importantly, in the transvaluation of the subtle and overt demeaning of women that centuries of patriarchy had produced, everyday life had been transformed for millions of women. Indirectly, the women's movement prefigured what would later become the Autonomen. Feminists were the ones who made "autonomy" their central defining point, and they passed it along to the next generations of activists. Their counterinstitutions were visionary and, like their illegal occupations of vacant houses that were then fixed up (*Instandbesetzungen*), subsequently became examples for larger movements. Before others did so, they began to work with immigrant Turkish women, and well before the Greens developed the slogan that they were "neither Left nor Right but in front," the women's movement had labeled Left and Right as patriarchal concepts having little to do with feminism.

On September 13, 1968, a critical date in the history of the German New Left and of German feminism, Helke Sander, a member of the Berlin Action Council for Women's Liberation, gave an impassioned speech at the national meeting of German SDS in Frankfurt calling an her male comrades to remove "the blinders you have over your eyes" and take note of their own sexism.[18] As expected by some, the meeting returned to business as usual as soon as she finished speaking. But when SDS theoretician Hans-Jürgen Krahl was in the middle of his speech (having nothing to do with the feminist appeal for support), another female delegate from Berlin screamed at him: "Comrade Krahl, you are objectively a counterrevolutionary and an agent of the class enemy!" She then hurled several tomatoes in the direction of the podium, one of which hit Krahl squarely in the face.

Many of the women in SDS were embarrassed by the action, but the deeds of the Berlin Action Council for Women's Liberation electrified feminists and are considered to be the beginning of the autonomous women's movement. Although it had formed while organizing among mothers with young children trying to cope with the scandalous lack of day care *(Kinderladen),* the Berlin Action Council's roots in the antiauthoritarian New Left defined its overly critical understanding of motherhood. In January 1968, it wrote: "The function of the mother is to internalize forms of domination and treat them as love." As many of these women were compelled to bring children to meetings and interrupt their own participation while their male comrades gave speeches about the "repressive nature of monogamy" and the need to negate *(Aufheben)* the "fixation of the children on their parents," women's self-critical comments were transformed into a mothers' movement around the issue of day care. While their subservience in SDS was initially ignored by their male counterparts, after they successfully organized kindergarten teachers, their groups began to be taken over by men.[19]

Initially, women saw their withdrawal from mixed groups as temporary, "to bring us to the point where we can come to our own self-understanding without hindsight and compromises. Only then will we be capable to unite with other groups in a meaningful fashion."[20] Like their male counterparts in the New Left, they believed that the class struggle was primary and women's liberation a "secondary contradiction." As women mobilized, crass male domination propelled militant feminists into ever more radical theory and practice. In November 1968, a group of SDS women from Frankfurt attempted to read a prepared statement at an SPD celebration of the fiftieth anniversary of women's right to vote, but they were physically prevented from doing so by SPD officials. They then formed a "Broad's Council" and prepared a now legendary leaflet for the next national SDS meeting a few weeks later. Entitled "Free the Socialist Eminences from Their Bourgeois Dicks!" the leaflet pictured six mounted penises with the corresponding names of male SDS leaders beneath them and a reclining female figure with an axe in her hand.

Nothing was more important to the new movement than the campaign to liberalize the abortion laws. Statutes criminalizing abortion had been on the books since 1871,[21] and at the turn of the century, intermittent struggles had failed to win significant reform. The specific statute that the second wave of feminists sought to repeal was paragraph 218 in the Basic Laws that outlawed abortion. On March 8, 1969, International Women's Day, the first of many demonstrations for deletion of paragraph 218 took place. The number of illegal abortions in West Germany was estimated at anywhere from half a million to a million (although the government's figure was only 1,005 for 1969). In the same year, a poll showed that 71 percent of German women (and 56 percent of the entire population) were against paragraph 218. As demonstrations and public pressure mounted, a shock wave hit Germany on June 2, 1971, when 374 women publicly declared, "I have had an abortion" in *Stern*, one of the country's main magazines. Initiated by Alice Schwarzer (who copied the action from the Women's Liberation Front in Paris, where 343 French women had published a similar declaration two months earlier), this public confession made abortion rights the country's number-one issue. Within two months of the *Stern* article, more than 2,345 more women signed on, 973 men admitted their "complicity," and 86,100 solidarity signatures were gathered.[22]

Women's movements in the United States, Holland, and Denmark were similarly engaged in feminist campaigns, and the international diffusion of action and thought was a noteworthy feature of this period. Forging connections with women's movements in other countries, feminism in Germany helped negate national chauvinistic tendencies. At a time when anti-Americanism was a growing force among leftists, women translated and read numerous texts from the United States. They also rediscovered the existence of a first wave of German feminism, a vibrant movement dating to the mid-nineteenth century whose history had largely been hidden.

As the campaign to decriminalize abortion gathered momentum, 450 women from forty groups came together in Frankfurt on March 11 and 12, 1972, for the first national women's congress. In plenaries and four working groups, women accelerated their pace of activity. The working group on families developed concrete demands, including division of domestic chores between men and women, equal pay for equal work, an end to traditional roles in the family, a year with pay for new mothers and fathers, unconditional twenty-four-hour kindergartens, and large dwellings at cheap rents to counter the isolation of the nuclear family. Working group "Action 218" prepared a new offensive against paragraph 218. Between twenty and thirty of the forty groups participating in the conference had originally been formed to legalize abortion, and the working group served to coordinate their future activities. The conference as a whole resolved that the women's question would no longer be subsumed beneath the question of class and that they would expand their autonomous organizations. Declaring their opposition to becoming an isolated "women's island," they promised to "struggle against the existing system."[23]

Besides helping illuminate the multifaceted meaning of autonomy, these definitions illustrate the continuity between the autonomous women's movement and the extraparliamentary opposition of the 1960s. Both formations were deeply suspicious of the co-optive consequences of entering into the established system. By definition, being autonomous for both feminists and the APO meant refusing to go into these institutions in order to change them. On the one side, the women's movement was on the offensive against paragraph 218, but simultaneously it created its own counterinstitutions "out of the extraparliamentary Left, that began in 1968 to build alternative structures, to live in group houses and to have its own presses and meeting places."[24] These two dimensions, opposition to the domination of the existing system and construction of liberated spaces within it, define the universe of discourse of autonomous movements.

In comparison to its counterpart in the United States, the German women's movement emphasized autonomy rather than equality.[25] After the US movement was able to win abortion rights, its energies became focused within the established political arena. One result was that liberal feminists led thousands of activists into pouring millions of hours into an unsuccessful campaign for the equal rights amendment. Despite de jure equal rights in Germany, the failure of German feminists to obtain commensurate abortion rights preconditioned their greater emphasis on autonomy. No central organization exists there, and liberal feminists have little influence. Identified primarily with radical feminists, the autonomous women's movement refers to local projects, a network of bookstores and presses, women's centers, and publications.

Müslis and Mollis: From the New Left to The Punk Left

In 1980, the dependence of local politics and economics on the world constellation of power was nowhere more clear than in Berlin. Then a divided city with occupation troops from the United States, Great Britain, France, and the Soviet Union in control, Berlin was home to hundreds of thousands of immigrant workers and their families from Turkey, the Middle East, and southern Europe. The "economic miracle" of postwar West Berlin—the city's gross national product increased tenfold from 1950 to 1973—owed much to national and international assistance and to the foreign workers who traveled far from home to take jobs that were too hard, too monotonous, too dangerous, too dirty, or too low-paid for Germans to have even considered. In 1931, West Berlin had the fifth largest Turkish population of any city in the world, and according to government statistics, more than two million foreign workers and their families resided in West Germany, a country with a population of 61.4 million.

By 1975, the economic miracle seemed to have a hollow ring as a deep recession set in. Many foreign workers went home as the number of unemployed in Germany topped one million for the first time since 1954.[26] In 1980, unemployment rose to include about two million Germans. West Berlin was particularly hard hit, not only as a result of the international economic downturn but also by a series of financial scandals as well. The magazine *Der Spiegel* put it succinctly: "The city is being made poorer because financial capital is plundering the government's bank account." The Berlin construction industry operated with a profit rate around 120 percent, but greedy developers and their politician friends were the subjects of three major scandals. At the same time, a housing crisis of immense proportion was touched off by an informal capital strike by big landlords after the passage of rent control and tough protection laws for tenants, which coincided with the beginning of the recession in 1974. The construction of new housing had peaked in 1973 because it was extremely profitable for landlords to abandon their buildings and thereby become eligible for low-interest city loans to build condominiums for the upper middle class. Seventeen thousand people without anyplace to live were registered with the local housing authority as cases of "extreme emergency," but well over fifty thousand Berliners were looking desperately for somewhere to live, even though estimates showed that there were between seven thousand and seventeen thousand empty houses and apartments,[27] and an additional forty thousand apartments were expected to be cleared out for renovation or destruction. Under these conditions, is it surprising that people without places to live simply moved into some of the scores of abandoned buildings?

The movement spontaneously constructed a base in Kreuzberg. Adjacent to the wall separating East and West Berlin, Kreuzberg had a sizable Turkish population and countercultural scene. Hundreds of abandoned buildings along the wall were an invitation for squatters, and beginning in the late 1970s, organized groups of fifty or more people successfully seized many buildings. At its high point, the squatters' movement in Berlin controlled 165 houses, each containing more than a dozen people. They restored abandoned buildings to liveable conditions, giving birth to a new word (*Instandbesetzen*, or rehab-squat). When their actions were construed as an attack on private property, the squatters responded: "It is better to occupy for restoration than to own for destruction." In March 1980, they formed a squatters' council (*Besetzerrat*) that met weekly. In the 1980s, thousands of adherents of an "alternative scene" established themselves in Kreuzberg, and by the end of the decade, they constituted approximately 30,000 of Kreuzberg's 145,000 residents. One estimate of Kreuzberg's composition was 50,000 "normal" Berliners, 30,000 to 40,000 from the alternative scene, and 40,000 Turks.[28]

For decades, young Germans had moved to Berlin. Since the city was not formally a part of West Germany (but governed by the Allies), young German men who lived in Berlin were exempt from mandatory military service. The city's radical tradition and comparatively liberal nature also attracted many youth, as did the Free University and the Technical University, two of Germany's best and largest universities. Out of the congruence of these various conditions, a radical Berlin "youth" scene appeared, largely composed of people who were either unwilling or unable to become integrated into middle-class German society. The city government estimated that this stratum of marginalized youth comprised at least 150,000 people in all of Berlin, and it expressed concern that many of them were not only opposed to the established parties, to the government, and to nuclear power and weapons but were also unable to accept as legitimate the middle-class values of their parents.[29] According to another government study, 20 percent of the squatters in Berlin in 1980 were marginalized people looking for an alternative lifestyle, and the other 80 percent were evenly divided between students and poorly paid industrial apprentices. Although viewed as a problem by government officials, the squatters actually fixed up their buildings and the neighborhoods they lived in. They helped turn sections of Kreuzberg from largely deserted ghost towns and no-man's lands alongside the "Iron Curtain" into vibrant multicultural enclaves.

The squatters' movement began where the APO had left off—with the fusion of a cultural politics. But this time, punk rock became the music of the movement. Punk was part of the breaking free of established routine and the constraints imposed by the cultural order. After mainstream rock 'n roll had become big money, punk was fresh. Because it was a marginal phenomenon, bands played for their friends at private parties, not in amphitheaters filled with masses. Punk music was a means of unleashing aggressive reaction against the dominant circumstances of conformity and consumerism.[30] If there was something hard-core about punk, the most hardcore of the new generation of activists felt duty-bound to defend imprisoned guerrillas. Rather than being rejected as sterile and counterproductive, the commando tactics that contributed to the New Left's demise were supplanted by anarchy and disorder as the specters raised by the movement's militant fringe. "No power to anyone," a popular slogan in 1981, sharply contradicted all brands of established politics, whether that of the young social democrats who ran for student government or that of the cadre of the new communist parties. The black leather jackets worn by many people at demonstrations and the black flags carried by others signaled less an ideological anarchism than a style of dress and behavior—symbols of a way of life that made contempt for the established institutions and their US. "protectors" into a virtue, on an equal footing with disdain for the "socialist" governments in Eastern Europe. Black became the color of the political void—of the withdrawal of allegiance to parties, governments, and nations. Nude marches and an unwillingness to communicate with politicians were facets of this phase of the movement, causing order-addicted German authorities more than a little consternation. When Hamburg Mayor Ulrich Klose invited the staff members of the city's high school newspaper to city hall, five of the students came and stayed only long enough to reveal circled "A"s painted on their bare behinds.

Such flagrant violations of the social code testified to the delegitimation already suffered by the nation's institutions, but a nihilistic moment of the opposition was reproduced within the movement. When a virtuous contempt for the social order is carried over into activist circles, it becomes highly destructive, especially when there are many deep divisions within the multifarious new movement. Of all the internal differences, the most commonly named one was between punks and hippies, or, as it was known in Germany, between *Mollis* (people who might throw Molotovs) and *Müslis* (a reference to a breakfast cereal that is a little softer than granola). Generally, the Müsli Left referred to long-haired, ecology-oriented activists who were into passive nonviolence, large-scale educational projects, communal living, and the development of a harmonious, liberated sensibility in relation to all life. The Müsli Left was considered "soft" in contrast to the Punk Left's cultural rebellion and professed affinity for violent confrontations, a politics quickly dubbed the "hard line." To generalize once again, the Müslis gravitated to the country (especially the area around Wendland, where scores of organic farms sprang up); the punks were inner-city dwellers. Punks were harder and colder, dressed in black, and were male centered, whereas Müslis were warmer, rainbow, and female oriented. These two strands were intimately woven together in the movement's political culture.

The squatters defied simple classification: from rockers with working-class roots to feminists, recent immigrants from Turkey to the elderly, students to single mothers, and born-again Christians to ideological anarchists, they were more a motley collection than a self-defined collectivity of mainly students like the New Left was. As living behind barricades became a way of life for many squatters, the illegality of their everyday lives radicalized their attitude toward the state and hardened their own feeling of self-importance.

When they moved against the squatters, German authorities adopted a course of action that sought to criminalize and punish hundreds of people whose only "crime" was having nowhere to live and moving into a vacant house. This hard-line approach further radicalized large numbers of young people, pushing many into desperate acts of resistance to perceived injustice. Beginning in December 1980, police attacks on squatted houses in West Berlin touched off an escalating spiral of mass arrests, street fighting, and further occupations. Over a hundred persons were arrested and more than twice that number injured there when barricade building and heavy street fighting lasted through the cold night of Friday, December 12. The squatters' movement quickly spread throughout West Germany and collided head-on with Bavarian order.

The conservative Christian Democratic government in southern Germany had long been critical of attempts to "compromise" with the squatters by its scandal-ridden Social Democratic colleagues in Berlin. The Christian Democrats showed their own method of governing when 141 young people attending a film about squatters in an occupied house in Nürnberg were rounded up by police after the building was surrounded. Even though many of those arrested were under sixteen years old and guilty of nothing more than going to a movie, they were held incommunicado for seventy-two hours or more, and in many cases, the police refused to tell concerned parents whether their missing children were under arrest. The resulting outrage among generally conservative middle-class Germans became the prime story of the nation's television stations and newspapers, but it did not stop the Christian Democrats from bringing criminal charges against some arrested minors and defending the largest mass arrest in Germany since World War II. As the number of house occupations continued to climb, police in southern Germany surrounded another squatted house, the "Black Forest House" in Freiburg, and again conducted mass arrests.

The Freiburg squatters called for a national day of solidarity demonstrations against the police attacks, and on Friday, March 13, 1981, rallies and demonstrations were held in every major city in West Germany, as well as in many other towns that had not seen a political protest for more than a decade. The biggest demonstration in the history of Freiburg—twenty-one thousand people was a festive affair; more than a thousand showed up in Bremen and Tübingen, and more than two thousand people marched in Stuttgart. In Hamburg, a peaceful demonstration of five thousand people was viciously attacked by police with dogs. On the same day, street fighting and trashing broke out in many cities. On "Black Friday," as that day was dubbed in Berlin, the downtown Kurfürstendamm (which caters to the shopping whims of chic, mainly upper-class customers) was heavily trashed, as it had been many times before. Unlike previous confrontations, the number of people in the streets reached fifteen or possibly twenty thousand, rather than the usual two to three thousand militants. There was a nude march at the same time as small, organized groups of marauders attacked at least thirty-nine buildings. They even set the Reichstag on fire—an ill-conceived attempt to replicate its 1933 destruction through arson, which touched off the Nazi reign of terror. (Although George Dimitrov and other Communists were blamed for the arson in 1933, it has long been suspected that the fire was set by the Nazis themselves as a pretext for seizing power.)

Die Tageszeitung (*Taz*), the independent radical daily newspaper, estimated that the widespread violence and massive participation in the squatters' movement of Friday the thirteenth greatly exceeded any high points of the late 1960s. Indeed, the defense of Kreuzberg was coordinated by the squatters' council, whose members developed elaborate plans for erecting which barricades to hinder the police's ability to cross canals and main thoroughfares leading into the neighborhood. After the street fighting of December 12, 1980, *Taz* had celebrated the barricades in the spirit of the barricades of 1848, 1919, 1929, and 1967. But on Black Friday, the newspaper's office in Berlin was raided by police and its new issue confiscated from kiosks throughout the country. To top it off, criminal charges were brought against its editors. For some, the political scenario became more reminiscent of the Nazi terror of 1933 than the democratic movement's temporary victory in 1848.

The December barricades and savage street fighting in Berlin set off a political whirlwind. The city's housing crisis was brought into the limelight of the nation's media, scandals rocked the city government, and what to do about the squatters became one of the major political questions in the country. Faced by the strong resistance of the squatters' movement to police attacks, the governing Social Democrats in Berlin put forth a plan to allow the squatters to remain in their occupied houses on the condition that they pay a minimal rent. This offer of compromise brought the Social Democrats under heavy criticism from conservatives, who accused them of condoning illegal occupations of vacant buildings. Within the squatters' movement, the compromise proposal drew the usual yawns, but it also caused a few sharp debates between those who saw it as a way of simply integrating the movement into the system and those who welcomed the opportunity for a short-term solution to their individual housing problems. Although a few groups of squatters collectively decided to begin paying rent, the vast majority did not.

As the number and frequency of occupations continued to grow, the police were instructed to raid only those houses occupied by activists who were suspected of being part of the leadership of the squatters' movement, particularly organizers of demonstrations or publishers of radical periodicals. A few people from each house overrun by the police were then charged under paragraph 129 with membership in a criminal organization—a legal statute carrying a possible life sentence that previously had been used to prosecute only suspected "terrorists." The government attempted to stop the movement's internal discussion and decision-making capacity. On April 7, 1981, the entire squatters' Council (128 people) was arrested. By August 1981, over three hundred people had been brought up on serious charges, the equivalent of conspiracy indictments in the United States.[31]

The squatters had prepared elaborate telephone, radio, and word-of-mouth communication networks through which hundreds of people could be instantaneously mobilized when the police gathered for their attacks, but because Berlin is so spread out, those who would have helped resist the police attacks arrived at the scene too late—long after the barricades inside the occupied houses had been broken through and the residents taken away by the police. With no other alternative in sight, the response of the movement was to begin a new round of street fights by late afternoon on the same day that the police had attacked. This escalating spiral of attacks and counterattacks culminated in the massive outbursts of Black Friday.

After the confrontations of Black Friday, German authorities launched a major national propaganda offensive against the squatters, attempting to isolate and criminalize them by linking them with guerrilla groups. Roman Herzog, then minister of the interior in Baden-Württemberg (and, beginning in 1994, president of the republic), charged that the RAF was infiltrating and recruiting from the squatters' movement. The West German interior minister, Gerhard Baum, claimed to be able to tie seventy of the thirteen hundred known squatters to armed groups. The media pointed out that Knut Folkers, serving a life sentence for terrorism, had been arrested in 1974 in a squatted house, and Susanne Albrecht (whose Face adorned the "Wanted for Terrorism" posters that hung in every post office and many other places in West Germany) had been part of a group that had moved into a vacant house in Hamburg in one of the first occupations in 1973. Positing links between the squats and armed groups was one of the government's chief means of trying to isolate the movement, which in turn refused to ignore the plight of the imprisoned "terrorists." During April 1981, another wave of riots was touched off in Berlin, this time in response to the death of an imprisoned RAF member on a hunger strike.

Although the German movement was under attack and its major daily news source was momentarily silenced on Black Friday, local calls for action aroused mobilizations that surpassed even the most optimistic expectations. After Black Friday, the number of occupied houses jumped from 35 to 160 in West Berlin and from 86 to at least 370 (possibly as many as 500) in all of West Germany.[32] The number of squatters was estimated at between five thousand and eight thousand.[33] Besides vacant apartment buildings, empty factories, breweries, and other commercial spaces cleared for demolition were taken over. These larger buildings provided even more room for groups to create regional cultural and action centers. At the KuKuCK in West Berlin, fifty people lived in a complex that included three stages, performance areas for ten theater groups, practice rooms for five bands, a studio, a café, and an auto repair shop.[34] Besides providing room for larger groups to live near their projects, such spaces were also ways for the movement to involve people at many levels. As one observer noted:

> Creating cultural centers—the Kukuckcentrum, Spectrum Cafe, Bobby Sands Café, [they] took it with the help of alternative mechanic collectives, printing collectives, plumbing collectives, took it with money collected from habitues of alternative cafés, with the help of "Patenschaften," literally "Godparent" groups, support groups of teachers, union members, artists, doctors, lawyers who created a moat around occupied housing, keeping the alligators at bay, pledging to sleep in when police came.[35]

The movement had moved into a new phase: instead of demanding alternative youth centers from the government (as in Zurich), they took matters into their own hands, defied the authorities, and defended their centers. Autonomy had become real, not simply an abstract aspiration or phase of rebellion against parental control trips. On March 29, over one thousand people converged on Münster for the first national congress of squatters. Vowing to fight the state's criminalization of their movement, the assembled squatters promised to spread the occupations further. In October, the squatters' council in Berlin wrote an open letter to the city's citizens. Asserting that without police attacks, there would be no riots, the letter provides an insightful exposition on the meaning of autonomy as it explains the motivation for squatting houses:

> When we occupied them, it was not only for preserving living space. But we also wanted to live and work together again. We want to put a stop to the process of isolation and destruction of collective living. Who in this city is not aware of the torturing loneliness and emptiness of everyday life that arose with the growing destruction of the old connections through urban redevelopment and other kinds of development of the city? This has driven more people out of their apartments than the war.[36]

The governing Social Democrats' inability to stop the new occupations led to a new hard-line Christian Democratic government in Berlin, but its offensive against the squatters proved of little value. The movement's response to an ultimatum issued by the new mayor demanding that the squatters clear out of eight houses was a poster of ten people mooning the government and an international call to *Tu Wat* (Do Something). Although some optimistically estimated that fifty thousand Autonomen from all of Europe would converge on Berlin to defend the squatted houses, at the appointed hour, less than five thousand people took to the streets—not an insignificant number when we remember that there were no more than a couple of hundred Weatherpeople in the streets of Chicago during the Days of Rage in 1969.

In 1981, the government's inability to defeat the squatters in the streets led to a tactical innovation: legalize the squatted houses in the large cities, thereby depriving the movement of a focus for action and, more importantly, of a sense of fighting against the existing system. Legalization meant that those who were previously living an everyday existence of resistance to a repressive order were suddenly transformed into guests of a tolerant big brother who provided them not only with low-rent houses but also with money to repair them. On the one side was the carrot—but the state continued to alternate its use with the stick, hoping not only to split off the movement's hard core from the marginal supporters but also to drive more militant activists into underground actions that would alienate and depoliticize the popular movement. As long as the struggle was between the forces of law and order and militant street fighters and "terrorists," the vast majority had little choice but to sit on the sidelines and take in the spectacle.

Of course, in the smaller cities and towns, places where the movement's activist base was small, the government's tolerance was never known. Squatted houses were simply cleared soon after they were occupied, and the local authorities were able to contain what militant opposition there was. In the larger cities such as Berlin, Hamburg, and Frankfurt, however, legalization was an important factor in the depoliticization of the movement. Even when the new city government in Berlin brought massive police power to bear against the squatters, they were not able to force the movement out of existence. Over a year of legalizations and intense police attacks succeeded only in reducing the number of squatted houses in West Berlin from 162 to 123, but the continuing crisis refused to disappear. The government estimated that only 25 of these 123 houses were active squats, the rest being composed of either "drop-outs" or peaceful squatters ready to negotiate. The hard-core squats were targeted by the police, while the rest were brought to the bargaining table.[37]

Despite the severe repression, the political impact of the squatters on the established system was far greater than anyone imagined. Although often overlooked, the relationship between extraparliamentary movements and the political system is worth exploring, particularly in the case of West Berlin, since its constellation of direct-action movements and establishment politics prefigured the alignment of national political forces a few years later.

Dynamics of Parliamentary and Extraparliamentary Endeavors

Parliamentary groups must operate according to the logic of the established political system. The first rule of any party must be to obey the law. To ensure members' compliance with existing rules for participation in the government, a structure must be maintained that is compatible with the state. Insurgent social movements aimed at limiting the power of government and creating autonomy seek forms of decision-making of a qualitatively different kind. The organic structures of the popular sources of the Autonomen (feminists, squatters, ecologists, and alternatives) were loose tactical organizations within which many people with diverse viewpoints could debate differences and democratically participate in formulating programs and making decisions. General assemblies open to all were the final decision-making bodies of the Berlin squatters, as were similar gatherings at Gorleben. Within these general assemblies, decisions were reached as often as possible through the consensus of hundreds of people, a process that sought to maximize participation and nurture the expansion of activists' political consciousness. Sometimes smaller groups were delegated by the general assembly, but only to carry out the will of the larger group.

In Berlin, the individual houses were the building blocks of the movement, serving as its eyes and ears. Democratic self-discipline among the squatters made it possible to avoid an overdose of centralism. Composed of representatives from each house who shared information and made strategic decisions, the squatters' council functioned as a forum where rumors and news were discussed, and it also linked the movement with its counterparts in other cities and countries. Self-discipline was evident in the special care taken not to produce media stars or individual leaders. More often than not, television crews could not find anyone willing to speak with them.

The antinuclear movement was similarly decentralized and bottom-up. Locally organized action committees put out the calls for both the Gorleben occupation and the actions at Brokdorf. Although national coordination existed for both mobilizations, there was no centralized antinuclear organization that developed a national strategy or steadied the movement's ups and downs. Apparently, such centralization was considered superfluous, since the antinuclear movement continued to build its mobilization capacities and popular support without it and ultimately stopped the construction of all new plants. As antinuclear weapons demonstrations grew more massive, two large national coalitions formed, one composed of independents, and the other dominated by Communists.

In the mid-1970s, autonomous groups first came together as vehicles for activists who were not organized into Marxist parties to discuss practical issues of tactics and strategy. By creating spaces in which fresh perspectives on militance and spontaneity could be articulated, these small autonomous groups helped steer the antinuclear and alternative movements clear of the ossified thinking of the traditional Left (although the same was not true of the disarmament movement and the Greens). Few if any Marxist groups showed up at Gorleben, a blessing in disguise that allowed the

The Black Bloc in West Berlin, June 12, 1987, led protests against US president Ronald Reagan. Photo: Berlin Ermittlungsausschusses

movement there the space to develop its own analysis and experiences (from which many people were further radicalized). The squatters' and antinuclear movements similarly constructed space in which popular initiatives governed by democratic forms of decision making and wide-ranging debates were possible. Even within these free forums, however, rigid thinking appeared, as illustrated in the following example. At the same time as the Free Republic of Wendland was in its first week of existence, over a thousand socialists, ecologists, activists from alternative institutions, and "nondogmatic" leftists gathered at a conference in Kassel to discuss "Ecology and Socialism." In one of the keynote speeches, Green member Rudolf Bahro (formerly an imprisoned critic of the regime in East Germany) maintained that the workers' movement could not and should not continue to be separated from the ecology question. This statement brought on hours of debate with the conference's orthodox Marxists, who expressed strong reservations about the "value of environmental politics as a part of the workers' movement."

Another source of the Autonomen was the alternative movement: a collection of self-managed institutions built up to serve the everyday needs of the movement. Bookstores, bars, free schools, ecology centers, food stores, cooperative living groups *(Wohngemeinschaften),* and day-care centers were created by activists throughout West Germany. In West Berlin, where the alternative movement was particularly strong, the movement entrenched itself in the Kreuzberg neighborhood. *Die Tageszeitung*, grew to a daily national circulation of over fifty thousand.[38] According to government statistics, in February 1982, anywhere from thirteen hundred to fifteen hundred new "self help" groups in West Berlin involved 15,000 volunteers in projects affecting 80,000 to 100,000 people.[39] These alternative institutions spawned a self-help network (*Netzwerk*). Each person put a small part of his or her monthly salary into the network, and these funds were then given or lent to various projects and new or needy alternative institutions. In its first year of existence beginning in October 1978, *Netzwerk* assembled a membership of over thirty-six hundred people and distributed about 300,000 marks (then over $150,000).[40] It quickly grew in membership and resources, and it served as a model in more than thirty-six other cities.[41]

Like the feminist movement, each of these sources of the autonomous movement (squatters, the antinuclear movement, and the alternatives) shared a similar decentralized, bottom-up form of organization as well as a common belief in immediate action decided upon by participants, not by commanders. In the contemporary world, is there a need for a Leninist centralized organization to bring scientific consciousness to the masses? Or does the conscious spontaneity of the Autonomen contain its own transcendental universality? The organized spontaneity of the squatters' council and other organically generated groups seems to prove that rigidly centralized organizational models are superfluous and even destructive. By creating forms of direct democratic decision making that necessitate popular involvement, autonomous movements unleash a process that, when allowed to proceed according to its own logic, continually enlarges its constituency and further radicalizes its adherents. Unlike the epoch in which Leninist centralism was formulated, we live amidst jet planes and global news broadcasts, developments that make international connections intuitively obvious to the most casual activist. Fax machines, tape recorders, and e-mail help integrate time and space, facilitating the sharing of experiences and making it possible to overcome regional isolation. Free radios and independent print shops make informational ties globally possible from the base.

Without centralized organization, however, political discussions at public meetings were seldom coherent enough to produce unity or to have an effect on anyone other than those who happened to show up at a given time and place. Despite clear similarities among the various incarnations of the decentralized impulse for autonomy (feminism, peace, squatters, alternatives, ecology), few attempts were made to understand their shared political content. Since there was no centralized organization of the movement, a fragmentation of the movement's consciousness and theory accompanied its multifarious activism. Worst of all, in the midst of escalating mobilizations and confrontations with the police, the movement's energies were often

Aftermath of the battle for Mainzerstrasse, Berlin, November 1990. Photo: Werner Schulze, imago.

directed by the most militant activists, whose presumably higher level of commitment and sacrifice gave them the moral high ground from which they pontificated on the need for armed resistance and on the facilely criticized tendencies from which they were distanced.

Ideally, the movement would have found a process whereby each of its parts would be strengthened by criticism. Instead, each wing of the movement considered itself in isolation from the others. All too often, spokespeople and articles sought to legitimate the "correct" nature of their position. In December 1980, for example, Wolfgang Pohrt wrote a review in *Der Spiegel* of the book *Wer Soll das alles Ändern?* ("Who Should Change It All?"), a portrayal and analysis of the German alternative movement by Joseph Huber. In a scathing attack on Huber and the alternatives, Pohrt accused them of having Nazi tendencies and of succumbing to what Adorno had named the "authoritarian syndrome." Rather than examining the sectarian character of Pohrt's attack on the alternatives, many militants in Berlin greeted the harsh rebuff of the alternatives as further proof of the rightness of their contempt for the "petit bourgeois" alternative institutions. *Radikal*, Berlin's local underground newspaper, whose editors were among those facing criminal charges, reprinted the review from *Der Spiegel* without even soliciting a response from Huber. A movement whose internal process involves glib slander of individuals without simultaneously providing means of discussion of such allegations is no more democratic than established politics. The coarse form and politically insulting content of Pohrt's review are examples of the paltriness of the inner life of the movement, a process in which friendly disagreements are turned into major antagonisms.[42] But Pohrt is only one example among many. At one point, the squatters' council was unable to continue meeting because fistfights broke out among the diverse participants.

Pragmatic activism and decentralization are certainly healthy qualities when counterposed to the totalitarianism of the Nazis, and they testify to the grassroots strength of the movement as well. However, the fragmentation and atomization of the youthful movement's theory and practice can also be seen as reflections of the centrifugal force of corporate capitalism and German culture. From this point of view, the anti-intellectualism and aggression of some activists are a spontaneous carrying over of some of the worst characteristics of present-day Germany, not the self-conscious or collective creations of a liberatory movement. In the contemporary context, self-defeating tendencies (what Herbert Marcuse called "psychic Thermidor") are extraordinarily important problems of social movements, and later in this book, I return to the issues of organization and internal reaction.

Another question posed by the forms of interaction discussed above is that of the movement's self-definition. Because some of the alternative institutions received financial support from the state, for example, some people questioned whether these groups were actually part of the autonomous movement. A few critical voices went further, asserting that the alternative institutions and the West Berlin scene (including the squatters) were nothing more than "political Disneylands" where young people could go through their adolescent rebellion, after which they would "come to their senses" and fill the niches of the bureaucracy and the offices of big corporations. Other autonomists responded that the building of a new society is not an abstraction or to be reserved for the distant future and that the abandoned inner cities were precisely where free space to begin building a new society was created. Because many radicals bitterly condemned the alternative institutions as "the middle class within the movement," it was difficult to even argue the possibility that alternative institutions (such as the distrusted and often spurned Greens) could have either liberatory or co-optive functions, in part depending upon their relationship to a larger social movement. So long as the movement is defined solely by its oppositional moments, it fails to offer alternative forms capable of sustaining it over the long term. Activists opposed nuclear power and weapons, housing policies based on profits for speculators, hierarchy, and patriarchy, but they did not develop to the point where they could offer a socially legitimate alternative that a majority of people could join. The alternative movement is positive insofar as it provides some activists with nonalienating jobs, creates nonhierarchical institutions, and provides a sense of community rooted in friendship. But the alternative institutions can serve as mechanisms of integration when they lead to the commercialization of previously uncommercialized needs, fulfill unmet needs within an oppressive system, help to fine-tune the established system by mitigating its worst excesses, and provide a pool of highly skilled but low paid social workers within "alternative" institutions. The criticism of alternative institutions by activists often helped depoliticize and isolate the alternatives, giving rise to individual and group power trips, greedy takeovers of their resources for individual ends, and authoritarian attempts to control their political content.

Despite their apparent shortcomings, oppositional moments were increasingly transformed from single-issue struggles into a coherent and vital movement. Besides being the driving force behind larger social movements and political adjustments, these militants succeeded in forging a new synthesis of theory and practice. Unknown in Europe since the heady days of Russia's Bolsheviks and Germany's Spartacists, a synthesis naming both capitalism and patriarchy as the structures to be destroyed galvanized itself across national and continental boundaries, as I discuss in the next chapter. More than a decade after the New Left, newly developed youth movements continued to question fundamental premises of industrial civilization. In this questioning was hope for a new kind of society based not on the accumulation of wealth and hierarchical politics but on the improvement of the quality of life for all.

Many Greens sympathize with the feminism and egalitarianism of such an autonomous vision, but others do not—nor are they required to in order to be part of a political party formally constituted to participate in government. Like all parliamentary groups, the Greens aspire to create legislation and allocate funds to meet the articulated needs of their base of support. Of necessity, they must conform to the hierarchy of the state on two dimensions: Within the context of carrying out governmental duties, they must accede to the dictates of higher officials. Within the party, some members arc elected representatives and sit in parliament, and others do not; millions pay dues to or cast votes for the few who are paid to carry out party policy. These hierarchical imperatives were recognized by the Greens even before they formally organized themselves. One of the threads woven into the discourse of this book has been the relationship of parliamentary and extraparliamentary forms of political engagement. In this section, I trace the history of the Greens and analyze some of the issues that animated their development from an "antiparty party" to the third largest party in Germany. Although the Greens grew out of the same milieu as the Autonomen, as time passed, the two formations became increasingly embittered and estranged from each other, and today few Germans treat them as connected. From my vantage point, they are each crystallization points within a diffuse continuum of opposition to behemoth nation-states and multinational corporations. Whether or not their efforts are successful depends, at least in part, upon their synergistic impact.

NOTES

1   Previous versions appeared in Z Magazine, September and October 1988. This essay was written in the 1980s, when the autonomous movement was still vibrant, which is no longer the case. Since the demise of East Germany, the Left Party has formed and run in German elections.

2   Winfried Kretschmer and Dieter Rucht, "Beispiel Wackersdorf: Die Protestbewegung gegen die Wiederaufarbeitungslage," in *Neue soziale Bewegungen in der Bundesrepublik Deutschland*, ed. Roland Roth and Dieter Rucht, (Bonn: Bundeszentrale für politische Bildung, 1987), pp. 142–3, 148.

3   Enno Brand, *Staarsgewelt* (Berlin: Verlag Die Werkstatt, 1988), pp. 259–60.

4   Bunte Hilfe Nordbayern, "Repression in der Provinz" (1989), pp. 87–8 (in the archives of the Institute for Social History in Amsterdam).

5   Monika Bauerlein, "Germany's Radical Counterculture: Are They Revolutionary Heroes or an Albatross for Other Activists?" *Utne Reader* (July/Aug. 1989), p. 32.

6   See Rob Burns and Wilfried van der Will, *Protest and Democracy in West Germany: Extra-Parliamentary Opposition and the Democratic Agenda* (London: St. Martin's Press, 1988), pp. 182–3.

7   For an analysis of this action and the mobilization at the international meetings of the World Bank and International Monetary Fund, see Jürgen Gerhards and Dieter Rucht, "Mesomobilization: Organizing and Framing in Two Protest Campaigns in West Germany," *American Journal of Sociology* 98, no. 3 (Nov. 1992), pp. 555–96.

8   Altogether, 475 different events were counted in one study. See Jürgen Gerhards, "Die Mobilisierung gegen die IWF— and Weltbanktagung 1988 in Berlin: Gruppen, Veranstaltungen, Diskurse," in *Neue soziale Bewegungen in der Bundesrepublik Deutschland*, ed. Roland Roth and Dieter Rucht, Zweite Auflage (Bonn: Bundeszentrale für politische Bildung, 1991), p. 219.

9   *Der Spiegel*, (Oct. 3, 1988), p. 132.

10 *Processo* (January 10, 1994).

11 See Dieter Hoffman-Axthelm, Otto Kallscheuer, Eberhard Knödler-Bunte, and Brigitte Wartmann, *Zwwei Kulturen? Tunix, Mescalero und die Folgen* (Berlin: Verlag AÄsthetik und Kommunikation, 1978), p. 86. Michael Ryan outlines a similar conception in his introduction to Antonio Negri's *Marx Beyond Marx: Lessons on the Grundrisse* (Brooklyn: Autonomedia, 1991), p. xxx. To Agnoli's two meanings, Ryan adds a third, "the multilateral productive potential" of the "subject in the communist society."

12 Although there have been few attempts made from within the Autonomen to define autonomy, one exception was made in preparation for the autonomist convention held in Berlin in April 1995. See *Eat It! Reader: Autonomie-Kongress-Reader Teil II*(Berlin, 1995), pp. 6–7.

13   See my *The Global Imagination of 1968* (PM Press, 2019).

14   This system assigns a proportional number of seats in parliament (the *Bundestag*) to any party that receives more than 5 percent of the vote.

15   In 1989, after I made a Black Rose presentation at MIT to several hundred people on the Autonomen, which included slides and copies of their magazines. One member of the audience confronted me with the charge that l had invented the whole movement, contending that the events I had described were simply part of the Greens.

16   Ingrid Damian-Hesser and Michael Damian, eds., *Handbuch: Bürgerinitiativen in Frankfurt* (Frankfurt: Verlag im Leseladen, 1978).

17   *Emma Sonderband: Schwestern Lust—Schwestern Frust: 20 Jahre Frauenbewegung* (Nachdruck, 1990; Einleitung, 1991), p. 4.

18   This speech is translated and excerpted in *German Feminism: Readings in Politics and Literature*, ed. Edith Hoshino Altbach, Jeanette Clausen, Dagmar Schultz, and Naomi Stephan (Albany: State University of New York Press, 1984), pp. 307–10.

19   Helke Sander, "Mütter sind politische Personen," *Courage* (Oct. 1978), pp. 38–45. The women's actions in Berlin transformed the groups that undertook them and led to women's councils being established in many other cities. In Münster, a group of sixty to seventy women quickly came together and developed campaigns using irony and defamation of men as key tactics. One of their members produced "The Cultural Revolution of Women," the first radical feminist text of the new wave of German feminism. As women met, they read texts from the US women's movement and adopted them for their own. For the most part, however, the movement was oriented to practice rather than theory.

20   Ann Anders (ed.), *Autonome Frauen: Schlüsseltexte der Neuen Frauenbewegung seit 1968* (Frankfurt: Athenäum, 1988), p. 11.

21   Alice Schwarzer, "Ewig zittere das Weib," in *Emma Sonderband*, p. 137. It should be noted that German law was a hodgepodge of various statures. After World War II, the United States essentially rewrote Germany's basic laws according to the US Constitution. In January 1949, the *Bundestag* approved an equal rights statute, but it had little enforceability. Another equal rights statute in 1957 modified rigidly patriarchal marriage and family laws.

22   Schwarzer was able to persuade only three groups to join her at first, women from Frauenaktion '70 in Frankfurt, the Socialist Women's Federation in Berlin, and one part of the "Red Women" of Munich. See Altbach et a1., p. 103.

23   *Emma Sonderband*, p. 61.

24   *Emma Sonderband*, p. 75.

25   See Ferree's discussion of this important topic.

26   Elmar Altvater, Jürgen Hoffman, Willi Semmler, *Vom Wirtshcafts wunder zur Wirtschaftskrise* (Berlin: Verlag Olle und Wolter, 1979), p. 100.

27   *Der Tagespiegel* (Berlin), June 8, 1980. The shortage of available houses resulted in standard nonrefundable deposits of around 6,000 DM (then about $3,000) for a small apartment. More than sixty thousand households—largely senior citizens—paid more than a third of their income toward rent. The West Berlin average was 20 percent of income for rent, heating, and electricity. Other major cities were equally bad. In Munich, for example, ten thousand people were registered with the housing office as emergency cases, and even by conservative estimates, an additional twelve thousand Germans were searching for housing there on the "free market."

    Although particularly severe, the housing crisis in West Berlin was also irrational, because the city had been depopulated by an exodus of Berliners after the war. Attracting Germans to work there was so difficult that even in the midst of the recession of 1974–76, a monthly average of ten thousand available jobs existed. For many, the city's geographical and political isolation from the rest of West Germany and its economic dependence on outside help were key reasons for Berlin's lack of appeal. Most West Berliners suffered acutely from "wall fever," and many left the city at least once a month. To help Berliners make life there more attractive, the government subsidized wages (8 percent was automatically added), paid birth bonuses to mothers, gave special allowances to the elderly (30 percent of the slightly more than two million West Berliners were over sixty years old in 1976), provided freely flowing student support money, and subsidized airfares to and from the city.

28 Haller, p. 104.

29 *New York Times*, (May 6, 1981), p. A–17.

30 See the discussion in Kriesi, p. 200. Internationally, much the same could be said of punk. See James Stark, *Punk '77: An Inside Look at the San Francisco Rock n' Roll Scene* (1977).

31 *SG*, p. 207. Quoting government statistics, Margit Mayer counted 54 police evictions, 410 police raids, 4,687 criminal investigations, and 2,287 arrests vis-à-vis the squatters' movement in West Berlin. See "Restructuring and Popular Opposition in West German Cities," in *The Capitalist City*, ed. M. Smith and J. Feagin (Oxford: Basil Blackwell, 1987), p. 353.

32 *Die Tageszeitung* (May 4, 1981), p. 12. Manrique counted 160 by the end of 1981 (p. 159). Kriesi maintained that there were over 500 (p. 170), a figure also given by Manrique (p. 168) for early summer 1981. The police referred to "about 700 known house occupations." See *Verfassungsschutzbericht* (1981), p. 71.

33 See Steven Katz and Margit Mayer, "Gimme Shelter: Self-Help Housing Struggles Within and Against the State in New York City and West Berlin," *International Journal of Urban and Regional Research* 9, no. 1 (1985), p. 33; also see Manrique, pp. 80, 118.

34 Manrique, p. 133.

35 Nanette Funk, "Take It," in *Semiotexte* vol. IV, no. 2, 1982 (German issue), p. 297.

36 *GAP*, p. 55.

37 By March 1984, only fourteen houses were still illegally occupied, the remainder having been legalized, cleared out by police, or abandoned. *GAP*, p. 54.

38 In 1995, *Taz* had a readership of 410,000 and printed just under 60,000 copies daily. Nonetheless, the end of the government's special subsidies for Berlin contributed to a financial crisis. *German Press Review* (Sept. 22, 1995).

39 Petra Kelly, *Um Hoffnung kämpfen: Gewaltfrei in eine grüne Zukenft* (Bornheim-Merten: Lamuv Verlag, 1983), pg. 180–1. Joseph Huber estimated the numbers involved in the national "active movement" at between 6,000 groups / 30,000 activists and 15,000 groups / 135,000 activism in 1980. *Wer soll das alles ändern? Die Alternativen der Alternativbewegung* (Berlin: Rotbuch Verlag, 1980), p. 29. Sarkar quotes numbers of 10,000 alternative self-help and service projects with 80,000 activists, and 4,000 alternative economic enterprises with 24,000 jobs in 1983 (*GAP*, p. 257). In addition, there were as many as 100,000 *Wohngemeinschaften* in the FRG in 1983 (*GAP*, p. 241).

40 Selbsthilfe Netzwerk Berlin, *Ein Jahr Netzwerk* (1979).

41 For an analysis of how *Netzwerk* fit into the overall movement and its context, see Mayer, p. 355.

42 Pohn's own contradictions were reflected years later in his advocacy of the use of nuclear weapons against Iraq during the Gulf War. He moved from attacking mild-mannered Joseph Huber as a Nazi to calling the antiwar movement in Germany "brownshirts." It was not only in Germany that "left-wing" personalities advocated such extreme positions. Problems such as these are universal and human in scope and are not contained within national boundaries.

The Extraparliamentary Left in Europe[1]

AFTER DISPERSAL of New Left social movements of the 1960s, media coverage in the USA included the electoral successes and failures of socialist governments in France, Spain, Portugal, and Greece; the rise and fall of Italian governments; and the emergence of the Green Party in West Germany (ecologists whose victories in elections could not be ignored). Occasional space was given to the spectacular actions and subsequent arrests of armed groups such as the Red Brigades in Italy, Direct Action in France, and Germany's Red Army Faction.

Left out of the news about Europe, however, were popular, direct-action movements in Italy, Holland, Denmark, Switzerland, and West Germany; movements composed of thousands of activists who refused to be confined to the ranks of main-stream politics or marginalized as guerrillas. They were a motor force driving both the parliamentary upsurge of the Greens and the armed struggle that has plagued German political life for more than two decades. Besides stimulating others, their militant resistance to the arms race, nuclear power, patriarchy, and a massive housing shortage transformed single-issue struggles into an autonomous movement whose aspirations were to transform the society as a whole. These social movements—known today as the Autonomen in Germany—are independent of political parties, and their adherents will have nothing to do with established forms of politics. They seek the subversion of nation-states and their representative structures of government and seek to replace the existing world system with anti-systemic forms of participatory democracy that they believe will facilitate greater individual and community control over everyday life.

As their international links developed, the Autonomen in many countries paralleled one another more than they conformed to mainstream politics or even to countercultural values in their own countries. Activists converged in conferences, friendships, and internationally coordinated campaigns, and a loosely linked network of "info-stores" or libertarian centers sprang up, functioning as the movement's eyes and ears.[2] For years before anyone dreamed of anything resembling the Autonomen, regional movements sprang up that punctuated local scenes with creative tactics and ironic interventions. In Holland, the Provos released chickens at rush hour in Amsterdam to have fun with traffic, and squatters were a huge presence. Copenhagen's flowerful counterculture was the darling of all Europe. By the end of the 1980s, however, the movements in these cities had adopted the features of the Autonomen, an intuitive and practical unity that transcended or even negated the nationalistically defined conceptions of self still inculcated in many young Europeans. As I discuss in this chapter, a remarkably coherent autonomous movement developed in Europe out of many disparate struggles. Their uniformity and unity had both positive and negative features. In Holland and Denmark, countries that, for a variety of reasons, had largely avoided violence of the German variety, the movements adopted tactics from Germany and became increasingly militant—to the point where their isolation hurt their own existence.[3] In Hamburg, Amsterdam, and Copenhagen, the central thrust of local autonomous movements was to create free spaces for everyday life—and there have been long and bitter struggles to defend these liberated territories. These two sides of Autonomen activism-campaigns against what they view as the system's irrationality and the buildup of their own "revolutionary dual power"—define complementary (and sometimes contradictory) dimensions of their existence. The former can easily lead to isolated small groups and prison, and the latter poses the dangers of integration and accommodation.

As European radicals became increasingly violence-prone, police actions were also internationally coordinated. In one month, police destroyed an Autonomen stronghold in Switzerland (the Zaffaraya encampment in Bern); evicted squatters in the German cities of Göttingen, Freiburg, Düssenldorf, Bochum, and Kiel; and mounted an unsuccessful assault on the Hafenstrasse squatters in Hamburg. The kettle tactic they used in Berlin was copied from earlier kettles in Hamburg and Mainz.[4]

In the 1980s, the "economic wonder" of postwar Europe turned into economic crisis, a continually developing erosion of economic prosperity that has not turned around in the 1990s. This economic downturn worried the guardians of *Pax* Americana long before their attention turned to the possibility of limited nuclear war or a breakdown in Western Europe's military and political alliances. During Jimmy Carter's presidency, the word "recession" became widely used in the United States, but in Western Europe, "depression" was how the economy was commonly described. In the period 1980–81, unemployment in Common Market countries rose 30 percent. After Margaret Thatcher came to power in May 1979, Great Britain's unemployment rate more than doubled to over 12 percent (about three million people), the highest unemployment rate there in over fifty years. Dutch unemployment rose to a postwar record of over 350,000. The expected turnabout never materialized, and unemployment remains the main economic problem of Europe.

An above-average—and climbing—unemployment rate for young people was a new phenomenon. Over the next decade, as these trends only intensified, unemployment among youth in Germany climbed to 9.6 percent in 1982 (over 20 percent in both France and the United Kingdom), and it remains above 9 percent into the 1990s.[5] Since the postwar baby boom in Germany was delayed until after reconstruction, the number of Germans between fifteen and twenty-nine years old in the workforce did not reach its apex until 1987.[6] The economic dimension of the crisis of youth is told in statistical surveys of shortages of housing and jobs, but another moment of the crisis accounted for the emergence of autonomous youth movements —a cultural-motivational dimension obvious in the unwillingness of young people to integrate themselves into what they considered to be the "middle class." The legitimacy of the family, the hegemony of the state, and the desirability of an everyday existence predicated on material comforts in exchange for hard work (the Protestant ethic) all became questioned. The new radicals were less concerned with material comforts for themselves than with creating a new relationship between humans and nature, with finding a way of life free from both capitalist exploitation and bureaucratic domination. Their aspirations for a nuclear-free, fully housed society seemed unattainable within the existing system: their aesthetic fight defied the logic of large-scale capitalist efficiency, and their notion of freedom as more than freedom from material want seemed incomprehensible in a world where starvation and war were still remembered by many older Europeans.

Amsterdam

From the 1960s into the 1990s, imaginative and playful countercultural movements in Amsterdam and Copenhagen connected with each other in a synchronous continuum of issues and tactics. Not burdened with the weight of reacting to nationalistic militarism, activists in these two cities shared a political culture of immediate actionism, and their actions often had direct national effects. In the 1980s, Amsterdam was a city being (post)modernized through a massive infusion of capital. Billions of guilders were pumped into urban revitalization programs, and as Holland became part of the homogenization process (widely perceived as the scourge of Americanization) sweeping Europe, its movement underwent a transition from a purely Dutch phenomenon, one replete with *provos, kabouters*, and *kraakers*, to a wing of the international Autonomen. In 1986, during a three-hour battle against police guarding the nuclear power plant at Borssele, the first Dutch group formed that referred to itself as Autonomen.

At its high point in the early 1980s, the *kraakers of* Amsterdam fired the imaginations of young people all over Europe. Between 1968 and 1981, more than ten thousand houses and apartments were squatted in Amsterdam, and an additional fifteen thousand were taken over in the rest of Holland. Many of these squatters (or *kraakers*

—pronounced "crackers") were organized into a network of resistance to the police and the government. In squatted "People's Kitchens," bars, and cafés, food, and drink were served at affordable prices. In occupied office buildings, neighborhood block committees set up information centers to deal with complaints against police and landlord brutality. A *kraaker* council planned the movement's direction, and a *kraaker* radio station kept people posted on new developments and late-breaking stories.

The single most important event in the life and death of the *kraakers* (and the most internationally publicized one) occurred on April 30, 1980, when riots marred Queen Beatrice's lavish coronation. *"Geen woning—geen Kronung"* ("No place to live, no coronation") was the slogan for the demonstrations, but it was meant more as a mobilizing call than a physical threat to the ceremony. The kraakers had originally hoped for a peaceful party day, although, like any other day, they had also planned to occupy a few more empty dwellings before beginning to party. They were against a coronation so lavish that it cost 56 million guilder (about $25 million). When mounted police attacked some of the street parties, people fought back, unleashing a storm that the police were unable to control. The police were so badly beaten that day that the next week, the police commissioner complained that many of his men could not continue to fulfilll their duties for psychological reasons.

In Amsterdam, a city with fewer than 800,000 inhabitants, more than 50,000 dwelling places were needed. When polled, a majority of the Dutch people repeatedly expressed sympathy for the squatters because of the dearth of reasonably priced places to live. Given the widespread sympathy enjoyed by the squatters, local authorities attempted to divide the movement by proclaiming only a few to be dangerous radicals who "led astray" thousands of "honest" squatters. Intense police attacks were then mounted on houses perceived to be the central leadership, but hastily assembled throngs of squatters, about one thousand within the first half hour, blocked the way to besieged houses in the Vondelstraat on March 3, 1980, and the Groote Keyser after the queen's coronation.

The *kraakers* were able to control the streets in the early 1980s, but their victories exacted a high cost: Dutch tolerance was tempered with a new edge of legal reprimand and revengeful violence. Citizens' committees formed to support the police, and football teams were recruited by landlords to clear out occupied buildings. These groups often did their dirty work dressed in American football gear (helmets and shoulder pads) and steel-tipped boots. In response to *kraaker* self-defense, the Dutch parliament reconsidered laws governing the vacant buildings. As previously liberal social security payments to students and young people were curtailed, the police were granted more money and more power. New laws were enforced to make it easier for landlords to evict squatters. Property owners had needed the names of specific

Philosopher Herbert Marcuse was one of the "3 M's" of 1968: Marx, Mao and Marcuse.

individuals in order to obtain authorization to call in the police, and because no self-respecting *kraaker* used his or her full name, it was all but impossible to evict them. The new laws waived the name requirement to obtain eviction papers and speeded up the time for actions to be sanctioned by the courts to less than a month. Also introduced were temporary rental contracts under which landlords did not have to show grounds for annulling contracts. When compared with laws in the United States and other European countries, Dutch law remained quite liberal in terms of squatters' rights.[7] Once a table, a chair, and a bed have been moved into a vacant apartment, the occupant is legally permitted to stay.

Although there continued to be new squats (in Amsterdam, a new squat per week was recorded), public opinion had turned dramatically against the squatters, and the police had inflicted a series of major defeats on them. One of the first battles lost by the *kraakers*—for the *Lucky Luiyk* (the Lucky Luke) in 1982—was fought against the police and members of one of the small but increasingly violent neo-fascist parties in Holland. The squatters repelled the fascists who assaulted the house, but they could not hold out against the police. When a streetcar was set on fire in this fight, schisms began to appear in the ranks of the movement, since many people questioned this extension of militant self-defense.

In truth, some *kraakers* were not interested in the radical transformation of society but merely needed individual solutions to their housing needs. To them, fighting the police was unnecessary, especially when it was possible to negotiate with the government and obtain a reasonable solution to their housing problems. From their point of view, the simultaneous existence of thousands of empty apartments and tens of thousands of people in need of housing was a technical problem that could gradually be solved by the existing system. Other *kraakers*—the radicals—saw the housing crisis as another example of the system's irrationality, an irrationality also evident in the increasing starvation in the Third World, the production of nuclear waste, and the transformation of cities into concrete jungles. From their point of view, using crowbars to occupy vacant buildings and barricades to defend them was part of the same struggle being waged with stones and slingshots in occupied Palestine and with AK-47s in Nicaragua. They felt that being afforded the luxuries of Dutch citizens was part of their national privileges as members of an affluent society in a corrupt world system. These *kraakers* understood the atomization and standardization of their lives as part of the price exacted by the world system, and they hoped to contribute to its global transformation.

By 1983, this division among the *kraakers* was no longer an internal matter. After doing all they could to distance these two wings of the movement from each other, Dutch authorities moved resolutely to eradicate the radicals. At the battle for the Groote Watering, the police used armored vehicles and construction cranes to evict the squatters. The cranes were used to hoist metal containers filled with half a dozen police onto the roofs of the building, where they could penetrate the elaborate defenses. At first, the *kraakers* were able to repulse these rooftop attacks, but the police used their imagination and loaded a police officer dressed as Santa Claus into one of the containers. His emergence so surprised the *kraakers* that the attack succeeded. The next police target was a building on Weyers, a huge stronghold with art galleries, coffee shops, and a concert hall. Despite five hundred defenders in the building and thousands of people in the streets, the massive police concentration and their use of overwhelming quantities of tear gas, armor, and cranes won the day. Today the new Holiday Inn at Weyers is a painful reminder of the police success, and February 1984 is remembered as a time when the movement was split beyond repair.

Despite these setbacks, the *kraakers* were not yet defeated. When the pope visited

Amsterdam in May 1985, millions of guilders had to be spent on his defense. Anonymous individuals offered a hefty reward to anyone who reached the pontiff, and in the riots that ensued, severe damage was inflicted on the city. The government reacted quickly. Using a specially trained unit, the police illegally evicted a woman and her child from a squatted house in a working-class neighborhood known as a *kraaker* stronghold. When hundreds of people attempted to resquat the house, the police panicked, shooting one person in the arm. The house was retaken by squatters. As riot police arrived to bolster the forces of order, hundreds more *kraakers* reinforced the ranks of their opponents. After the police took the house for the second time, they badly beat all thirty-two people inside and put them in jail without bedding, food, or medical care. The next day, Hans Koch, one of those who had been beaten, was found dead in his jail cell. For the next three nights, angry groups of *kraakers* attacked police stations, torched police cars—some in front of police headquarters—and smashed city offices. City authorities stonewalled any response to the death of Hans Koch, and even a year later, the government still had not completed its inquiry into his death. In December 1986, when the report was finally released, it blamed the victim, claiming that his drug addiction had caused his death. Although the *kraakers* swiftly responded by firebombing more police stations, the government had chosen a violent solution in the struggle to reclaim Amsterdam.

The next month, when the new law governing housing went into effect, the balance of forces shifted. With yuppies on the ascendancy, the movement moved underground, and those committed to a vision of change developed new forms of resistance. Alternative institutions, previously incidental offsprings of a vibrant popular movement, were compelled to tie themselves more intimately to their only remaining constituency: the international Autonomen. Increasingly cut off from the younger generation in Holland, the *kraakers* replenished their ranks with activists from England, Germany, and as far away as Australia. The internationalization of the movement only intensified the reaction of the Dutch Right. Portraying the *kraakers* as foreigners, they recruited Dutch football teams to join with neo-fascist groups and attack squatted houses, often in full view of police. In one such confrontation, a team known as the Rams arrived in full American football gear, and although the occupants tried to surrender peacefully, they were severely beaten, to the point where one of them had to spend two weeks in the hospital with multiple fractures of the legs and arms and severe facial lacerations.

With the intensification of the attacks against the movement, a greater commitment to practical resistance seemed needed. With a declining popular base, secretive small-group actions, particularly by people using the signature of RA RA (Anti-Racist Action Group), became more common. RA RA grew out of the *kraaker* movement, and like the squatters, it became part of a wider European movement. By the late 1980s, RA RA was part of a militant anti-imperialism movement on the rise in European circles. In 1985, RA RA began its most successful campaign—to force MAKRO supermarkets, a chain owned by one of the largest corporations in Holland, to divest its investments in South Africa. After a series of firebombings caused over 100 million guilders in damages to these supermarkets, the corporation withdrew its money from South Africa. Emboldened by success, RA RA then attacked Shell, Holland's largest corporation, one of the world's largest multinationals, and the Dutch queen's main source of income. In one night, thirty-seven Shell stations were torched in Amsterdam alone. Despite more than a hundred such attacks on its gas stations, Shell increased its investments in South Africa and simultaneously launched an extensive public-relations campaign against the domestic "terrorists."

The Dutch royal family is one of Shell's largest stockholders, and the police were eager to show their loyalty. On April 11, 1988, Dutch police raided ten houses, seizing address books, diaries, and computers and arresting eight people on suspicion of belonging to RA RA. Although the press immediately declared that the hard core of RA RA had finally been apprehended, five of the eight were quickly released for lack of evidence, and the cases against the remaining three were undeniably weak. Moreover, in response to the arrests, Shell stations were sabotaged in Utrecht, Apeldoorn, Tilburg, Baarn, Almere, and Haaksbergen, a clear sign that the infrastructure of RA RA remained intact. At the same time, the popular movement declined. We see here a stark subcycle within the better-known synergistic dynamic of repression and resistance: secretive conspiratorial resistance helps minimize the possibility and impact of open popular forms of resistance; guerrilla actions replace massive mobilizations; and the impetus to increasing democracy is lost as the bitterness of confrontation becomes primary. In such contexts, the forces of order thrive while popular movements become weakened and vulnerable.

In Holland, the police first crushed the *kraakers* in Nijmegen, their second greatest redoubt. A large vacant building owned by Shell—the Marienburcht—had been resquatted on April 24 by over a hundred people wearing masks, helmets, and gloves, and armed with clubs. They quickly scared away the few policemen at the scene and barricaded themselves inside the building. At 5 A.M. the next day, hundreds of riot police retook the building, arresting 123 people. Three weeks later, another building, originally squatted by a women's group in 1980, was also attacked by police enforcing the city council's declaration of the city as a "*kraaker*-free zone."

The government's success in Nijmegen encouraged the police to take action in Amsterdam, where the squatters were strongest. On July 18, hundreds of riot police launched a combined assault from the canals and the streets on the last big *kraaker* bastion in Amsterdam on the Konradstraat. Hundreds of people defended the building, an old textile mill used for years as an alternative workplace for artisans and home for 140 people. At one point in the battle, the building caught on fire, causing a giant cloud of smoke to rise ominously over the city. In the aftermath of their eviction, one of the *kraakers* expressed his frustration: "We were disappointed not because we didn't carry our own plan of defense, but because the police came at us much harder than we anticipated." At the time, homelessness and unemployment were severe problems in Holland, and the Dutch state was throwing money at them. Few people expected the huge attack on the Konradstraat, particularly because its occupants had put forth a proposal to renovate the building at a low cost. The squatters' plan would have provided double the number of apartments and jobs that eventually were created, but the fate of that building revealed that the Social Democrats governing Amsterdam had another priority: destroying the *kraakers*.

By 1990, massive police attacks and modification of the laws covering squatters succeeded in displacing thousands of them from the center city, areas that were reclaimed by yuppies and sanitized for tourists. In 1993, fewer than a thousand apartments and houses were occupied in the entire country. What had been a feeling of empowerment in 1980 had been transformed into marginalization and paranoia. Whereas conflicts with the system had once been paramount, as with all movements in decline, the most pressing problems became internal ones. Such splits were so severe that a "traitors" list was published, a booklet entitled "Pearls Before Swine" containing the names of about two hundred people found guilty of informing to the police, negotiating with the government for their own personal gain, or becoming yuppies.[8] The movement had cut itself off from its own membership. One of the participants explained: "Once paranoia sets in, every new person is suspect, and you're left with 200 militants in your friendship circle. Then the rest of society has been insulated from the movement, and the 200 gradually become 150, then 50."

Copenhagen

In September 1971, a former army base on Christiania Island in Copenhagen was occupied by fifty activists, and during the years since, a diverse group of nearly a thousand inhabitants has made the 156 abandoned army buildings into homes. Christiania has long been a focal point for a cultural-political opposition in Denmark, and its residents have repelled attacks from police and an invasion of bikers in 1976. They have created more than two hundred jobs in self-managed institutions and provided foreigners and Danes alike with a countercultural haven.[9] The Christiania squat grew out of the same 1960s impetus that produced the "children's power" movement in Copenhagen. Danish society took care of every Dane's needs, but left out of the smoothly functioning system was any consideration of young people determining how to live their own lives. To create alternatives for themselves, teenagers squatted several empty houses in the late 1960s and were heard to shout: "Free us from our parents!" In March 1972, they established the Children's Liberation Front, a decentralized organization that had groups living in several parts of the city. They dedicated themselves to providing a sanctuary for battered, abused, and bored young people. In response to complaints from concerned parents, the police raided some of the houses in the summer of 1973. Trying to maintain a safe refuge, the group kept its campaign going by squatting one of the buildings in Christiania.[10]

In the Free Republic of Christiania, hundreds of people illegally live in an alternative community where no authority counts except that of the *Ting*, an ancient Danish form of consensual decision making. One of the central buildings is known as the *Tinghus* (Ting house). Sitting in a circle at meetings of the communal council, each resident may go to the center and speak, and decisions are made by the eventual agreement of all through consensus rather than a majority vote. Direct democracy within the Danish movement does not have to be explained—it is almost second nature—nor is it limited to occasional gatherings of political groups who use it as a formal method of decision-making. In other free areas besides Christiania, the *Ting* has been the way of life for over a thousand people since 1971.

Social atomization in the United States has advanced far beyond Europe, and our cultural heritage is young and diffuse. Consensus often means that dissenting individuals exercise veto power over a group, making it impossible to formulate a common will and fomenting internal strife. In contrast, the bonds between those who live in Christiania are reinforced by the *Ting*. As one communard explained Christiania's structure to me:

> If a problem comes up, it is first discussed in the house where it originates, where it hopefully will be resolved. Only if the issue is still not taken care of will a neighborhood meeting be called to discuss it. This way, the house and then the neighborhood must fail to deal with the problem before it becomes necessary to have a community meeting, and by then, most people have already heard about the matter and considered the various options. We never vote at community meetings nor do we have a council, because then some people make decisions for others. We only have community meetings when we need to—sometimes not for years, other times once a week.

Although Christiania is squatted, rent is collected for community projects and utilities. Every neighborhood has a person who collects a minimal payment (about $100 per resident per month, or 400 kroner, in 1990), and each of the bars, restaurants, and shops pays something to the "big box," as the community fund is known. "Little boxes" for each neighborhood spend about half of the collected money, a structure that keeps decision-making at the base and also guarantees the availability of funding for grassroots ideas and initiatives. Residents have created a variety of shops: blacksmiths and metalworkers produce ecological ovens and a unique Christiania-designed bicycle; jewelers, potters, candle makers, and shoemakers labor side by side in other workshops; and there are numerous alternative healers and restaurants. The hundreds of people who work in Christiania's shops have a workers' council with regular meetings open to all who labor in the alternative institutions. The council also funds a child-care center.

Although many people live in Christiania for only short periods of time, some have stayed together through the years. At a particularly tense moment in their relations with the authorities, the long-term residents formed a "Rainbow Army" (committed to nonviolence) designed to deal with repeated threats by the authorities to evict them, to keep the collective buildings in good repair, and to meet other communal needs. The call in the Christiania newspaper, *Ugespejlet* (Daily Mirror), read:

> By creating a Rainbow Army of nonviolent, hardworking people who all collaborate with each other, every individual in his or her own way, we can stand united, one for all and all for one, and overcome the threatening situation we are facing. Because we love each other, we can organize ourselves practically, in spite of our differences.[11]

On April 1, 1976, Danish authorities had promised to clear out the communards, but the imaginative campaign mounted by the Rainbow Army brought twenty-five thousand supporters to Christiania on the appointed day. Some of the best bands in Denmark had produced a Christiania record, and the Christiania Action Theater had toured the country with a production of *April Fool's Day*. Evidently, the Rainbow Army won a decisive victory, because the planned eviction was first postponed and finally canceled altogether in favor of legalization. Christiania thereby was transformed from a free space in which laws did not exist to a charming village throwback to feudal Europe, where autonomous principalities existed only with the consent of the lord.[12] In this case, Christiania pays the Ministry of Defense over $500,000 annually for water, electricity, and other services and has been recognized officially as a "social experiment."

Like any community in formation, Christiania has problems, particularly drugs and police incursions. Over the years, the most severe internal issues Christiania has faced have been profit-hungry heroin dealers who moved into the "liberated" zone and refused to leave, even though at every entrance to Christiania, signs posted by the residents read: "Speed, coke, heroin etc. are forbidden to be sold, used or possessed in Christiania." Christiania's position on drugs is the same as that of the Black Panther Party and the Metropolitan Indians: life drugs (marijuana, hashish, mushrooms) should be cheap and legal, and death drugs (speed, cocaine, heroin) should be unavailable. Not only does this sensibility contradict mainstream understanding of psychopharmacology, but its realization represents the de facto enactment of dual power regarding everyday life. Outdated, hypocritical regulations governing individual decisions on drug use are a revealing dimension of the obsolete character of the existing criminal justice system. Christiania's existence as a center for life drugs is civil disobedience in everyday life. In this context, being a dealer should not simply be understood as individual criminal behavior. Since the community tacitly accepts the use of life drugs, making them available at a reasonable price is part of the process of living according to self-determined norms and values. The existing government's laws are at best, a nuisance, and at worst, a giant conspiracy supporting corporations that manufacture alcohol and market tobacco. Between January and October 1975, over a thousand people were arrested in police sweeps aimed at hashish dealers and petty thieves.[13] These police intrusions come in waves, but the Christiania communards are left to fend for themselves when confronted with death drugs. Twice they used the *Ting* to convince motorcycle gangs who were dealing heroin to leave Christiania, although several people suffered injuries while persuading the bikers to leave.[14] Unless the movement is able to deal with the drug issue collectively, Christiania will be destroyed from within like Haight-Ashbury in the 1960s. Despite public support for an "Amsterdam solution" (i.e., turning a blind eye to hashish as—long as heroin is not sold), in the summer of 1987, there were fourteen days of fights with the police, numerous searches, and many arrests before the authorities finally relented. The threat of renewed hostility remained, but the police returned to their old policy of tolerating hashish dealers as long as the quantity they carry is less than 100 grams.

In the mid-1980s, RA RA's anti-Shell campaign spread throughout Europe. In Denmark, on November 23, 1986, twenty-eight Shell stations were simultaneously attacked, causing damages of about $200,000. Although the international cycle of repression and resistance was not yet fully synchronized, these actions were one indication that the targets and tactics—particularly the turn toward small-group destruction of property—were increasingly coordinated across national borders. Years earlier, the struggle in Switzerland for an autonomous youth center had profoundly affected emerging Danish movements. In August 1981, thousands of people signed a petition requesting the use of a vacant bread factory to create a youth house "managed by those using it through direct democracy." For two months, the group raised money, canvassed the neighborhood, and negotiated with the city council. When they were unable to achieve even the slightest positive response from Copenhagen's politicians, the *Initiv-gruppen* decided to take matters into their own hands—they squatted the factory. But within two hours, the police evicted them.

A week later, after hours of meetings with city officials and debates among themselves, the *Initiv-gruppen* squatted an abandoned rubber factory in the same neighborhood. This time the police response was quite violent. The hundred or more people in the building, ranging in age from ten to twenty-five, were shelled by massive quantities of tear gas, the first time gas had been used against demonstrators in Denmark since the 1930s. The police violence led to an intensification of the struggle. Five days after the gassing, hundreds of people converged on an abandoned convent and barricaded themselves inside (and made preparations to repel even a heavy gas attack). Public support was with the squatters, and the police could do little more than encircle the building and await the outcome of neighborhood elections, which happened to be scheduled for that week. The Left Socialists, a small radical party that grew out of the New Left of the 1960s, won control of the borough and quickly sanctioned the use of the convent for a youth house. During the next four months, however, the dream of a youth center turned into a nightmare. Drug addicts from the neighborhood used the convent as a shooting gallery, and a biker club, the Black Panthers, beat up the youthful occupants on several occasions without having to worry about police intervention. After months of such problems, the *Initiv-gruppen* disbanded themselves in disgust, leaving behind only twenty activists, who were soon evicted without incident.

Despite the disappointing outcome, a new group emerged—the BZ (Occupation Brigade)—and a month later they squatted a vacant music museum, the Mekanisk Musikmuseum, in an upper-middle class neighborhood. This time the police were unprepared to deal with the escalation of the confrontation. For the first time, the squatters fought back when the police arrived, throwing anything and everything—including a toilet—out the windows. The stubborn resistance mounted by BZ was initially successful, but after several hours of fighting, the police retook the building and arrested all 147 people inside. The ground rules of confrontational politics in Denmark were forever changed. After the battle for the music museum, a militant squatters' movement emerged in Denmark's cities, and although it was never as massive as the one in Holland, it forged significant ties to groups of retired elders and linked up with the "free areas" of Christiania and Thy camp in northern Jutland.

Christiania provides a living example of the fusion of work and play—of the organizing principles for a new society—and its effect on Denmark's movement has been unmistakable. As one communard explained, in much of Europe, political activists generally emerge from the tough punk rock milieu, whereas in Denmark, many people who become active were first hippies whose earliest experiences with self-determined actions were in Christiania. Christiania is a safe back area to which evicted squatters can escape and from which new actions can emanate, it provides a respite from the turmoil of urban repression and stress; and it also acts as a brake on the reduction of popular movements to small-group actions and martyred heroes. In one such example, a BZ base of four squatted houses in one block was under attack. As the police massed for their final assault, the squatters saw the handwriting on the wall and made use of an elaborate network of tunnels to escape. After the police had battered down door after door in the adjoining squats, much to their public embarrassment, they found no one in the buildings: the BZers had vanished. Although no one would say for sure where they went, Christiania was a common guess.

Perhaps the most well-organized single action of the international Autonomen was accomplished by BZ in September 1986, when hundreds of people took over part of the Osterbro neighborhood in Copenhagen and held it for nine days despite repeated attacks by police and fascists. The fight for the Ryesgade, as this action became known, grew out of the housing crisis but was also an extension of the politics of anti-imperialism. Inside the "cop-free zone," one of the first acts was to torch a building owned by Sperry Corporation, a US multinational involved in the production of Cruise and Pershing missiles. As one BZ activist explained: "It's not enough to talk. Love is a battle. We are fighting homelessness and gentrification, but also the USA, South Africa, and capitalism to show our solidarity. Many of us have been to work in Nicaragua. Now the battle comes home."

To call the Ryesgade action a battle is a slight misstatement. Actually, it was a series of street fights, all of which were won by the squatters. It all began on Sunday, September 14, when a thousand people gathered in the center of the city for what was supposed to be a march to a park. The demonstration suddenly broke away from the "planned" route, and following prearranged scheme, hundreds of people ran to the Ryesgade area, completely fooling the police. In the words of one of the participants, when the police finally massed and marched on the barricades: "It was a vicious fight. As hundreds of riot police attacked, we threw Molotovs, fireworks, bricks, and slung catapults, driving them back." When the police counterattacked from the other side of Ryesgade, hundreds of masked Autonomen repulsed them. When the police retreated for the final time that day, the barricades were reinforced and a huge street party began. Hundreds of people slept at the barricades in preparation for the next attack. In the morning, the police were again greeted with "concrete rain" when they charged, but this time the police attacked on two sides simultaneously and broke through on one. As someone described the scene: "All seems lost, then at the last moment, over a hundred supporters from the city come charging in from the rear, attacking the police from the rear and forcing them to flee! The riot cops run away and don't try to break through again. We reinforce the barricades."

Even though the situation in the neighborhood resembled martial law, the local residents remained supportive of the BZers. During the nine days of fighting, BZ members went food shopping for elderly residents of the neighborhood who were afraid to venture out beyond the barricades because of possible police reprisals. As the city government met in emergency sessions, the Danish autonomists discussed their options. They easily reached a consensus that reformist solutions—such as the offer of a Danish rock star to buy the buildings and give them to BZ—were out of the question. BZ did not recognize the legitimacy of the government, and BZ members resolved to prove that they were beyond its powers. In Amsterdam, a solidarity demonstration attacked the Danish consulate, and there were marches in Aarhus (Jutland) as well as in Germany and Sweden. The network of free radio stations in Denmark provided support for the four hundred people in the Ryesgade by sponsoring open mike debates and calling for food, blankets, and supplies to be delivered to the "liberated area." After nine days, the city finally called on the army for help, and a bloody finale seemed imminent. The squatters called a press conference for 9 A.M. on Monday, September 23, but when the media arrived, they found the houses deserted, prompting the two negotiators working for the city to ask: "Where did the BZers go when they left? What did the town hall learn? It seems the act can start all over again, anywhere, at any time. Even bigger. With the same participants."

After the Ryesgade action, the police tried unsuccessfully to locate the leadership of BZ. At the same time, the movement began to attack targets related to South Africa. Besides an increasing number of small-group sabotage actions, particularly against Shell, another tactic became widely used: "compulsory relocations." A large group of people would suddenly arrive at a corporate office, bank, or travel agency guilty of some wrongdoing, such as having ties to South Africa. People would quickly remove everything, piling typewriters, computers, desks, and furniture in the street while others handed out letters of explanation to the workers and to onlookers. Finally, as quickly as the action began, everyone vanished, leaving the office relocated. These quick and peaceful compulsory relocations enjoyed wide public support and, because they were accomplished so quickly, afforded little opportunity for the police to attack. The same could not be said of the attacks on Shell. In the fall of 1987, activists accidentally damaged a gas station's underground tanks and caused hundreds of gallons of fuel to leak into the earth. Taking advantage of the movement's apparent blunder, Danish police raided homes, offices, and the youth house, arresting people and confiscating property.

Internationally, the Autonomen borrowed tactics and targets from one another, and in May 1988, Danish BZ copied a page from their German counterparts and put together an action week like *Tuwat* in Berlin and *Tag X* in Hamburg. The actions began on May 12, when the door of city hall was painted with the word *Amandla* (African National Congress' slogan for victory) and Israeli, NATO, and Confederate flags were burned from a makeshift gallows. On Friday the thirteenth, small groups carried out attacks throughout Copenhagen. Supermarkets carrying Israeli produce were spray-painted to remind shoppers of the boycott of Israeli goods; a street was barricaded and a house quickly squatted; spontaneous demonstrations fought off police attacks. Although such tactics helped activists feel good, they did little to help broaden their base of support. Prior to the action week, it was already clear that the autonomous movement was increasingly isolated. The meager number of votes garnered by the Left Socialist Party when it used a slingshot as its campaign logo was one such sign. (It failed to receive even the 2 percent needed to gain parliamentary representatives.)

Like their counterparts throughout Europe, the more the Autonomen relied on militant small-group actions, the less popular support they got and the more they came to rely on a small circle of people. As the rise of anti-imperialist politics created a set of priorities focused on the Third World, many activists did not care whether they received popular support within their own societies. As the movement became increasingly violent, it lost whatever sympathy it had, making it an easy target for the forces of repression to hit. Finally, on May 18, 1993, militant isolationism reached its climax when several hundred demonstrators, reacting to the Danish electorate's approval of closer European union, went on a rampage in Copenhagen. As cobblestones and bricks were thrown at police, the order was given to fire on the crowd, and that night ten people were wounded by police gunfire.[15] During the subsequent trials, riot participants received little public support, and long sentences were meted out to many activists.

Hafenstrasse: International Symbol

By 1988, the international focal point of the Autonomen was undoubtedly the set of houses first occupied in 1981 in Hamburg's Hafenstrasse. At the same time as the squatters' movement reached its high point in Berlin, several empty houses in the St. Pauli district of Hamburg were quietly taken over. These eight houses on the harbor gradually became the single most significant focal point of the struggle waged by autonomous movements in Europe. Repeated attempts by the city government and police to dislodge the squatters failed as the Hafenstrasse squatters mobilized thousands of sympathizers and hundreds of street fighters to protect their liberated space. They enacted elaborate defense plans in the face of repeated police assaults; put together lightning-like retaliatory raids on city offices and corporate targets after assaults on the squatted houses; dealt with severe internal problems; and walked a thin line between the state's programs of legalization and criminalization. Moreover, they hosted international Autonomen gatherings in their houses, thereby strengthening the movement's international vitality by providing a forum where the movement could discuss its options and plan its actions.

When the squatters' movement elsewhere suffered a series of defeats, the Hafenstrasse's capability to remain intact made it a symbol of almost mythic proportions among Europe's Autonomen. As one leaflet put it: "Everything is present in this struggle: militant resistance, the fight to live together in communes, internationalism, the struggle for self-management and collective structure. The Hafenstrasse has shown that resolute struggle can become the path for many." Unlike their counterparts in Berlin and elsewhere, who were often ex-students or of respectable working-class origins, the Hafenstrasse drew heavily from the lumpen proletariat (the criminal clement and blackmarket entrepreneurs). Part of the squatters' murals painted on the side of one of the houses transformed the famous call made by Karl Marx ("Workers of the World, Unite!") into "Criminals of the World, Unite!"

Klaus Dohnanyi, then mayor of Hamburg, was unable to control the Hafenstrasse *Chaoten*. He sent his police to clear out these houses four times without success. In 1986, after the Hamburg electrical utility documented the yearly "theft" of more than $50,000 worth of services by the squatters, hundreds of police were called in and were able to clear out a few of the buildings, although eight houses clustered together in three large buildings remained in the hands of the Autonomen. In response to these attacks, the movement unleashed its own counteroffensive, marching more than ten thousand strong around a "black block" of at least fifteen hundred militants carrying a banner reading "Build Revolutionary Dual Power!" At the end of the march, the black block beat back the police in heavy fighting. The next day, fires broke out in thirteen department stores in Hamburg, causing damages estimated at almost $10 million. Over the next months, while the city government floundered, the movement kept the pressure up.[16] On "Day X," April 23, 1987, small groups of Autonomen again retaliated, attacking houses of city officials, court buildings, city offices, and radio Hamburg. In all, more than thirty targets were hit in a fifteen-minute period.

The city then declared the occupied houses "Public-Enemy Number 1," and the squatters braced themselves for fresh attacks. Steel doors were installed, bars were mounted in the windows, and barbed wire was hung on the sides and roofs of the buildings. In early November, the city promised to clear out and tear down the houses within fourteen days. The squatters painted a new slogan on the side of the one of the houses—"Don't count our days, count yours!" —and barricaded the houses. Rumors spread that a network of underground tunnels had been dug for resupply or escape. Netting was hung on the second stories of the houses to ward off the use of ladders, and patrols on the roofs guarded against helicopter landings. Four thousand police arrived from all over Germany, and the country's borders were closed to suspicious-looking tourists headed in the direction of Hamburg.

On Friday, November 13, 1987 (less than two weeks after the shootings at Startbahn West), the squatters' radio station began broadcasting for supporters to join the fight. Police helicopters were chased from the rooftops by a few shots from flare guns, and loudspeakers blasted the song "It's war, war in the city," as the fight began in earnest. After a night of fighting, the barricades were still standing, and rush-hour traffic had to be rerouted because part of a nearby bridge had been borrowed to help build them. Adopting a Spanish Republican and Sandinista slogan, the banner hung on the outside of the houses said "No pasaran!"

Over the next week, as the Autonomen celebrated their victory, two thousand police reinforcements arrived, posing an even uglier confrontation. Mayor Dohnanyi, however, had had his fill, and he succeeded in averting a final battle by mobilizing support for a new plan: legalize the Hafenstrasse squatters by creating a corporation composed of liberal city council members and some of the squatters. The building would then be leased to the squatters, and the city would provide funds for renovations, thereby creating needed "alternative" housing. Most importantly, by providing government approval, these measures would have the effect of ending the illegal occupation of the Hafenstrasse. Although Dohnanyi's plan gave the Hafenstrasse and their supporters a victory, he vowed to clear out any new squats in Hamburg within twenty-four hours (Berlin's solution to militant squatters).

At first, conservative politicians resisted Dohnanyi's plan, but they reluctantly agreed to support it in order to defuse the crisis. After the approval of Dohnanyi's proposal by the city government, the jubilant Autonomen dismantled their street barricades, stripped the houses of their defenses, and even sent the mayor a bouquet of flowers. For his efforts, Dohnanyi was awarded the prestigious Theodor Heuss medal. After six months of peace, however, conservatives in the city government blocked the new corporation in May 1988. Rather than participate in a new round of fighting, Klaus Dohnanyi resigned as mayor, leaving the future of the Hafenstrasse in doubt. Years of negotiations led to a long-term agreement under which the former squatters can remain in the buildings, and in the early 1990s, residents drew up blueprints for major renovations rather than for militant self-defense.[17]

Although they were victorious, the Hafenstrasse's residents paid a high price for their years of continuous resistance to state assaults. Among the earliest occupants, children were driven out, and the internal relationships among those remaining were strained. One of the lowest points was reached in June 1984, when three squatters (two women and a man) beat and raped a visitor in one of the buildings.[18] The collective decided to take matters into its own hands: the three were beaten up, their heads were shaved, and they were thrown out in the street. In a leaflet explaining their actions, the residents wrote: "It was clear that we could not work with the bulls [the police] and the judges in order to deal with the problem. If we had, that would have meant going to precisely the same forces that never missed an opportunity to trick us, and with them in control, they would have tried to do us in." Because they exercised their own brand of revolutionary justice, the squatters were accused of creating a space outside the law, a common conservative charge employed over the following years to justify the use of massive police force.

The psychological price paid by those who lived in the Hafenstrasse was all too evident in their paranoia and crisis mentality. As Hamburg's eight-hundredth birthday celebration approached and more and more new construction was completed along the waterfront, the future of the Hafenstrasse remained contingent upon constant alertness and the willingness of hundreds—possibly thousands—to fight for their free space. Although the Autonomen's continuing resistance to anything approaching middle-class respectability should have resulted (at least by US standards) in a decisive offensive against them, the costs of clearing out the houses would have been unacceptably high by European standards.[19] For more than a decade, the squatters' stubborn refusal to accept the inevitable succeeded in transforming the idea that the imposition of the system's will is inevitably the outcome of the popular contestation of power.

The Hafenstrasse inspired the conscious spontaneity of the autonomous movement. Their continuing existence symbolized militant resistance, and they were the cutting edge of an autonomous movement that existed in a series of militant confrontations. To be sure, the Autonomen remain a diffuse collection of militant counterculturalists who assemble sporadically and whose identity is far from fixed. Their strength is not in their overwhelming numbers. In June 1987, for example, when President Ronald Reagan visited Berlin, the autonomous "black bloc," identified by their black ski masks and militant disposition, numbered only three thousand of the fifty thousand anti-Reagan demonstrators. And in 1988, when seventy-five thousand protesters gathered at the meeting of the International Monetary Fund and the World Bank in Berlin, only a small fraction could be counted as Autonomen. In both cases, however, the initiative of the Autonomen resulted in larger actions, and they were the militant organizers creating a context in which other forms of participation (signing petitions, attending programs and rallies, publishing informational leaflets, and so forth) had meaning.

After the shootings at Startbahn West in Frankfurt and the wave of arrests throughout Europe in November 1987, however, public opinion dramatically swung over to the states' side. Criminalizing the autonomous movement, as had been done a decade earlier in Italy, caused many people to drop out of political activism altogether. Yet the structure—or, to be precise, the lack of formal structure—of the autonomous movement made it difficult to obliterate the movement. No matter how many times the police raided offices or arrested people, they could not seize the leaders of the movement—since there were none—or destroy its organizations—since they were fluid and changing. The Autonomen occupy a nebulous territory of oppositional forces located somewhere between the clandestine red underground and green corridors of parliament, and the counterculture nourishes and creates a context out of reach of political repression.

Feminism

In 1981, the feminist movement was extremely critical of the "male violence" and "penis politics" of the extraparliamentary movement, and the Autonomen were still a movement in formation, clearly unprepared to deal with issues raised by feminists. Seven years later, the greater role played by women in the movement made it impossible to argue against violence solely from the perspective of sexual politics. The very existence of the Red Zoras was an indication of the transformation of this new generation of German women and profoundly affected the ground rules upon which feminism and the politics of gender in general are evaluated by men and women alike. The very notion that some inherent peacefulness in women's nature makes them naturally disposed to resist domination was viewed as part of the system of patriarchy by the Red Zoras:

> When sections of the feminist movement ingenuously return to norms of feminine behavior to find in "the nature" of women all the characteristics that find parallels in the peace movement in the form of the will to sacrifice, humility, refusal of confrontation and combat, they favor the biological theory of "femininity" which for a long time has been known and understood as a product of power.

The autonomous women's movement had long worked with Turks, but given the cultural contrast between punks and newly arrived immigrants from Turkey, feminist connections, beyond those forged by working together in cooperative food stores selling organic produce or learning German, took time to develop. When Turkish and German women first began to meet, obstacles seemed insurmountable. German women, for example, could not understand why their Turkish counterparts insisted on retaining the traditional scarfs worn by Islamic women to cover their heads in public. Turkish women could not convince the Germans that public lesbian leadership and gay banners at marches on International Women's Day made it almost impossible to justify their own participation to their communities. Despite such cultural divergence, common needs led to a women's crisis center being established. The Gray Wolves, Turkish fascists who have long attacked leftist Turks in Germany and in Turkey, issued warnings to Turkish women to stay out of the center. When these warnings were ignored, a gunman assaulted the center in 1984, shooting a Turkish woman dead and severely wounding one of her German coworkers. Along with the Gray Wolves, the police also treated Kreuzberg as enemy territory, frequently entering punk bars such as the Pink Panther and Turkish coffeehouses to arrest people.

By May Day of 1987, the stage was set for a reaction to police brutality, and when it finally came, everyone seemed surprised by its intensity.[20] What began as the traditional street party in Kreuzberg's Lausitzer Platz quickly turned into a full-scale riot. Although the police has initiated the confrontation, they quickly realized that they did not have the strength to control the crowd, and they hastily retreated. Store after store was looted—or, as some insisted, became the scene of "proletarian shopping." One of the participants jubilantly remembered: "From Heinrichplatz to the Gorlitzer Bahnhof, a liberated territory was held for most of the night. It was not just the Autonomen who participated but also 'normal' people: youth, grandmothers, Turks. It was fantastic."

A year later, with thousands of police massed on what seemed to be every side street, demonstrators formed spirited contingents of women, Turks, and a "black bloc" of ski-masked militants ready for action. The banner leading the march, "We fight internationally against capital and patriarchy," indicated the growing influence of the women's movement on the Autonornen, as well as the ascendancy of anti-imperialism as the defining content of the current generation's politics.

May Day 1988: a Personal Note

As the sun set and the full moon rose on May Day 1988, I sat with friends at an outdoor table at a Greek tavern in Kreuzberg. Police sirens began what would be their night-long wail, and a line of more than thirty police vans, each containing half a dozen helmeted riot police, pulled past the bar and headed for the street party at Lausitzer Platz. After they passed, someone strolled over to the corner and returned with a report: "The bulls [police] are going nuts. They must still be smarting from last year." We quickly discussed our options: leave the scene, go and fight the police, or stay and drink some more beer under the full moon. We chose the latter.

Given the police preparations, none of us felt any possibility of winning the streets, but we did not want to head home in case we had not evaluated the situation properly. Gunther quickly improvised a spontaneous modification of our plan. He strolled back to the corner and moved a trash barrel into the middle of the street. Udo went next, carrying a broken chair from the back of the bar, followed by Renate, who picked up a cement block and tossed it on the growing pile. Before long, the street was flimsily blockaded.

We ordered another round, and I asked Gunther if we should reconsider our decision not to move back to Lausitzer Platz. "Look," he began, "we're driving the bulls up the walls. They don't know what to expect from us. Years ago, when we were fighting them every day on the Ku'damm [Berlin's main shopping street], there were a few thousand of us ready to go at it. It was such a hot day we couldn't stand it, and you know if we were hot, it might have been hell in full riot gear. A few people took of their clothes and before you knew it, people were jumping into the Hallensee [a nearby lake] to cool off. Then we all stripped and jumped in. Thousands of us were enjoying ourselves at the beach, while the bulls stood by sweating like pigs not knowing what was happening. The city government, the media, and the bulls could never figure out who gave the order to jump in. They still can't understand our politics or our culture, especially when we don't lose our sense of humor. Right now there are hundreds of bulls looking for us and here we sit, enjoying ourselves drinking a beer. Look at that moon!"

As we sat watching the arc of the moon, I recalled my last night in Berlin in 1981. No matter where in Kreuzberg you went, vicious street fights erupted when the police savagely—and unsuccessfully—attempted to stop the squatters' movement from occupying more vacant houses. After their brutality against nonviolent protesters at Gorleben, the police had suddenly found themselves unable to maintain order in any of Germany's big cities, and Berlin, of course, was in the forefront of the movement. I will never forget the transformation of Hans. He and I had gotten to know each other fairly well in the eighteen months I'd lived in Berlin. He'd patiently explained nuances of German politics to me, while I, perhaps not so patiently, had questioned his assumptions regarding the propriety of pacifism. After a few hours of back and forth with the police in Hermannplatz one night, our roommate Anna and I had grown weary of the effort and were determined, to head home. When we found Hans, he was incredulous that we were leaving. "What?" he shouted. "You're leaving now? I'll be here until there are no bulls left in the streets or no more rocks to throw at the bulls!" Hans's radicalization was symptomatic of thousands of people who followed a similar trajectory in 1981, as the cycle of resistance and repression had intensified.

Around two in the morning, the riot was apparently over, and we headed home, taking the indirect route through Lausitzer Platz. Evidently, not all the partygoers had had time to pack up their belongings before heading home. There were many abandoned items of clothing in the streets. The city had cleared the streets of anything that looked like it could be used to build barricades, but the charred remnants of wood lying in the streets indicated that the state's preparations had not been entirely successful.

The next day, as we read the newspaper reports on the previous night's events, several people stopped by the commune looking for friends who had not made it home. Renate was quite concerned about the fate of Arnt, since he was nowhere to be found. As she searched for him in the neighborhood, we read *Die Tageszeitung*. Apparently, the police had moved against the street party when a small campfire had been lit. The ensuing confrontation involved fifteen hundred Berlin police against the remnants of six thousand demonstrators, most of whom had chosen not to participate in the resistance to the police assault. The Pink Panther had been raided again, and by the end of the night, more than a hundred people had been injured and a total of 134 people were under arrest—most of them with the equivalent of felonies that might bring some jail time.

On the bright side, Arnt was discovered sleeping in the commune next door, and among the casualties of the previous night's police riot were none other than Berlin's chief of police and two of his top aides. These gentlemen had been observing the police action from the edge of the crowd when, from another direction, they were confronted with newly arrived members of the riot squad, who proceeded to bash heads without warning. When the police officers exclaimed that they were in charge of the riot squad and that one of them was the chief of police, the response was indicative of the demeanor of the police that night: "Yeah, and we're the emperors of China!" That remark was followed by blows, which sent the three to the hospital.

When Gunther finally came downstairs and heard the news, he bellowed, "You see, who says there isn't justice in this world?" As he drank his morning cup of coffee, he continued, "This whole system is destroying itself—killing off the rivers and the forests, poisoning the air, stockpiling nuclear waste, and building the ugliest buildings imaginable. No wonder they're beating up their leaders. They can't even take care of Germany's two and a half million unemployed."

"Where's the alternative?" one of us rejoined. "It's certainly not in the anti-imps [anti-imperialists], who would just as soon see Germany go down the tubes, and the Greens are part of the system, no?" For the first time, Gunther looked serious: "The alternative won't appear ready-made overnight, my friend, but we see it growing in the Hafenstrasse, in the resistance to Wackersdorf, to Startbahn West, and in our street parties. An army of lovers cannot lose."

NOTES

1   An earlier version of this article appeared in *Monthly Review*, September 1982: 31–45.

2   In 1989, the German government counted such centers in more than fifty cities. See *Verfassungsschutzbericht* (1989), p. 62.

3   There were points at which Dutch movements rejected tactics from Germany. In 1988 and 1989, discussions in Amsterdam questioned the idea of wearing black ski masks at militant demonstrations. See Val, "Liebe, Krieg und Alltag," in Geronimo, *Feuer und Flamme 2: Kritiken, Reflexionen und Anmerkungen zur Lage der Autonomen* (Berlin: Edition ID-Archiv, 1992), pp. 34–5. In Denmark, however, the ski masks became part of an autonomous uniform.

4   Brand, pp. 259, 262, 266.

5   *OECD Employment Outlook* (1984, 1985); *Amtliche Nachrichten der Bundesanstalt für Arbeit* (Bonn: 1991).

6   Elmar Altvater, Jürgen Hoffman, and Willi Semmler, *Von Wirtschaftswunder zur Wirtschaftskrise* (Berlin: Verlag Olle und Wolter, 1979), p. 263.

7   See Martin Moerings, "Niederlande: Der subventionierte Protest," in *Angriff auf das Herz des Staates*. Zweiter Band (Frankfurt: Suhrkamp, 1988), pp. 321–2.

8   See ADILICO, *Cracking the Movement: Squatting Beyond the Media* (Brooklyn, NY: Autonomedia, 1994), p. 205.

9   Heiner Luft Kastell, *Christiania: Selbts-organization von Nichtangepassten* (Copenhagen: 1977), and Doris Teller, Heiner Gringmuth, and Ernst-Ullrich Pinkert (eds.), *Christiania: Argumente zur Erhaltung eines befreiten Stadtviertels* (Werdorf: Gisela Lotz Verlag, 1978).

10   Michael Haller, "Schwesterlichkeit: Über die 'Kindermacht' in Kopenhagen," in *Aussteigen oder rebellieren: Jugendliche gegen Staat und Gesellschaft*, ed. Michael Haller (Reinbek bei Hamburg: Rowohlt Spiegel-Bush, 1981).

11   Ria Bjerre, "For Christiania with Love," in Alberto Ruz Buenfil, *Rainbow Nation Without Borders: Toward an Ecotopian Millennium* (Santa Fe, NM: Bear and Co., 1991), p. 89.

12   See Bjerre, pp. 99–100.

13   Michael Haller, "Das Dorf in der Stadt: Über 'Christiania' in Kopenhagen," in Haller, p. 143.

14   For one account of what was involved, see Mark Edwards, *Christiania: A Personal View of Europe's Freetown* (Photographers Gallery of London, 1979).

15   "Danish Police Fire at Anti-Unity Mob," *New York Times* (May 20, 1993).

16   See Andrei Markovits and Philip Gorski, *The German Left: Red, Green and Beyond* (New York: Oxford University Press, 1993), p. 224, for an analysis of the parliamentary dimension of the Hamburg government's weakness as related to a strong showing by the local Greens (GAL) in November 1986 and Dohnanyi's subsequent jockeying to form a coalition with the Free Democrats.

17   See *Die Tageszeitung* (Sep. 3, 1993) for drawings and an interview with the architect, Wolfgang Dirksen.

18   See Michael Hermann, Han-Joachim Lenger, Jan Philipp Reemtsma, and Karl Heinz Roth, *Hofenstrasse: Chronik und Analysen eines Konflikts* (Hamburg: Verlag am Galgenberg, 1987), p. 147. Additional materials for this chapter were found in the archives of the Schwarzmarkt Buchhandlung in Hamburg.

19   Many Americans find it hard to understand how the Hafenstrasse could resist the police. After all, around the same time (on May 13, 1985), a similar group in Philadelphia (MOVE) as well a the entire neighborhood in which they lived—was wiped out by a massive police firebomb, and squatters in the United States are routinely evicted brutally by overwhelming police force. Unfortunately, the delicate nature of authorizing deadly force in Europe finds no parallel in the United States.

20   See *1. Mai 1987–12. Juni 1987* (Berlin: Ermittlungsausschuss, 1988), *1. Mai 1987–1992* (Berlin: Umbruch-Bilder, 1992).

Marcuse as an Activist: Reminiscences of His Theory and Practice[1]

HERBERT MARCUSE was not a famous man nor was his writing well known until late in his life. When it became his fate to be blessed (or cursed) with public attention, fame quickly turned into notoriety, and he became more well-known than many people might now recall. In 1968, students and young radicals the world over read and discussed the three M's: Marx, Mao and Marcuse. Wherever he went, he was attacked by both the left and the right—at least in terms of the Communist left. In Germany, he was blamed for the wave of guerrilla attacks in the 1970s. In the United States, then-Governor Ronald Reagan denounced him for complicity in campus violence, and after a concerted campaign against him, one replete with pounds of hate mail, death threats, vilification in the media, and an offer by the American Legion to buy his contract from the university, he was retired unceremoniously and denied the opportunity to continue teaching courses. In his own words, he was "lucky to still have a mailbox" at the University of California, San Diego.

On at least three continents, he was taken to task for subversion of the young—the same charge leveled at Socrates. He was denounced by Pope Paul VI for "theory that opens the way to license cloaked as liberty, and the aberration of instinct called liberation." He was attacked perhaps most vehemently by Soviet Marxists, who considered him a representative of the "reactionary petty bourgeoisie." The British left's interpretation of Marcuse's life is very similar to the Soviet analysis, at least in Perry Anderson's opinion. Anderson mistakenly characterized Marcuse as living a bourgeois life-style in La Jolla, far removed from the exigencies of struggle and the poverty of the lower class.

A lesser man would have been seduced (or broken) by his worldwide notoriety, yet through it all, Marcuse's inner sense of self prevailed. His confidence in his convictions remained unswerving, and although he was denied scheduled classes, he participated in a series of activist study groups, accepted as many of the constant speaking invitations as his time allowed, and, to my good fortune, worked individually (in my case on a regular basis) with selected students who sought him out. Behind closed doors, he was an active participant on campus and in community groups. Not only was he a public spokesperson for us, twice drawing over a thousand people at Socialist Forum lectures, conducting a seminar of sorts with 35 community activists on the need for utopian vision at the Left Bank (an alternative bookstore/craft center), hosting a fundraiser with Fred Jameson there, and debating Kate Millet at Stanford, he also involved himself in our struggles and dilemmas—or perhaps I should say that he let us drag him into some of our less than refreshing personal acrimony, recriminations, and crises. He did live in La Jolla near UCSD, so near that he could walk to work, a necessity because he rarely—if ever—drove a car at that point in his life. He never told me why, but I heard that the entire Frankfurt school nearly perished in an automobile accident when a bee flew into a car full of them while Adorno was driving.

Despite extensive tributes to (and critiques of) Herbert Marcuse, little has been written concerning the relevance of his work for future social movements, nor has his activist involvement been widely understood. What I seek to do in the following pages is provide an image of Marcuse based upon seven years of friendship and political collaboration, experiences that refute some assessments of him and provide insight into the character and interest of his theoretical work.

For many of us, Herbert was more than a respected philosopher or well-known academic. He was someone whose experiences and insights provided a living link with the practice of twentieth century revolutionary movements and the theory of radical critique that has developed since the beginning of history. For his friends, he affirmed that nexus between biography and history which C. Wright Mills dubbed "the sociological imagination." Reacting calmly and with humor in my own moments of dire personal crisis, Herbert was able to situate my concrete dilemmas in a larger historical-psychological context, helping me transcend the painful insecurity of self-doubt by affirming the necessity of living "the examined life." More than once, an evening of scotch and home cooking during which I vented my frustrations at the absurdities of academic life kept me from dropping out of graduate school.

What I recall most vividly from these early days of our friendship was Herbert's quiet insistence on the necessity of theory and the omnipresent nature of modern anti-intellectualism. When we first met, I was driving a cab at night and an activist in the anti-war movement and counterinstitutions in Ocean Beach, one of the last havens of the radical counterculture. To my present embarrassment, although I had heard of him, I had read none of his books nor heard him speak publicly. I was surprised at his immediate delight when I invited him to visit me at Red House, a well-known political commune and police/FBI target.

We immediately developed an affinity for each other—from my side because I liked his sardonic wit, his amusement at the uncomfortable personal acrimony that accompanies political activism in the United States, but most importantly because he was able to formulate radical statements in the most unlikely situations. We once found ourselves arguing the merits of monogamy and the appropriateness of his wearing a tie to work (a practice he later all but abandoned) when Herbert quietly announced that the more straight one's attire, the more possible it was to speak one's non-conformist political viewpoints—a hypothesis I have since tested many times and found to be true. On another occasion, I found myself asserting the need to preserve our ancient cultural heritages, particularly our philosophical tradition but also ethnic customs and identities, until Herbert put an end to my prattle with a wave of his hand: "Human beings are capable of creating cultures far superior to those based on Judeo-Christian values. There are enough people working to preserve the past. What about the future?"

A story I like to relate about Marcuse occurred in 1976 when we were demonstrating against CIA involvement at the University of California. I enrolled there in 1974 to work more closely with Herbert. With the help of friendly secretaries, activists had uncovered several university based CIA projects: dolphins in Point Loma at an institute affiliated with UCSD were being trained to attack underwater divers and blow up ships below the water line; a weather modification project was being studied that was supposed to seed clouds over Cuba during the harvest season, thereby destroying the ripe sugarcane; an economics professor had set up a private research institute using CIA money in Sorrento Valley behind the university. For months, we met, held teach-ins and published proof of the CIA's presence on campus. A wide debate ensued, and in response to a proposal by Herbert, the faculty voted to condemn CIA involvement. Nonetheless, the administration remained impassive, choosing to ignore the many voices of protest as though we were less than worthy of response. In complete disregard of our existence, several administrators traveled to Langley to attend a CIA conference on affirmative action, and they scheduled David Saxon, president of the eight-campus UC system, to speak at a public forum on the same topic at UCSD.

As we debated what course of action to take—the militants argued for tomatoes, while the moderates favored a silent vigil—I consulted Herbert, and together we discussed plans for a militant but non-violent protest. A wide array of campus groups—Chicanos, black students and the anti-CIA coalition—drew together to confront Saxon. Marcuse was looking forward to the demonstration and we agreed to meet there. I remember distinctly that as David Saxon was being introduced, Herbert came over to my side. As Saxon went on about the role of the university in society, we began a chant picked up by the hundreds of assembled students: "Bull-Shit! Bull-Shit!" Saxon ended up not finishing his prepared speech, and as tried to he walk off, he was surrounded and followed by the throng who pressed him on the CIA's presence at the university. The campus police moved in, shoving some of us aside. We shoved back, without anyone being arrested. At one point, Saxon was pushed down, and someone spit on him while he squirmed to get back up. We had not really planned any of this, but we all felt very positive about the determination of so many to force the issue. As we did plan, our actions at UCSD, one of the campuses at the largest university in the world when it is considered as one entity including UCLA, Santa Barbara, Berkeley, etc., were widely covered, making the front page of *Excelsior* in Mexico as well as many dailies in the US. Anti-CIA protests soon occurred all over the country.

Our next step was to call a conference in San Diego for public discussion of the direction the movement would take. Although Herbert assented to being one of our main presenters, he didn't want it to be announced that he was going to speak because, as he pointed out, many other people would come just to hear him. He preferred to speak directly to the activists who made their way to San Diego for the movement. For several hours, he was the center of the conference. In his talk, he affirmed the importance of what we as students were doing—trying to organize in the universities. It should be remembered that at this point in time, the movement (not only on the West coast) was dominated by sectarian workerists who insisted that students were "petty bourgeois" and of no political importance. Some of the existing Marxist-Leninist groups were actually opposed to our protests on the campuses—saying that we diverted attention from the "real" issues—and one wrote and circulated a booklet exposing us as agents of the CIA because we had invited Marcuse, a well-known "counter-revolutionary agent-guru" who had worked for the OSS (which later became the CIA).[2]

I remember being offended and angered when I found a copy of this booklet one morning on the Red House steps. I showed it to Herbert, and he seemed to enjoy listening to me read it aloud, amused by the absurdity of its language and content. When he came to my initials and his name in the text, he laughed aloud. "Oh! How these people love us!" At that moment, I couldn't quite understand the ease with which he handled insult, but in looking back, I can now appreciate a skill all of us in the movement have had to cultivate.

It would be wrong to infer that Herbert was always able to handle attacks on him without feeling hurt. It depressed him when he was painted as someone who was against democracy, who thought there should be less democracy, as when his essay on repressive tolerance was misconstrued. He seemed taken aback when his book on aesthetics was given abominable reviews in major German newspapers. And he never forgot the rude reception given him by Maoists in Berlin in 1968. Somehow, however, when the left attacked him, he derived some satisfaction from it. Perhaps it had to do with his understanding of who the real enemies of freedom were. The numerous threats made against his life, threats so real that student groups voluntarily established a sort of watch over him to insure his safety, were a grim reality of to all of us around him.

Less than a year after it was founded, the Anti-CIA Coalition was dissolved by a majority vote of its members. Internal differences and mistrust had compounded our problems. Around the same time, a coup was accomplished within *Natty Dread*, the campus newspaper that had been the movement's voice (Marcuse never liked the name). The new editors refused to print any part of an article I wrote (with Herbert's help) summing up the legacy of the year's political struggles. Needless to say, I was crushed. Once again, it was Herbert's insight and wit that helped me get through a difficult time. "What's become of your article?" he asked with a sheepish grin on his face and a copy of the *New Indicator*, as the paper had been renamed, in his hand. "That newspaper is the organ of one fraction of the movement," I replied, "if indeed we can still speak of a movement." Disgusted and depressed, I went on: "What's the point of putting all this energy into creating organizations when they don't last?" In one of those rare moments when Herbert answered me directly rather than asking another question, he said quite plainly: "Marx never created a lasting organization. Besides, organizations that last seldom remain revolutionary. Political experience and education are cumulative, and with enough time, their quantity produces qualitative leaps."

However struck I was by his logic, I remained unconvinced. "What of us?" I demanded. "Without a unifying organization, how do we help each other move ahead personally and politically?" I reminded him of the animosity one of our most active members faced from her family because, in their eyes, her political involvement had hurt her education and career. I questioned whether or not her political involvement had been a positive force in her life. Neither of us spoke. Finally, Herbert relit his cigar, and as he puffed on it, we let our minds wander. Some questions apparently have no answers, some concerns are not easily put to rest, although I am happy to report decades later that this person we discussed is teaching and writing in the field of mass communications at a major university.

As the above experiences testify, Marcuse's life after 1968 was extraordinarily tied to radical politics. Despite his fame, his modesty forbade him from believing the prominence given him by the media. He was exceptionally receptive to visitors, and about once a week, when someone from a distant part of the planet would show up and want to meet with him, he would make time. He always disavowed the role of guru or father-figure in our activist circles, and he did his best to subvert our daily routines, questioning our motives and direction while raising theoretical issues designed to create another reality for us. While he was working on his book on aesthetics, we had a small group that engaged some of the issues with which he was involved. I recall now that the majority was Mexican artists—all in the United States illegally. As we read Marquez's *One Hundred Years of Solitude*, Herbert, more than any of us, was able to keep straight the names of the characters. One of his last lectures was in Mexicali, a small border town across the border from Calexico in the eastern part of southern California. One of the members of the aesthetics group accompanied him, serving as translator and companion in a trip few Norteños of any age would have made.

Like many of us, Marcuse was transformed by the global movement of 1968, but his political experience began much earlier. When World War I was ending, his fellow enlisted men elected him to a soldiers' council in Germany. He told me of standing with a rifle in Alexander Platz and pondering the fate of the revolution. He noticed that it was increasingly officers who were getting elected to representative positions and came to the conclusion that the revolution had been lost within the councils themselves because the class structure was being replicated.

This was not the first time his prognosis would be correct. He was able to read historical events with an uncanny accuracy. When *Counterrevolution and Revolt* was published in 1972, (which I regard as Marcuse's best political book and which Perry Anderson confirmed to me in 1981 that he had not read even though he had published a major study of Marcuse), many of us were running around with thoughts of radical change, revolution, international uprisings, and declining US military power in our heads. Marcuse contradicted all that, stating clearly that what was occurring was not radical change, but a preventative counterrevolution in response to an already defeated revolt. In our discussions in the late 1970s, he questioned whether it was revolution or fascism that was transpiring in the Third World, and he repeatedly asked who would be militarily mightier than the US. At this time, Poulantzas and Castells were predicting the dominance of the Soviet Union.

Another example of his predictive capacity is contained in *Soviet Marxism* (published in 1958). In 1956, in response to the 20th Party Congress of the Soviet Union, uprisings in Poland and Hungary had been suppressed, and there was a great deal of speculation that Khrushchev would have to roll back his program of de-Stalinization and crack down further. Marcuse differed: "The Eastern European events were likely to slow down and perhaps even reverse de-Stalinization in some fields; particularly in international strategy, a considerable 'hardening' has become apparent. However, if our analysis is correct, the fundamental trend will continue and reassert itself throughout such reversals. With respect to internal Soviet developments, this means at present continuation of 'collective leadership,' decline in the power of the secret police, decentralization, legal reforms, relaxation in censorship, liberalization in cultural life." If one rereads Soviet Marxism in light of perestroika and glasnost, it was a powerful analysis of the Soviet Union, one that understood the fundamental direction of Soviet communism. Long before anyone else, Marcuse perceived that the structural conditions of Soviet society, unlike the advanced capitalist ones, indicated that it would not be necessary to use violence to transform them.

As his health deteriorated, we had several discussions about religion and death. At the time, there was something of a revival of Judaism and religion in general among many people who previously had been content with secular utopianism as their metaphysical orientation. Ricky Sherover was active in one of the Jewish groups that met regularly, and we often arranged for Herbert and me to spend that evening together. As Ricky left one night, Herbert challenged me to explain the interest so many of our friends had developed in their religious background. My first response was that anti-Semitism and the insecurity of Israel were probably behind it, but that did not suit him. He asked when Israel had lost a war, and if I could name one incident of anti-Semitism in our circles, which came close to any of the cases of racism, which were common knowledge. I fell back to a position asserting that whites needed an identity as oppressed rather than oppressors, to which he countered with two other questions: Why had such an identity not been necessary in the sixties? How could I explain the conversion of Eldridge Cleaver? In his own way, Herbert was helping me realize that the movement's ascendancy (along with that sense of common purpose and solidarity) was long past—a simple fact that I stubbornly resisted (and sometimes still refuse to accept fully).

On more than one occasion, Marcuse said to me that he really did not care what happened to him after he died. During this period of time, Tito fought death for weeks—was it months?—even while unconscious, and we agreed that way of dying was not one we would choose—if we could help it. I asked him what he thought would become of our movement. He looked me squarely in the eyes. "The revolution will not come in your lifetime," he said, "unless you live to be a very old man like me, which I expect you to do."

Herbert was always after me to have him help me secure a real job—as he referred to a tenure-line academic position (which he liked to remind me were getting harder to find). I resisted his pressure for many reasons; among them that I sensed it would mean I had finished being his student. As I tired of San Diego, I finally gave in to his wishes that I make a move by convincing him that what I really should do was go to Europe for a year, during which time I could think about my future. I applied to go to Madrid for a year, and when notified of my acceptance, I rushed over to his office. "Madrid?" he asked. "What are you going to do **there**? You'll be bored in no time." Somewhat flustered, I asked where he thought I should be going. "Why Germany, of course, to Berlin. There's a lot going on there." I protested that my German was not at the level of my Spanish and that UCSD had no programs in Germany. Herbert assured me both these issues would easily be taken care of, and then and there, he began to acquaint me with the recent history of German social movements.

It is difficult to understand why in the United States there has been very little interest in his works since his death. The same is not the case in Germany. There a popular movement continued to develop after the mid-1970s and Marcuse is still considered to be important reading. His final German book has never been published in English. To refer to *Time Messages* as a book is not entirely accurate because it is three essays and an interview with Hans Enzensberger. The essays include "Marxism and Feminism,"[3] "Theory and Practice" and "Failure of the New Left?"[4] . The interview with Enzensberger deals with the question of revolutionary organization in the United States. While some argue that his books are academic, not political, my understanding is different. In 1978, after I had read all his books, I surmised that his life's project had been to prepare the theory for future revolutionary movements. I called my interpretation to Herbert's attention. He seemed quite pleased. "Yes," he said, "you could say that."

Marcuse's Theory and Practical Action

Despite his relative obscurity in the US, Marcuse's theories remain quite relevant, particularly for those concerned with social transformation. Several of the concepts he developed have been extraordinary helpful to me, and I discuss them below to indicate further his orientation to political change, not only in his everyday life but also in his writing. Central to Marcuse's writings throughout his life is the concern that liberation is not abstract (as in Sartre) but depends on sensuous human beings. Rationality has a soul to it, a body that goes along with it. His dialectical thought united mind and body, finding unity in seeming opposites. What seems to be greater individual freedom in modern society may simultaneously be greater enslavement, since it is now the individual who must enslave (or free) him/herself.

Even in moments of revolution, Marcuse argued, our own personalities limit our possibilities, a reality he discussed with me through the concept of psychic Thermidor. (Thermidor was the month of the French revolutionary calendar during which reaction set in.) Psychic Thermidor refers to an internally conditioned reaction which revolutionaries suffer, a syndrome Marcuse accounted for in the changed material conditions of advanced capitalism: "The economic and political incorporation of the individuals into the hierarchical system of labor is accompanied by an instinctual process in which the human objects of domination reproduce their own repression... The revolt against the primal father eliminated an individual person who could be (and was) replaced by other persons; but when the dominion of the father has

As he traveled, Herbert Marcuse was sought out by activists in many parts of the world.

expanded into the dominion of society, no such replacement seems possible and the guilt becomes fatal."[5]

For Marcuse, the key to unlocking the nascent revolt might not be in the ripening of objective conditions, but in a radical restructuring of our psychology. He tried to locate the kind of psychic structure that would characterize a free society and found it in societies in which the pleasure principle organizes society, not the performance principle. Surplus repression was the concept he developed to explain the mechanism by which the emergence of the pleasure principle is internally diminished.

In *Civilization and Its Discontents*, Freud made the case that each of us must internalize mechanisms to repress our instinctive desires and needs and that the superego develops methods of repression that allow city life. Marcuse went further, arguing that the superego has become so great a constraint on the ego in mass society (in which the father is replaced by institutions as the domineering force) that this new personality structure imposes far more repression on people (i.e. people impose far more repression on themselves) than is actually needed for civilization to exist.

Marcuse's emphasis on human beings as the center of the universe, not just as the subjects but simultaneously the objects of liberation, led him to ask whether there is a biological basis for freedom. Do human beings have an instinctual need for freedom? His answer was affirmative. For hundreds of years, Western progressive thinking

posited the irrational as opposed to freedom. The Enlightenment, the French and
American revolutions took as their goals increasing rationality and limiting irrationality
—at least to the extent that we generally think of the irrational as meaning something
evil and uncontrollable. By locating the movement for freedom in the instinctual
structure, Marcuse was able to anticipate the coming of the green movement, long
before people began to talk about Nature as our ally. When he talked about inner
nature as a reservoir of revolutionary impulse, making a point subsequently taken up
by the German Greens, he differed from Habermas, who regards the psychic as "inner
foreign territory."

Moreover, in response to a feminist study group in which he took part, he
extended his discussion to deal with feminism, which he called the movement's most
radical subversive potential: feminist socialism. He said that the radical subversion of
values could never be the mere by-products of new social institutions. "It must have
its roots in the men and women who build the new institutions... Socialism, as a
qualitatively different way of life would not only use the productive forces for the
reduction of alienated labor and labor time, but also for making life an end in itself,
for the development of the senses and the intellect, for pacification of aggressiveness,
the enjoyment of being, for the emancipation of the senses and of the intellect from
the rationality of domination: creative receptivity vs. repressive productivity. In this
context, the liberation of women would indeed appear as the antithesis to the
Performance Principle, would indeed appear as the revolutionary function of the
female in the reconstruction of society."[6]

He had long written on sexuality, developing the concept of repressive
desublimation in his synthesis of Marx and Freud in what he thought of as his best
book, *Eros and Civilization*. The problem he was trying to understand is this: How
can a society in which sexual restrictions are so low still exhibit the characteristics of
a sexually repressed society? His answer is that the quantity of sexual activity does
not necessarily alter the quality of connections between individuals (sexual or
otherwise). This is particularly the case when sexuality has been transformed into a
mechanistic act, into a commodity, into part of an entire cultural infrastructure based
on the fetishization of commodities. Marcuse argued that the psychic structure of
society has remained very similar despite the change in its outward appearance. The
Hegelian/Platonic differentiation between essence and appearance is applied here but
with a Freudian/Marxist twist, one that understands cooptation as the mechanism
assuring the smooth functioning of the social order.

Like repressive desublimation, repressive tolerance requires understanding the
difference between essence and appearance, between quality and quantity. Developed

out of his understanding of art, particularly how the Dada/Surrealist revolt against modern scientific society was integrated into that society to become a means of entertaining it, repressive tolerance asks: How can a government maintain order and at the same time appear to allow the free expression of opinion? How can there be so little genuine political opposition in the United States when in fact we appear to have freedom of expression? Marcuse's answer has two dimensions. In the first place, he called attention to the problem that revolution (in his view, a necessity for the realization of freedom) is illegal. If we dispense with the assumption that fundamental change in the social structure can evolve within the normal course of events, then it is important to question the ways in which tolerance—adherence to the rules of normal discourse—makes revolutionary change impossible.[7]

Secondly, Marcuse asked whether we are free because we think we are free. Is there a level on which our psychic structure and our intellectual assumptions are anesthetized and standardized by the institutions of mass society? As he put it: "...the democratic argument implies a necessary condition, namely, that the people must be capable of deliberating and choosing on the basis of knowledge, that they must have access to authentic information, and that, on this basis, their evaluation must be the result of autonomous thought."[8] Just because people are granted the right of freedom of expression does not mean that information and thought are true.[9]

His argument was construed as elitist and anti-democratic, but a different interpretation is also possible, namely that education and truth are vital preconditions for freedom. And who, he never tired of asking, will educate the educators? For many people, it is very difficult to read Marcuse simply because his prose is an obstacle. He wrote small books, yet their ideas are immense—in stark contrast to books today that are huge and contain so much pulp in their content.

The demise of the thinking individual as opposed to the mass-mediated individual able to deal with vast quantities of information is characteristic of our age. Marcuse couldn't deal with information overload. If we were having a conversation, he would ask politely for the music to could be turned off. Either we listened to the music or had a conversation, but not both simultaneously. My generation loves to have the music on, with the television turned down, and have something else going on as well. Yet we are unable to read Marcuse. "Debilitating comfort" was Marcuse's poetic way of talking about how consumer society actually is harmful to human beings. The increase in the quantity of material goods is not necessarily linked to an increase on the quality of our lives. If we agree that the concepts with which he concerned himself (the nature of freedom, the character of thought) lie in a domain beyond the satisfaction of "material needs" (the dominant discourse of consumer society), then it would be surprising if his discussion were facilely accessed by people conditioned to buy and consume rather than ponder and transcend.

In preparing this article, I've spent time with Herbert in my dreams and realized how much I miss him—as a friend and as a progressive human being. He had an inner sense of himself in relationship to history that put me at ease. He was somehow at peace as few people are, a very rare quality, particularly in an individual whose intellect was so keen. His passing in 1979 is the passing of an entire generation in which the synthesis of the sacred and profane was possible. Yet his written legacy remains a powerful tool for future revolutions.

NOTES

1   This is a revised version of a talk given at M.I.T. for the Black Rose lecture series on November 1, 1991. It was originally published in *New Political Science* 36-7, Summer/Fall 1996.

2   During World War 2, Marcuse did work for the Office of Strategic Services, the forerunner to the CIA, eloquent testimony to his understanding of the relation of theory and practice. His job was to analyze Nazi propaganda and to give the American authorities an understanding of what the internal dynamics of the Nazi party might be. As he told me, the group that assembled in that office was one of the finest bunch of intellectuals that he has ever worked with, very dedicated people, and every one of them became a full professor or a writer of note. He also said that most of their research found its way into file cabinets and not into policy-making circles.

3   Originally published in the New Indicator, "Marxism and Feminism" was reprinted in *City Lights Anthology*, edited by Lawrence Ferlinghetti (City Lights Books, 1974).

4   A talk he gave for the Socialist Forum, "Failure of the New Left?" was translated from the German version and printed in *New German Critique* 18 (Fall, 1979).

5   *Eros and Civilization*, p. 91.

6   "Marxism and Feminism," op. cit.

7   "Under a system of constitutionally guaranteed and (generally and without too many and too glaring exceptions) practiced civil rights and liberties, opposition and dissent are tolerated unless they issue in violence and/or exhortation to and organization of violent subversion. The underlining assumption is that the established society is free, and that any improvement, even a change in the social structure and social values, would come about in the course of normal events, prepared, defined, and tested in free and equal discussion, on the open marketplace of ideas and goods." *A Critique of Pure Tolerance*, pp. 92-3.

8   Ibid. pp. 94-5.

9   The concept of repressive tolerance caused Marcuse immense problems in Germany, particularly since the authorities used it to lump him with guerrillas. Despite their opinions, Marcuse was in no way a believer in such tactics, as I found on many occasions when we discussed this issue at length.
    At the same moment, however, he did not believe in extending the right of free speech to Nazis or the Klan, since in his mind the distance between thought and deed was so short. In today's Germany, however, there are many who argue that even fascist demonstrations openly goose-stepping in front of residence houses for foreigners should be allowed free expression. In Germany, of all places, they argue, every political party, particular ones like the Republicans (or AfD) that have won seats in elections, must have the right to demonstrate in public. Even when anti-fascist protestors assemble to prevent neo-Nazis from gathering, many on the left oppose them.

Eros and Revolution[1]

IN HIS LAST three books, *Counterrevolution and Revolt*, *Essay on Liberation*, and *The Aesthetic Dimension*, Herbert Marcuse concerned himself as never before with questions raised by contemporaneous social movements. His work on Nature in these three books was central to his notion that there may be a "biological foundation for socialism," that Nature—not only external Nature but our own inner human nature—is an "ally" in the revolutionary process. As Marcuse so clearly formulated it, humans have an instinctual need for freedom—something that we grasp intuitively.[2] Unlike Habermas, who considered the unconscious "inner foreign territory" as part of his overly rationalistic model of humans, Marcuse's understanding embraced the erotic and unconscious dimensions of human nature as central to the project of liberation.

Following Marcuse's formulation of political eros, I developed the concept of the eros effect in my book on the global imagination of 1968 to explain the rapid spread of revolutionary aspirations and actions.[3] The eros effect is crystalized in the sudden and synchronous international emergence of hundreds of thousands of people who occupy public space and call for a completely different political reality. Other dimensions of this phenomenon include: the simultaneous appearance of revolts in many places, the intuitive identification of hundreds of thousands of people with each other across national and ethnic dividing lines, their common belief in new values, and suspension of normal daily routines like competitive business practices, criminal behavior, and acquisitiveness. In my view, it is the instinctual need for freedom that is sublimated into a collective phenomenon during moments of the eros effect.[4] After 1968, other such moments are evident in the Arab Spring and the Occupy Wall Street protests that spread to more than 1,000 cities globally as well as in the less well-known wave of Asian uprisings in the 1980s and 1990s.

The eros effect first appeared to me as I completed a decade of research on social movements in 1968. As I sat over looking the Pacific in Ocean Beach, California, I had a Eureka moment as I uncovered the specific synchronic relations to each other of spontaneous uprisings, strikes, and massive occupations of public space. During this world-historical period, millions of ordinary people suddenly entered into history in solidarity with each other. Their activation was based more upon feeling connected with others and love for freedom than with specific national economic or political conditions. No central organization called for these actions. People intuitively believed that they could change the direction of the world from war to peace, from racism to solidarity, from external domination to self-determination, and from patriotism to humanism. Universal interests became generalized at the same time as dominant values of society (national chauvinism, hierarchy, and domination) were negated.

When the eros effect is activated, humans' love for and solidarity with each other suddenly replace previously dominant values and norms. Competition gives way to cooperation, hierarchy to equality, power to truth. During the Vietnam War, for example, many Americans' patriotism was superseded by solidarity with the people of Vietnam, and in place of racism, many white Americans insisted a Vietnamese life was worth the same as an American life (defying the continual media barrage to the contrary). According to many opinion polls at that time, Vietnamese leader Ho Chi Minh was more popular on American college campuses than US President Nixon. Moments of the eros effect reveal movements' aspirations and visions as embodied in actions of millions of people, a far more significant dimension than statements of leaders, organizations, or parties.

European philosophers of the seventeenth and eighteenth centuries sought to understand the structure of individual thought and to classify it according to its various dimensions and historical unfolding. Using a similar analytical method, we can today comprehend social movements as the logical progress in history which unfolds within the praxis of thousands—and sometimes millions—of people as they rise up to change their lives. The inner logic in seemingly spontaneous actions during moments of crisis—particularly in events like general strikes, uprisings, insurrections, and revolutions—constitutes the concrete realization of liberty in history. People's collective actions define the specific character of freedom at any given moment. By reconstructing the actions of hundreds of thousands of people in insurgencies and uncovering concrete dynamics of the unconscious, we can contribute to a philo-sophical history not simply from an individual mind but from the actions of thousands of people. As Susan Buck-Morss put it, what is needed is to "construct not a philosophy *of* history, but a philosophy *out* of history, or (this amounts to the same thing) to reconstruct historical material as philosophy."[5]

One after another, insurgencies at the end of the twentieth century illustrate that ordinary people's collective wisdom is far greater than that of entrenched elites, whether democratically elected or self-appointed. Whether we look at France in May 1968, the Prague Spring, or Occupy Wall Street, people's common sense is greater than the "rational" knowledge of elites. Throughout the world, throngs of ordinary citizens who go into the streets and face violence and arrest, endangering their own lives and their families' futures, have visions of freedom writ large. Empirical analysis of the actions of hundreds of thousands of ordinary people—millions if we sum the total number of participants—reveals that ordinary people want peace, greater democratic rights, equality and simple forms of progress, while elites are more concerned with cutting taxes on the rich, extending national sovereignty, and protecting corporate profits. In the transformed reality constructed by people power, mobilized throngs have newfound capacities to enact change. Inspired by previous movements of common people to overturn elites at the apex of power, popular movements continue to enlarge the scope of human liberty. Without highly paid trainers, insurgent activists adapt new technologies (such as the fax machine in China in 1989, the cell phone video in Burma, and social media in Egypt) and bring them into use far faster than the corporate or political elite.

Forms of direct democracy and collective action developed by the New Left continue to define movement aspirations and structures. This is precisely why the New Left was a world-historical movement. In Gwangju, South Korea in 1980, people refused to accept a new military dictator and stayed in the streets for democracy. When the army brutally attacked the city, outraged citizens beat back a vicious military assault and held their liberated city for a week, using general assemblies and direct democracy to run their commune. Abetted by the US, the South Korean military crushed the commune with tanks and helicopters, killing hundreds of people (at the time, Human Rights Watch estimated the carnage in the thousands). Within the Zapatistas, in the protests in Seattle in 1999, and in the more recent wave from Tahrir Square to Wall Street, general assemblies and direct democracy remain movements' modus operandi.

Alongside participatory currents, the history of social movements is also the history of popular insurgencies being placated, accommodated and sold out by reform-minded parties and organizations of all kinds—whether French and Italian Communists, Czech or Bangladeshi democrats, and Korean or US trade unions. Ritualized protests organized by top-down groups with "progressive" leaders no longer suffice to bring the "masses" into the streets. Apparently, after 1968, centrally controlled elites, like Leninist-style parties, are no longer needed to transcend the reformism of spontaneously formed movements since these movements are themselves capable of developing a universal critique and autonomous capacities for self-government. Since World War 2, humanity's increasingly awareness of our own power and strategic capacities has continually manifested itself in sudden and simultaneous contestation of power by hundreds of thousands of people.

A significant new tactic in the arsenal of popular movements, the eros effect is not simply an act of mind, nor can it simply be willed by a "conscious element" (or revolutionary party). Rather it involves popular movements emerging as forces on their own as ordinary people take history into their own hands. The concept of the eros effect is a means of rescuing the revolutionary value of spontaneity, a way to stimulate a reevaluation of the unconscious and strengthen the will of popular movements to remain steadfast in their revulsion with war, inequality, and domination. Rather than portraying emotions as linked to reaction, the notion of the eros effect seeks to bring them into the realm of positive revolutionary resources whose mobilization can result in significant social transformation.

Limits of the Eros Effect

Uprisings may be powerful vehicles for overthrowing entrenched dictatorships, but they are also useful to global elites whose interests transcend nations. Massive occupation of public space was clearly effective in overthrowing existing regimes (such as Marcos in 1986, Korea's military dictatorship in 1987, and Mubarak in 2011), but the system has become adept at riding the wave of uprisings to stabilize its operations. The wave of Asian people power uprisings from 1980 to 1992 helped to incorporate more of the world into the orbit of Japanese and US banks.[6] The South Korean working class's heroic struggles for union rights became useful to neoliberal economic penetration of the country.[7] In democratic South Korea and Taiwan, as in the Philippines after Marcos (and elsewhere), newly-elected administrations accelerated neoliberal programs that permitted foreign investors to penetrate previously closed markets and to discipline workforces of millions of people in order to extract greater profits.

Although Egypt's future has yet to be written, the military's control after Mubarak's imprisonment is another example of how dictatorships in danger of being toppled—and possibly taken out of the orbit of the US—can be salvaged by deposing a few men at the top while retaining the core of the system. Egypt's military leaders enforce Mubarakism without Mubarak, a more stable system ruled by an elite friendly to the US. As we saw in the Philippines without Marcos, Korea without the military dictatorship, and Taiwan without the White Terror, unstable countries were turned into fertile grounds for US and Japanese banks and corporations. An end to "crony" capitalism meant the expansion of transnational corporate markets and profits.

Humanity's unending need for freedom constitutes the planet's most powerful natural resource. In the struggle to create free human beings, political movements play paramount roles. Uprisings accelerate social transformation, change governments, and revolutionize individual consciousness and social relationships. Most popular insurgencies result in expanded liberties for millions of people; when they are brutally repressed, the regime's days are numbered. Uprisings' enormous energies transform people's everyday existence and continue to energize long past their decline. Uprisings activate civil society and mobilize subaltern groups, such as the working class, students, minorities, and women. After uprisings, autonomous media and grassroots organizations mushroom, feminism strengthens, and workers strike. Even among non-participants, bonds are created through powerful erotic energies unleashed in these exhilarating moments. These instances of what Marcuse called "political eros" are profoundly important in rekindling imaginations and nurturing hope.

Revisiting the Eros Effect

Although contemporary rational choice theorists (who emphasize individual gain as the key motivation for people's actions) cannot comprehend instinctual motivations, even George Kennan, who famously started the Cold War with an essay written under the pseudonym Mr. X, found the anti-nuclear wave of protests in the early 1980s to be "expression of a deep instinctual insistence, if you don't mind, on sheer survival... This movement is too powerful, too elementary, too deeply embedded in the natural human instinct for self-preservation to be brushed aside."[8]

A similar basis for action was also gleaned by social scientist Choi Jungwoon in reference to the Gwangju Uprising. As an established scholar unfamiliar with what had transpired in 1980, Choi was subsequently approached by his professional academic association to investigate the uprising. After extensive research, he concluded that Gwangju citizens had crystallized an "absolute community" in which all were equal and united by love.[9]

So impressed was Choi with the solidarity he uncovered in Gwangju, he believed, "The most basic human values travel beyond history and culture; they began with the birth of humankind and will continue into the unknown future...The term to refer to this primeval instinct has not been found in South Korea's narrow arena for political discourse and ideology." The empirical history of crowd behavior in the late twentieth century—most clearly in Gwangju—demands a reevaluation of the frozen categories of crowds, through which they are viewed as emotionally degraded, when Gwangju's people were passionately intelligent and loving.[10]

For Choi,

"...it was not 'mobs' of cowardly people hoping to rely on the power of numbers. The absolute community provided encounters among dignified warriors. The absolute community was formed only from love...In Western Philosophy, reason is derived from solitary individuals. However the Gwangju uprising demonstrates that human beings who were conscious of being members of a community achieved reason. Reason was the capability of the community, not that of individuals...."[11]

The connective threads running through grassroots movements around the world are often intuitively woven together in innumerable strands of what might seem like very different struggles. In the 1970s, Italy's Metropolitan Indians, the most spectacular of dozens of autonomous groups that constituted Italian *Autonomia*, adopted very similar notions to the US Yippies and Black Panthers, Dutch Provos, and Christiania's communards.[12] No organizational means of communication tied together these communities of struggle; rather, intuition and common sense made the same conclusions flow naturally from people's hearts.[13]

Diffusion—what Samuel Huntington called "snowballing"—can help us to trace how one movement causes another.[14] Snowballing is a postmodern version of "Domino Theory" that guided American anti-communism in the 1950s. Based upon the assumption that there is a single point of origin for insurgencies, this concept expresses the paranoid fears of a center for social control that perceives itself to be surrounded by enemies, not the wondrous joy at the simultaneous emergence of freedom struggles. Tied as Huntington was to Washington policymakers, his ideological presuppositions blinded him to the emergence of polycentric grassroots movements. The distance between his theory and law enforcement officials is not great. As the US civil rights movement accelerated in the 1960s, sheriffs and police continually blamed Martin Luther King or Malcolm X for their own city's problems, and campus administrators often insisted that "outside agitators" caused university protests.

What Huntington called snowballing has been described by others—even by progressive academics in what Barbara Epstein dubbed the "social movement industry"—through terms like demonstration effect, diffusion, emulation, domino effect, and contagion. The sheer number of labels is one indication of this phenomenon's recent emergence as a significant variable. The concept of diffusion and Marxist notion of the circulation of struggle are valuable because they show that struggles impact each other. Leaving aside the difference in values embedded in disease-laden labels like "contagion" and less pejorative terms like "diffusion" and "demonstration effect," they all assume a single, external point of origin. None of these concepts comprehends the *simultaneous* appearance of insurgencies among different peoples, even across cultures. It's not simply a chain reaction, not just that A causes B which causes C. Events erupt simultaneously at multiple points and mutually amplify each other. They produce feedback loops with multiple iterations. To put it in terms of a mathematical analysis, we could say that diffusion and the circulation of struggles describe the process of movement development geometrically, while the eros effect describes these same developments in terms of calculus.

While the influence of one event upon another is no doubt substantial, to comprehend movements as externally induced—much as a collision of bowling balls—is to miss something essential about their inner logic and meaning. Simultaneous emergence and mutual amplification of insurgencies are alternative understandings, ones embedded in the notion of the "eros effect." Rather than a simple monocausal process of protest, the eros effect provides a way to comprehend the polycentric—indeed decentered—source of movements' energies. For Huntington, simultaneity was "impossible," and he excluded it in advance.[15]

Out of a series of struggles in France, activists developed a very similar notion to the eros effect: "Revolutionary movements do not spread by contamination but by *resonance*…An insurrection is not like a plague or a forest fire—a linear process which spreads from place to place after an initial spark. It rather takes the shape of music, whose focal points, though dispersed in time and space, succeed in imposing the rhythms of their own vibrations, always taking on more density."[16] In many places, grassroots activism made possible "discoveries" of this same phenomenon with a simultaneity and autonomy that defied "scientific" understanding.

Long before the social media, simultaneous tactical innovations occurred in different places. To name just one example, in May of 1970, after the US invaded Cambodia and killed college students on its own campuses, activists from all across the country simultaneously blocked highways. There was no central organization directing people to do so. People didn't obstruct highways simply because they heard that people elsewhere in the country were doing it but because people thought they should do something effective to stop a society destroying hundreds of lives every day in Vietnam. Without direct lines of communication, activists on the West Coast clogged Route 5 while, at the same time, activists in other parts of the country stopped traffic on Route 95. Tactics may move in a line from point A to point B through a process of diffusion, but we can't ignore how tactical innovations can also happen simultaneously.

Carl Jung and Synchronicity

How can we understand simultaneous emergence of freedom struggles in many places? One avenue was explored by Carl Jung, for whom synchronicity was so abstract and "irrepresentable" that he insisted we abandon completely the notion that the psyche is connected to the brain.[17] Instead, through archetypes, he understood that unconscious impulses could influence consciousness. Such instinctual impulses originate in the deep layers of the unconscious, in what Jung called the "phylogenetic substratum."[18] They function to return our unknown lives from a distant past to consciousness—from the world of communalism at the dawn of human existence. For Jung, "…in addition to memories from a long-distant conscious past, completely new thoughts and creative ideas can also present themselves from the unconscious—

thoughts and ideas that have never been conscious before. They grow up from the dark depths of the mind like a lotus and form a most important part of the subliminal psyche."[19]

The unconscious may not be rational, but it can certainly be more reasonable than "rational" thought. Consider the intuitive revulsion everyone feels for the wanton destruction of Nature caused by "rational" industrialization.[20] When the unconscious is aroused, it flows toward consciousness—a psychic process very similar to what I understand as the eros effect.[21] Jung refers us to something that "indwells in the soul" and has the power to transform things, especially in moments of "great excess of love or hate."[22] We should note that by love, he meant eros in all its forms, not simply sex. According to Jung, Freud attempted to understand the inner erotic necessities emanating from our instincts according to that one dimension. Freud sought to "lay hold of unconfinable Eros within the crude terminology of sex."[23] In our age, when reversal of commodification of the life-world is paramount, can we reclaim eros from the throes of its reification as sex?

For Marcuse, political eros was "Beauty in its most sublimated form."[24] The eros effect emanates from the instinctual reservoir, the collective unconscious, and is a form of sublimation of instinctual drives into erotic channels of human solidarity and love of freedom. Despite his conservative political orientation, Carl Jung also recognized ways that instinct makes rebellious actions necessary on our part: "The growth of culture consists, as we know, in a progressive subjugation of the animal in humans.[25] It is a process of domestication which cannot be accomplished without rebellion on the part of the animal nature that thirsts for freedom. From time to time there passes as it were a wave of frenzy through the ranks of humans too long constrained within the limitations of their culture."[26] For Jung, these internally necessary drives for change manifested themselves in the European Renaissance and other forms of cultural expression. Under certain conditions they could produce social eruptions: "Separation from his instinctual nature inevitably plunges civilized humans into the conflict between the conscious and unconscious, spirit and nature, knowledge and faith, a split that becomes pathological the moment his consciousness is no longer able to neglect or suppress his instinctual side. The accumulation of individuals who have got into this critical state starts off a mass movement…"[27]

The eros effect rests on intuition, an unquantifiable quality that may make its simultaneity impenetrable to the social control center (the police)—as well as impossible to verify "scientifically." For Jung, synchronistic phenomena are akin to magic, and are not statistically verifiable.[28] "Meaningful coincidences" cannot be explained by rational cognition, but to recall them is to prepare the ground for their future recurrences. Just as keeping a dream journal enhances remembering dreams, so recalling instances of the eros effect prepares the ground for further episodes. Revolutionary spirit for Jung would arise outside the realm of sense perception: "The hallmarks of spirit are, firstly, the principle of spontaneous movement and activity; secondly, the spontaneous capacity to produce images independently of sense perception and thirdly, the autonomous and sovereign manipulation of these images."[29]

When time and space are drastically altered in moments of the eros effect, explanations that assume linear conceptions cannot comprehend what is happening. Thus, the cause of the eros effect may not be capable of being understood within the framework of academic social science. As Jung describes such moments: "There I am utterly one with the world, so much a part of it that I will forget all too easily who I really am. 'Lost in oneself' is a good way of describing this state. But this self is the world, if only a consciousness could see it."[30] In a similar vein of thought, Marcuse understood primary narcissism as "more than autoeroticism; it engulfs the 'environment,' integrating the narcissistic ego with the objective world."[31] He derived his understanding of this "oceanic feeling" from Freud's realization in *Civilizations and Its Discontents* that "narcissism survives not only as a constitutive element in the construction of the reality." For Freud, the content of the ego-feeling was "limitless extension and oneness with the universe." In our feeling of merger with all of humanity, time does not exist, which may help us understand why outbursts of insurgencies so often appropriate past movement identities as their own.

Being "one with the world" implies bonding with those around us, a process similar to what Gaetano Mosca conceived as a human "instinct" for "herding together" that underlies "moral and, sometimes, physical conflicts."[32] Such smart group behavior —containing no centralized control yet eliciting appropriate responses to local situations—is present already among caribou, birds, bees, and ants. Swarm theory seems an appropriate means to comprehend protests like those in Seattle in 1999, when cell phones, texting, internet, and people's common sense created a "smart mob" that came together, dispersed, and reconstituted "like a school of fish."[33]

Eros' Aesthetic Dimension

Seldom do self-appointed theorists of the working class mention women or minorities, and only in rare cases (as Herbert Marcuse did in his final book) do they even consider the possibility of freedom meaning to live without the compulsion to work.[34] At a time when it is possible for human beings to work 20 hours per week for 20 years and to retire with enough money to live decently, the state-capitalist system demands we work longer hours and for more years in order for governments and corporations to continue to function. The Soviet Union's variety of state socialism was little better. Indeed, that variety of Marxism was rightly perceived as wanting to make the entire world into a factory.

Much like medieval theologians who debated how many angels could dance on the head of a pin, idealistic categorical imperatives define many leftists' means of analyzing the strategic value of sectors of the population and long-term goals. For mainstream democratization theorists, a bias exists in favor of the middle class as the vehicle of democratization, while academic Marxists insist rigidly that the working class is key, even to the point of excluding from conferences and journals those they regard as outside lines they draw in the sand.[35] In our world where humanity is the identity of movements emerging across the world and where Nature's destruction approaches a tipping point, species is key. For many Marxists, however, the "working class" functions as a collective father figure, a thing-in-itself fixed once and for all time in a frozen metaphysic universally "valid" yet nowhere relevant.

The history of recent uprisings provides a rich empirical resource from which to evaluate the political positions of sectors of the population, to gauge the concrete historical meaning of "class-for-itself." Revolutionary subjects reveal themselves in concrete praxis, not in the obscure calculations and charts of "analytical Marxians." As Marcuse formulated it, "The search for specific historical agents of revolutionary change in the advanced capitalist countries is indeed meaningless. Revolutionary forces emerge in the process of change itself."[36] Proletarian dogmatism of the Left leaves it playing in the academic sandbox or searching the refuse bin of history for a non-existent "master class."

If Marxists reify categories of production and seek to make the whole world into a factory, reducing humanity to the proletariat, feminism is a vital counterforce that organically constitutes human life in domains other than work. As Marcuse so eloquently reminds us: "In a free society…existence would no longer be determined by life-long alienated labor…"[37] If Soviet Marxism turned art into an instrument of the state, Marcuse offered a different interpretation. At a time when consumerism envelops the continent of Desire and weapons of mass destruction destroy the foundations of the Beautiful, art's own autonomous logic might be its salvation. The resolution of this apparent contradiction is the understanding that within art's formal aesthetics, a truth is contained that transforms society. For Marcuse:

> "Art can express its radical potential only *as art*, in its own language and image…. The liberating 'message' of art…is likely to persist until the millennium which will never be, art must remain *alienation*…Art cannot represent the revolution, it can only invoke it in another medium, in an

aesthetic form in which the political content becomes *meta*political, governed by the internal necessity of art."[38]

The call for art to obey the dictates of the political struggle would mean "the imagination has become wholly functional: servant to instrumentalist Reason."[39] Especially in an era when the system delivers the goods so that people live to work in order to buy into consumerism, art's role may even be that of "An Enemy of the People" as it seeks to change the world.[40]

Activating the Eros Effect

People's intuition and self-organization—not the dictates of any party—are increasingly keys to the emergence of global protests. While political leadership based upon authoritarian models of organization has withered among freedom-loving movements, the power of example and synchronicity of uprisings are increasingly potent— especially when their promulgators are among the poorest inhabitants of a world capable of providing plenty for all. Actualized in the actions of millions of people in 1968, the eros effect continues to define an essential core of movements, and as such it is a weapon of enormous future potential. Both the disarmament movement of the 1980s and the alterglobalization movement of the 1990s experienced periods of rapid international proliferation. With the Arab Spring and Occupy Wall Street protests currently spreading, transnational eruptions of protests have become widely visible.

   Instances of the spread of movements across borders, involving a process of mutual amplification and synergy, are significant precursors for future mobilizations. In the period after 1968, as the global movement's capacity for decentralized international coordination developed, five other episodes of the international eros effect can be discerned:

1. The disarmament movement of the early 1980s
2. The wave of East Asian uprisings in the 1980s and 1990s
3. The revolts against Soviet regimes in East Europe from 1989 to 1991
4. The alterglobalization wave and anti-war protests on February 15, 2003
5. The Arab Spring and Occupy Movements of 2011

Continuing global upsurges pick up from the international synchronicity and expanding popular involvement of movements since World War 2. The next generations of protests—drawn from the trajectory of Chiapas, Caracas, Gwangju, Berlin, Seattle, February 15, 2003, and the Arab Spring—will surpasses these other waves in a cascading global resonance. As the global tendencies of the world system intensify in their impact on millions of peoples' everyday lives, internationally coordinated opposition is more and more a necessity.

For the eros effect to be activated, thousands and then millions of people who comprise civil society need to act—to negate their existing daily routines and break free of ingrained patterns. This process is not simply enacted by the will power of a small group—although ones may help spark it. Without help from anyone, the global movement is building toward a protracted people's uprisings that breaks through regional cultures and confronts the planetary constraints on people's freedom. As the target is fixed, its bulls eye will be reached: the hundred billionaires who greedily hoard humanity's collective wealth, an even smaller number of gigantic global banks and corporations, and militarized nation-states armed with weapons of mass destruction. People used to think that it took a vanguard party to provide this kind of coordination, but these recent episodes of the eros effect prove otherwise. The multitude has its own intelligence, an intelligence of the life-force, of the heart. The eros effect is not an intelligence of Cartesian duality, yet is a moment of extraordinary reasonability.

The twentieth century will be remembered for its horrific wars, environmental devastation, and mass starvation amid great prosperity. It will also be known as a time when human beings began a struggle to transform the entire world system. Uprisings at the century's end reveal people's attempts to enact global justice. From the grassroots, millions of people around the world in the past three decades have constituted a protracted people's uprising against capitalism and war. Without anyone telling people to do so, millions of us in the alterglobalization movement have confronted elite meetings of the institutions of the world economic system—practical targets whose universal meaning is profoundly indicative of people's yearnings for a new world economic system. No central organization dictated this focus. Rather, millions of people autonomously developed it through their own thoughts and actions. Similarly, without central organization, as many as thirty million people around the world took to the streets on February 15, 2003 to protest the second US war on Iraq. As the global movement becomes increasingly aware of its own power, its strategy and impact are certain to become more focused. By creatively synthesizing direct-democratic forms of decision-making and militant popular resistance, people's movements will continue to develop along the historical lines revealed in 1968 and subsequent Asian uprisings: within a grammar of autonomy, "conscious spontaneity," and the eros effect.

As we move into the twenty-first century, the Arab Spring and Occupy protests provide empirical evidence of the growing consciousness of ordinary people who go into the streets to change history. In 1968, "the whole world was watching." Today, it is increasingly the case that the whole world is awakening. Our ultimate goal should be to forge permanent popular assemblies as forms of governance, to enlarge and solidify the kinds of small general assemblies proliferating from the grassroots. Previous historical examples of such forms of governance can be found in the 1871 Paris Commune and the 1980 absolute community in Gwangju.[41]

   No one could have guessed that the suicide of a vegetable vendor in a small Tunisian town would set off the Arab Spring. Not even Mohamed Bouazizi himself had any idea that his solitary act of despair and anger would resonate among so many people. It appears that leaderless conjunctures most often produce the eros effect. Like falling in love, enacting the eros effect is a complex process. Can we make ourselves fall in love? Can we simply will ourselves to remain in love? If the eros effect were continually activated, we would have passed from the realm of prehistory, to a world in which human beings for the first time are able to determine for themselves the type of society in which they wish to live.

NOTES

1   Originally prepared for the Critical Refusals Conference of the International Herbert Marcuse Society, Philadelphia, October 28, 2011. Earlier versions appeared in *Radical Philosophy Review*. Special Double Issue — 16.1 and 16.2. 2014. Republished in *Spontaneous Combustion: The Eros Effect and Global Revolution* edited by Jason Del Gandio and AK Thompson (Albany: State University of New York Press, 2017) 37-52.

2   See "A Biological Foundation for Socialism?" in *Essay on Liberation* (Boston: Beacon Press, 1969) pp. 6-22.

3   See *The Imagination of the New Left: A Global Analysis of 1968* (Boston: South End Press, 1987) and *The Subversion of Politics: European Autonomous Social Movements and the Decolonization of Everyday Life* (Oakland: AK Press, 2006) for development of the eros effect. For another early theoretical formulation, see my 1989 paper at http://www.eroseffect.com/articles/eroseffectpaper.PDF. The concept is expanded in *Asia's Unknown Uprisings* (Oakland: PM Press, 2012).

4   For Marcuse's formulation, see *Essay on Liberation* (Boston: Beacon Press, 1969).

5   Susan Buck-Morss, *The Dialectics of Seeing: Walter Benjamin and the Arcades Project* (Cambridge: MIT Press, 1989) pp. 77, 55.

6   See Vol. 2 of my *Asia's Unknown Uprisings* (Oakland, PM Press, 2012).

7   See Loren Goldner, http://libcom.org/history/korean-working-class-mass-strike-casualization-retreat-1987-2007.

8   George Kennan, "On Nuclear War," *The New York Review of Books*, January 21, 1982 as quoted in Marc Nerfin, "Neither Prince Nor Merchant: Citizen—An Introduction to the Third System," *Development Dialogue* (1987) p. 175.

9   Choi Jungwoon, *The Gwangju Uprising: The Pivotal Democratic Movement that Changed the History of Modern Korea* (Paramus: Homa and Sekey Books, 2006) pp. 85, 131. For background on the uprising, see "Remembering the Kwangju Uprising," http://eroseffect.com/articles/rememberingkwangju.pdf

10 See my chapter, "Remembering the Gwangju Uprising," in *South Korean Democracy: Legacy of the Gwangju Uprising* (London: Routledge, 2006).

11 Choi Jungwoon, *The Gwangju Uprising: The Pivotal Democratic Movement that Changed the History of Modern Korea* (Paramus: Homa and Sekey Books: 2006) p. 134.

12 See Mary Anne Staniszewski, Dara Greenwald, and Josh MacPhee, editors, *Signs of Change* (Oakland: AK Press, 2010).

13 Compare with Habermas' negative assessment in *Toward a Rational Society*, pp. 35-6

14 Samuel Huntington, *The Third Wave: Democratization in the Late Twentieth Century* (Norman: University of Oklahoma Press, 1991) p. 46. Hereafter *Third Wave*.

15   Huntington, *Third Wave*, p. 33

16   The Invisible Committee, *The Coming Insurrection*, http://www.bloom0101.org/thecominginsurrection.pdf, p. 6.

17   Carl G. Jung, *Synchronicity: An Acausal Connecting Principle* (Princeton: Princeton University Press, 1973) p. 89.

18   Jung, *Archetypes*, p. 286.

19 J ung, "Approaching the Unconscious," in *Man and His Symbols* (New York: Dell, 1968) p. 25.

20   Teodros Kiros considers a "rationality of the heart" an antidote to contemporary civilization's misuse of reason. See *Zara Yacob: Rationality of the Human Heart* (Trenton, NJ: Red Sea Press, 2005).

21   Jung, *Synchronicity*, p. 30.

22   Jung, *Synchronicity*, p. 32. As Jung notes, the concept is originally Avicenna's. Three hundred years later, Ibn Khaldun similarly discussed forms of cognition outside the realm of rational thought. See my essay, "Ibn Khaldun: A Dialectical Philosopher for the New Millennium," in *African Philosophy: Critical Interventions* edited by Teodros Kiros (New York: Routledge, 2000).

23   Carl Jung, "The Eros Theory," p. 28.

24   Herbert Marcuse, *The Aesthetic Dimension: A Critique of Marxist Aesthetics* (Boston: Beacon Press, 1978) p. 64.

25   The text uses "man" and I have substituted "humans" in three places.

26   Carl Jung, "The Eros Theory," in *Collected Works*, Second Edition (Princeton: Princeton University Press, 1966) Vol. 7, p. 19.

27   Carl Jung, *The Undiscovered Self* (New York: Signet, 2006) p. 79.

28   See Jung, *Synchronicity*, pp. 95, 103, 106-7.

29   Jung, *Archetypes*, p. 212.

30   Jung, *The Archetypes and the Collective Unconscious* (Princeton: Princeton University Press, 1990) p. 22.

31   Marcuse, *Eros and Civilization* (Boston: Beacon Press, 1955), p. 168.

32   Gaetano Mosca as quoted in Mancur Olson, *The Logic of Collective Action: Public Goods and the Theory of Groups* (Cambridge: Harvard University Press, 1971) p. 17.

33   For more on swarm theory, see Peter Miller, "Swarm Theory: Ants, Bees and Birds Teach Us How to Cope With a Complex World," *National Geographic*, July 2007, p. 146.

34   Herbert Marcuse, *The Aesthetic Dimension: A Critique of Marxist Aesthetics* (Boston: Beacon Press, 1978) pp. 28-9.

35   A recent example is American Sociological Association President Erik Olin Wright's refusal in 2011 to approve a panel on autonomous social movements because he considered them not to be "working class."

36   *Essay on Liberation*, p. 79.

37   Marcuse, *The Aesthetic Dimension*, pp. 28-9.

38   Herbert Marcuse, *Counterrevolution and Revolt* (Boston: Beacon Press, 1972) pp. 103-4.

39   Marcuse, *Counterrevolution and Revolt*, p. 107.

40   Marcuse, *The Aesthetic Dimension*, p. 35.

41   See my article, "Comparing the Paris Commune and the Gwangju Uprising," in this book.

Eurocentric Understanding of Civil Society[1]

IDEALIZATION OF European forms of civil society has impeded Western comprehension of social and political development in other societies. To overlay Europe's specific historical formation onto the rest of the world, as Eurocentrists do, is not simply an academic or theoretical problem. Not by coincidence, in these same regions where it is often claimed that "civil society" does not exist, the West continues to wage major wars. Disastrous US wars in Asia, based upon the idea of bringing "democracy" and "freedom" to the Philippines, Korea, Vietnam and Iraq, have killed no fewer than ten million people since 1898.

Not so long ago, Euro-American expansionism was driven by now obsolete notions like Manifest Destiny, the White Man's Burden, and Civilizing Mission (*mission civilisatrice*). Today, more subtle but no less condescending conceptions of superiority and universal applicability fuel the West's appetite to universalize its form of "democracy" and "freedom." The scholarly establishment's exogenous understanding of civil society is a modern equivalent to antiquated racist categories that justified colonialism and genocide. With war looming over Iran and a new cold war underway with China, the time is long overdue to reconsider policies predicated upon global applicability of Western values.

The original conception of civil society was grounded in the specific historical form it took in Europe, an insight upon which Herbert Marcuse built a non-Eurocentric understanding in *Reason and Revolution*.[2] Rather than deploring its absence in other parts of the world or seeking to export it, Marcuse noted the specificity of "bourgeois" society to European history and sharply criticized its "one-dimensional" humans. In the thoughts that follow, I question the West's cultural superiority and indicate possible alternative forms of civil society.

If we are to create a world in which diversity is celebrated and people are truly blessed with the autonomous space to determine their own forms of governance and daily life, then we must conceptualize civil society in very different forms than its uniquely European embodiment. A brief survey of Western Europe's historical development will help clarify its unique character.

Origins of Western European Civil Society

After the Roman Empire divided into East and West in 285 CE, two very different social systems were consolidated. Rome was overrun and sacked in 410 and 455. The city fell by the wayside and was depopulated to the point where fewer than 15,000 people lived there in 1300—even before the Black Death killed half of Europe's urban population. In the East, the "Roman Empire" (Byzantium) continued to exist for a millennium after the sacking of Rome. With Christianity as the state religion, Constantinople was the capital of a wealthy merchant empire where the emperor was both supreme military leader and in control of the church (*caesaropapism*). Although he recognized the bishops of Rome, Constantinople, Antioch, Alexandria, and Jerusalem as local religious authorities, Justinian (who ruled from 527-565) reserved for himself sovereignty over all matters of religious doctrine. He governed according to the notion of "one state, one church, and one law."

Under Justinian, everyday life in Constantinople was tightly regulated. He consolidated Roman law and promulgated severe moral proscriptions. Gambling was outlawed. Male homosexuals had their genitals removed. Astrologers were publicly whipped and paraded on camels through the city. As Procopius tells us, "in his zeal to gather men into one Christian doctrine, he recklessly killed all who dissented."[3] Justinian abolished all dissenting forms of worship ("heresies" such as Samaritans, Montanists, Sabbatians, and Arians) and confiscated their vast wealth "beyond telling or numbering." He empowered priests to rob even the very rich. With a firm grip on power, he sent his army to reconquer Rome in 537 and commissioned the magnificent domed church, Hagia Sophia, to commemorate revitalization of the empire.

The Byzantine reconquest of Rome was short-lived. A range of powers came to control Italy, only one of whom was the Bishop of Rome, whose elevation to "Pope" divided the Christian church in 1054, when Catholics and Orthodox mutually excommunicated each other. Although the Pope proclaimed himself to be infallible in religious matters, he was often an appendage of political power—of secular autonomous centers of military might. In Western Europe, no particular government could claim absolute authority over the church, unlike the Byzantine emperor's control of the universal church. In 1203, Byzantium itself was devastated when the Venetian-financed fourth crusade sacked Constantinople, forever hallowing out the empire until its conquest by the Turks in 1453.

In the West, three centuries after Rome was sacked, hundreds of political entities and ethnicities were amalgamated into a confederation that became known as the Holy Roman Empire. In 800, the Bishop of Rome crowned Charlemagne, a Carolinian king of the Franks, as emperor, a title that rivaled the ruler of Constantinople. Free cities, kingdoms, duchies, and principalities all enjoyed varying degrees of independence and privileges within a weakly unified state. So amorphous was its character that Voltaire famously declared that it "… was in no way holy, nor Roman, nor an empire." In 987, the Carolingian empire fragmented, and the country of France emerged. Almost at the same time, the kingdom of England was consolidated, where in 1215, a rebellion led by nobles compelled the king to sign the Magna Carta. Revolutions in 1688 in England and 1789 in France further expanded the rights of citizens and the space for civil society. So dispersed was political power in the West that dozens of principalities existed in Germany when Napoleon rose to power at the beginning of the nineteenth century.[4] Nation-states in both Italy and Germany were only forged in the late nineteenth century.

Dispersal of power in western Europe had been further propelled by Protestant Revolutions in the sixteenth century. Wars against entrenched Roman Catholic powers created social spaces in which individual citizens could assert their rights outside the rules of religious dogma and the power of feudalism. As German cities grew alongside aristocratic estates, any serf who could find urban sanctuary for more than a year and a day could legally be released from the bonds of feudal servitude. Newly found merchant wealth, the Renaissance, and the Enlightenment led to acceleration of technical innovations, colonial conquests, and revolutions whose combined effects thrust Europe into world leadership in the modern era.[5]

The origins of "*bürgerliche Gesellschaft*" ("bourgeois society"—which became known as civil society) can be traced to the long historical process of ever-growing autonomy of citizens from church and state. For Eurocentric theory, the West's civil society is its sole genuine form. The particular historical outcome of Western Europe's social development is frozen as the model that all societies must take in order for "democracy" and "freedom" to flourish. A corollary of this glorification is the elevation of European individualism to a universal model with which no other culture's "individual" can compare.

Whether we conceptualize civil society as an arena where people pursue their own interests as individuals or as groups (as classes, interest groups, ethnicities, races, gender identities, families, or regionally-based clusters), a central defining element is that the terrain is autonomous of state power (although various individuals and groups may use the government to further their aims).

According to Jürgen Habermas' theory of civil society, an informal "public sphere" developed in the late seventeenth century in England, Germany and France, creating arenas distinct from political power. As capitalist markets and nation-states became ever increasing forces of system integration, the public sphere was "structurally transformed."[6] In the twentieth century, during the same period of time that C. Wright Mills discussed the rise of mass society and the decline of the "public," Habermas observed that the boundary between the state and civil society had collapsed, rendering the concept of civil society problematic.

From Civil Society to Life-World

Despite its structural transformation, civil society is preserved in the "life-world," an autonomous space where "rational will-formation" free of distorted communication can lead to "collective self-determination of the public sphere." For Habermas, rational will formation requires certain conditions, including freedom from distortions of communication, coercion, and pressure to not speak up within a shared ethical culture. Outside the capitalist market and nation-states' dynamics of system integration, the informal sphere of everyday life in the family, voluntary organizations, and interest groups is a private domain uncontrolled by public authorities.[7]

Building upon his analysis, Habermas' followers have posited a list of require-ments in order for undistorted communication to be said to exist: a free press and literacy, individual rights, and avenues for communication free of coercion in sites for collective deliberation (such as cafés and salons).[8] For Habermas, undistorted communication must be *reasoned* between free and equal citizens. Western European privacy and the "bourgeois individual" stand in sharp contrast to Asia and the East, where he claims the autonomous individual did not develop. He considers privacy and individual rights in Germany as fundamentally different than in Asia's densely packed cities.[9] In Habermas's view, coffee houses and salons in eighteenth-century Europe were central sites for new forms communication between free individuals, who built a new web of relationships into civil society. Many people have asked whether or not Asia's teahouses might be considered similar domains. For those who hold European society in high regard, the answer is "no." The argument is made that tea house discussions may not have fostered "a certain quality of relationship."[10]

There are two problems here: the ideal type employed by Habermas poses a pure form of civil society rather than envisioning a variety of existing forms. A more serious problem is derivation of this ideal type solely from Europe, where bourgeois society facilitated the emergence of an urban capitalist class essential to civil society. Do other parts of the world have to follow precisely in that historical development pattern in order for them to have a civil society? If so, that would exclude in advance the possibility of non-Western forms of civil society.

By reifying Western categories into universal ones, Eurocentric theory seeks to refashion what are regarded as antiquated anti-democratic social systems. If the West could learn to celebrate diversity, and not seek to impose the European model onto the rest of the world, would other cultures be left free to fashion their own autonomous norms, values and institutions? Despite the bold assertions of Francis Fukuyama and

American triumphalists at the end of the Cold War, modern representative democracy, dominated by huge money and powerful interests, is neither the final form of democracy nor genuine freedom.

When imposed by military force, the brutal victimization of non-Western countries reveals the system's dependence upon violence to create "democracy" and enforce "freedom." Harvard University political scientist Samuel Huntington is an extreme case in point. Seeking to "democratize" Vietnam, he advocated "forced-draft urbanization"—massive bombing and defoliation of the countryside of Vietnam to force the rural population to migrate to cities, thereby creating "preconditions for democracy." According to Huntington's "rational" logic and misinformed history, all democracies have originated in cities; by urbanizing Vietnam he was bringing it the preconditions for democracy.[11] Following his lead, the US waged the largest chemical warfare program in world history (euphemistically dubbed "Agent Orange") at the cost of monumental destruction of all forms of life.

Huntington never stopped to consider existing rural culture in Vietnam as participatory and consensual. For him, it was an obstacle to American aims, all the more so since the guerrillas regularly raised more tax revenues in the countryside than did the US-created Republic of Vietnam. Even after one-third the population of southern Vietnam was forcibly relocated to "strategic hamlets," people's hearts and minds were never won by the US.

*   *   *

Habermas' universalization of European civil society leads him to envision a "functioning global public sphere" where humanity can be said to be "advancing toward a perpetual peace." This phrase is taken from Immanuel Kant, whom Habermas seeks to bring into the present because Kant "…could not foresee the structural transformation of this bourgeois public sphere into a semantically degenerated public sphere dominated by the electronic mass media and pervaded by images and virtual reality."[12] Within the universal framework of a "single representative polity," Habermas explicitly "must reject collective rights and survival guarantees."[13] He anticipates mobilization of an "international civil society" to confront nation-states to end war, ecological devastation and poverty. For him the political public sphere can "prevent the implementation of 'shady' policies" through public criticism.[14] He believes the League of Nations and the United Nations indicate that the World Spirit has "lurched forward."[15]

Habermas' Eurocentric bias is explicit: "Only the states of the *First World* can afford to harmonize their national interests to a certain extent with the norms that define the halfhearted cosmopolitan aspirations of the UN."[16] He believes that for a perpetual peace to exist, there needs to be: "… a normative agreement concerning human rights whose interpretation of the moment is a matter of dispute between the West, on the one hand, and the Asians and Africans, on the other…"[17] By privileging Western notions of human rights, it appears that Habermas does not include the right to life of more than ten million people killed in US war in Asia, nor the two million prisoners currently being held in the United States, many of whom suffer severely deprived and depraved conditions of life. Denied elementary guarantees of personal safety, many prisoners' food provisions are below minimum standards established by government agencies.[18]

Can the United Nations formulate the universal interests of humanity? The UN is an international confederation of militarized nation-states armed with weapons of mass destruction, which its members feel entitled to produce, sell and use against both foreign and domestic "enemies." In the nineteenth and twentieth centuries, Europe carved the world into national entities as colonial powers conquered the planet and needed local authorities to assist imperial domination. Created in the name of "progress" and "enlightenment," today these nation-states are part of the problem facing humanity. A genuine perpetual peace lies outside the domains of nation-states, singly or in combinations.

From the grassroots, federations of self-governing, autonomous communities have been envisioned and created in the last fifty years. First formulated in 1970 by Black Panther leader Huey P. Newton as "Revolutionary Intercommunalism," anarchist Murray Bookchin recast it as "Libertarian Municipalism" in 1991. More recently, Kurdish national liberation leader Abdullah Ocalan transformed the struggle of his people to become "Democratic Confederalism" rather than the creation of a nation-state.[19] The fact that a very similar goal was formulated by revolutionary leaders with such different ideologies reveals that the history has brought us to the point where such a form of democracy is precisely what is needed. In Rojava, Syria, implementation of post-patriarchal, secular, participatory governance is living testimony to its viability. Dismissed by Habermas as "communitarian," such alternatives to nation-states contain the universal in their particular existence. Habermas' universal proves to be empty except in the existence of the "World Mind." Sensuous, living human beings first must love and respect themselves and their neighbors before being able to actualize a world of "perpetual peace."[20]

Habermas makes the claim that world society exists because "communication systems and markets have created a global network."[21] His earlier work had supplemented Marx's understanding of the self-formation of the human species through labor to include the dimension of communication,[22] yet he continues to disregard revolution (what Marx considered creation of the "class-for-itself") as an important domain of species self-creation. Habermas' explanation of the origins of "world society" ignores massive protest movements, such as on February 15, 2003, when more than thirty million people went into the streets around the world to oppose an Iraq war that had not yet begun. Nowhere does he mention the global uprising of 1968, the disarmament movement of the early 1980s, Asia's string of democratic uprisings from 1986 to 1992, the regional overthrow of authoritarian regimes Eastern Europe in 1989, the alterglobalization upsurge from the Zapatistas to Seattle in 1999, and Occupy Wall Street/the Arab Spring in 2001—all of which were factors in the formation of world society —and to which we must add the uprising of 2020.[23]

Unlike Herbert Marcuse, who remained closely connected with social movements throughout his life, Habermas and other members of the Frankfurt School opposed insurgent movements in key moments. During the 1960s, Max Horkheimer gave a highly publicized speech at an American army base in Germany thanking the US for liberating Germans from Nazism and comparing that effort to the US war to save Vietnam from Communism. Theodor Adorno called on the Frankfurt police to help control his classroom. After the murder in Berlin of student activist Benno Ohnesorg on June 2, 1967, the movement gathered in Hannover for his funeral. Rudi Dutschke gave an impassioned speech calling for militant resistance. Habermas dismissed Dutschke's comments as "Left Fascism." Although Habermas later retracted the comment, his affiliation with movements was thereafter never viable.

Herbert Marcuse's Understanding of Civil Society

Unlike many of his contemporaries, Herbert Marcuse did not consider Europe a model for the rest of the world. Dialectically comprehending the relationship of freedom and slavery, of progress and domination, Marcuse, following Hegel, understood that individuals seeking to maximize their own interests in civil society led to the West's bloody quest for world domination.[24] For Marcuse, European civil society contained inherently destructive dynamics that drove it to incessant expansion and conquest of new markets through global colonization. As Marcuse wrote:

> Significantly enough, it is in this discussion of the police that Hegel makes some of his most pointed and far-reaching remarks about the destructive course that civil society is bound to take. And he concludes with the statement that 'by means of its own dialectic the civil society is driven beyond its own limits as a definite and self-complete society.' It must seek to open new markets to absorb the products of an increasing over-production, and must pursue a policy of economic expansion and systematic colonization.[25]

Although Hegel is often misunderstood as not having paid attention to economics, Marcuse emphasized Hegel's analysis of the "economic foundation" of civil society. Hegel recognized that the relations of civil society could never provide for perfect freedom and perfect reason owing to the particular mode of labor on which they were based. Within civil society, humans are "subject to the laws of an unmastered economy, and had to be tamed by a strong state, capable of coping with the social contradictions."[26] Hegel predicted that the vast wealth of society would not be able to prevent immiseration and poverty. In 1821, he foresaw that this imploding dimension of civil society would lead to economic collapse, with millions of people thrown out of work. He understood that "this society, in the excess of its wealth, is not wealthy enough…to stem excess of poverty and the creation of paupers."[27] As a result, Hegel believed that civil society would inevitably lead to "an authoritarian system, a change that springs from the economic foundations of that society itself, and serves to perpetuate its framework."[28]

Hegel measured progress by human freedom. As Hegel understood it, the world was governed by reason, and history was the practical realization of the "universal mind" over time. For Hegel, progress was "the self-consciousness of freedom" that operated through the world mind, better known today as "world spirit" (*Zeitgeist*). Hegel defined three historical epochs of freedom:

1. Oriental, in which one, the despot, is free
2. Greco-Roman, in which some humans, but not slaves, are free
3. German-Christian, in which humans are free

It is precisely this "freedom" of all individuals to maximize their economic interests which becomes the cause of society dividing into billionaires alongside hundreds of millions of paupers.

Turning to the specificity demanded by Hegel's *Logic*, Marcuse insists that bourgeois society is a particular form applicable to the West:

Hegel's system is necessarily associated with a definite political philosophy and with a definite social and political order. The dialectic between civil society and the state of the Restoration is not incidental in Hegel's philosophy, nor is it just a section of his Philosophy of Right; its principles already operate in the conceptual structure of his system. His basic concepts are, on the other hand, but the culmination of the entire tradition of Western thought. They become understandable only when interpreted within this tradition.[29]

Unbridled individualism, the central organizing principle of European civil society, creates the need for a universal authority to constrain individual excesses. Marcuse understood that abstract generalization of particular interests is problematic. When individual interests conflict with collective rights, then the rights of the whole collide with those of the individual. Individuals' interests therefore do not correspond with what is just: "The [universal] right, however, holds the higher authority because it also represents—though in an inadequate form—the interest of the whole. The right of the whole and that of the individual do not have the same validity."[30] To secure the rights of the individual, the state stands outside civil society to enforce the "unselfish needs of the whole."[31]

*　　*　　*

In our epoch, rationality itself has become unreasonable. Overwhelmed by constantly expanding technical and institutional powers, progress has turned into its opposite:

- instead of the state safeguarding individual rights, government violence is a key problems today. Hegel's idealized police, upholders of justice in the interests of the whole society, are today all too often murderers of innocent youth, disproportionately people of color. For years now, something like three Americans every day are killed by police.[32] Deadly use of force is the reason for the global uprising of 2020 under slogans like Black Lives Matter and Defund the Police.

- instead of developing the free individual, society today produces conformity and standardization of thought. Progress is measured in material goods and the "standard of living."

- instead of greater freedom from the state, contemporary society shrinks autonomy and expands heteronomous domination. In the US and many other places, religious values are imposed upon on entire groups such as women and gays. Moslem women in France are legally prohibited from wearing their hijabs.

- instead of expanding life possibilities, the system demands we work longer hours for more years for less money, despite the economic possibility of far greater free time. In 1930, John Maynard Keynes predicted a work week of only 15 hours by 2030 because of "science and compound interest."[33] Yet today, "making a living" through a lifetime of toil rather than living freely remains nearly everyone's preoccupation, from cradle to grave. Indeed, hundreds of millions of marginalized wretched of the earth barely have enough food or medicine. Well-fed dissident voices are increasingly denied jobs and public platforms. Part-time positions proliferate with low wages, leaving fewer families with opportunities to make ends meet.

- instead of expanding academic freedom, the state has remolded it into a means to support and celebrate war criminals like Samuel Huntington. The original meaning of academic freedom was intellectual freedom from government and religious control. In our society, public intellectuals vanish, and critical thinking is devalued.

Like Karl Marx, Marcuse considered the subject of history to be sensuous human beings whose actions are determined by their own needs for freedom. By integrating Freudian psychoanalysis into his analysis, Marcuse was able to proceed far beyond Marx.[34] While Habermas treated the unconscious as inner foreign territory, Marcuse clarified the role of the individual in social development:

"In the case of capitalism, the individual needs above the (unsublimated) biological level are shaped by the conditions of alienated labor, and by their recreation and compensation in leisure time and in inter-personal relations. Hegel (*Philosophy of Right* , pp. 189 ff.) speaks of the "system of needs" established by "civil society"(= *bürgerliche Gesellschaft*) into which the individual is born and which, as the concrete universal, operates through his particular needs. This system derives from the general competition of the individuals in (alienated) labor, and requires, for its functioning, an apparatus of domination."[35]

Marcuse went beyond economic benefits to discuss how colonialism also satisfies deep-rooted instinctual needs:

It seems not inappropriate to sharpen Hegel's conception by focusing it on the repression and aggressiveness mobilized and made socially useful in this system…The brutal satisfaction of the social need for dominating and "pacifying" ever more areas of the globe (and of outer space) also satisfies deep-rooted instinctual needs of the individual – together with his material and cultural needs.[36]

A well-known advocate for those marginalized from the material privileges of the world system, Marcuse's advocacy did not arise solely from his emotional solidarity with the "wretched of the earth" but also from his intellectual comprehension of the relationship between instincts and society. As opposed to glorifying European civil society, he called for "counter-behavior" among a new subject in the advanced capitalist societies "aiming at abolishing the conditions which gave rise to the closed mental structure."[37] He made no attempt to transpose Western models onto the entire world or to fetishize bourgeois civil society as its only form. He insisted upon the need for liberation from the very system glorified by Eurocentrists.

While bourgeois profitability and unbridled individualism became the predominant form of interaction among Europeans (and subsequently, much the rest of the world), group ties in Asia reveal complex networks of civil society that play important roles in regulating behavior. Yet for generations, an uninterrupted intellectual disparagement of Asia has accompanied popular fear of the "Yellow Menace."

Western Myths

Asian values, including survivalisms of Buddhism, Confucian, Daoism and Islam, continue to infuse moral and ethical constraints on everyday life. Instead of locating Asia's heritage of values and relations as a resource, many Western observers point to the dearth of American-style voluntary groups and conclude that there is no civil society. John Keane notes that, "in early modern usages, 'civil society' was typically contrasted with the 'Asiatic' region, in which, or so it was said, civil societies had manifestly failed to appear."[38]

So greatly were Asian societies devalued that democracy has been formulated solely as a European (Greek) invention, even though research has revealed republican forms of government in ancient Sumerian cities.[39] In India, from approximately 600 to 300 BCE, republics arose in the Ganges plain with elected leaders and assemblies, which gave rise to egalitarian breakaways from the Hindu caste system such as Jainism and Buddhism.[40] Commenting on Asian philosophers like Lao-tzu, Mencius and Confucius, South Korean president and Nobel prize recipient Kim Dae Jung persuasively postulated Asia's cultural traditions as possibly providing a contemporary basis for new "global democracy" to be constructed.[41]

Evidence of civil society in Asia defined even by European standards abounds. In China between 1905 and 1949, no less than 100 disparate women's papers were published in Beijing. Chinese chambers of commerce in market towns were said to number at least two thousand in 1912, with about 200,000 merchant members, and an additional 871 associations in larger cities.[42] As early as the thirteenth century, Marco Polo noted charity for the poor and a high level of social solidarity in the Chinese city of Hangzhou. A more recent account described that the poor were cared for by "private charity on the part of the rich merchants who wanted to make a name for themselves by doing good works."[43]

"Asian despotism" has long been exaggerated, while problems of crime and savage relations in the West have been minimized. In my view, many teahouses and even street corners in Asia might be considered as much a public space in which individuals can develop as the interiors of Europe's finest cafés. The gentleness of Confucian public space, in which individuals are relatively safe from the kinds of public criminal intrusions that Westerners have long since accepted as normal, provides a safety that leads to reasoned discussions rather than to violent settlement of disputes, to social relations and individual thinking that could flower in non-capitalist contexts. So "normal" were fraud and crime in Europe that Hegel called them "unpremeditated or civil wrong [*unbefangenes oder bürgerliches Unrecht*]." He specifically considered them to be "a material part of civil society."[44]

Famously, Hegel enunciated the phrase "Oriental despotism": "The Orientals have not attained the knowledge that Spirit—man as such—is free; and because they do not know this, they are not free. They only know that one is free . . . that One is therefore a despot, not a free man."[45] Over the years, Hegel's formulation has continued to be repeated, notably by his student Karl Marx, who regarded the Asiatic mode of production as despotic and unchanging.[46] He believed all societies would follow the same stages of economic development through which Europe had passed: from "primitive" communism to slave society, feudalism, and capitalism, before being able to achieve socialism and communism.

Scholars like Max Weber also chastised Far Eastern cultures for being despotic and feudal, lacking the ingredients for organizational success, and outside the grand narrative of Western civilization. Max Weber believed the West exclusively knew rational law and rational personal ethics. In 1956, Zbigniew Brzezinski wrote that in the Orient, "despotic forms of government have been the rule for thousands of years." The following year, Karl Wittvogel published his technologically-determinist explanation of "oriental despotism," attributing the phenomenon to central control of hydraulic systems.[47]

Nor are anarchists immune from prejudice against Asians. Gentle and poetic anarchist prince Peter Kropotkin had many virtues, yet one encounters passages in *Mutual Aid* with consternation. His use of "savages" and "barbarians" is curiously antiquated. Moreover in his *Memoirs*, we find oblique, racist references to "Asiatic schemes" as well as phrases like of "an Oriental fashion, in an abominable way" and "oriental amusements were looked upon with disgust."[48] I assume that Kropotkin would have outgrown his bias, although in his own day, it was seldom questioned.

Communist policymakers in the Soviet Union similarly distrusted Asians. In 1937, under Stalin's orders, some 200,000 Koreans living in eastern Siberia near Korea and Japan were deported to Central Asia (Kazakhstan and Uzbekistan) for fear they would support Japan, even though Koreans were waging a mighty independence struggle against Japanese occupation. In the same period of time, many Korean Communists were summarily executed for fear they might be Japanese spies.[49] Even progressives like former Czech president Vaclav Havel made racist remarks when he off-handedly equated Asia with despotism and Europe with democracy. Jürgen Habermas has also associated Asia with evil during the German "historians' debate."[50] Ernst Nolte's 1986 article had challenged the unique character of Nazi crimes and labeled the Holocaust an "Asiatic" deed perpetrated by Hitler and the Nazis. Nolte attributed their motives to fear of becoming potential victims of Stalin's gulags and class murders—which he also considered "Asiatic." In response, Habermas challenged Nolte's conclusion denying the uniqueness of Nazism's crimes, but he never challenged the "Asiatic" label of these crimes against humanity. Habermas' acceptance of Nolte's term is part of a substantial bias against Asians.[51]

Since many Western theorists believe civil society produces economic development, they therefore expect the trajectory of the West and its particular kind of civil society to be the future of "less developed" countries.[52] Such pro-European bias can be located in the work of conservative commentator Lucian Pye, who posited Protestantism as an ideal basis for civic culture and suggested Asia's lack of it might mean it would be the last continent to democratize.[53] Where once Confucian values were blamed for lack of business acumen and the ease with which Western businesspersons took advantage of polite Orientals, today Confucian culture is positively correlated with wealth.[54]

As Asia's economies grew rapidly in the 1970s and 1980s, Singapore's Lee Kwan Yew and Malaysia's Mahathir Mohamad embraced "Asian values" as a reason for their success. They believed that unlike the West, Asians prize family above individual, social order over individual freedom, and hard work over leisure. Yet for all the talk of "Asian" values, the continent is incredibly diverse, embracing lands from Iraq to Korea, Siberia to Sri Lanka. Even if we limit ourselves to eastern Asia, diversity is much greater than many people appreciate. Among ten places united in a wave of Asian democratic uprisings from 1986-1998, two are Islamic (Bangladesh and Indonesia), one is Hindu (Nepal), three are Confucian (China, Taiwan, and South Korea), one is Catholic (Philippines), and three are Buddhist (Thailand, Burma, and South Korea).[55] South Korea also has many Protestants, possibly one-third of its population.

Conservative American anti-communism obscured the existence of civil society in Eastern Europe by insisting the "totalitarian" state had swallowed all autonomous elements of society, yet there seems to be general agreement today that uprisings there at the end of the twentieth century which overthrew Soviet rule emanated from civil society. As the cunning of history invalidated much Cold War propaganda on both sides, the political practice of *Solidarność* in Poland (a predominantly Catholic society) caused Polish dissidents to talk of "the rebellion of civil society against the state."[56]

Traditional civil societies, so different from the West's, have been great sources of strength for social movements. From the tree and the drum, which Korean villagers could use to announce grievances and to find consensual means of resolving them, to Chinese people's right to petition for redress of grievances, and to Nepalese understanding of the dharma's meaning that kings should rule justly, cultural traditions were operative means of rallying opposition against ruling powers. If Asia only had weak civil societies, how could democratization movements have succeeded? As Larry Diamond and others point out, "civil society has played a crucial role in building pressure for democratic transition and pushing it through to completion."[57] Nowhere was this more apparent than in South Korea.

Korean Civil Society

Korean neighborhoods and villages created a fundamentally different civil society than that which appeared in Western in European cities. Many scholars insist that Korea has no history of democracy, that civil society only appeared in the late twentieth century as a result of "American democratization." Not only do such accounts ignore US opposition to democracy in South Korea from 1945 to 1993, but such assertions minimize the courage and sacrifices endured by indigenous partisans of freedom. Even before the twentieth century, Koreans enjoyed longstanding autonomous forms of consensual decision-making and often resisted the central government when thy did not agree with royal decisions. In pre-modern Korea, alongside *yangban* (royal) tyranny, communal village government worked by consensus. In many localities, representatives coordinated neighborhood needs, and daily forms of cooperation patterned the tapestry of people's lives. Folk drama reinforced group ties at the same time as it gave occasion to ridicule rulers. Beyond the power of governing authorities, shamanistic rituals invoked higher powers to sustain and empower people. Villagers autonomously shared labor with each other through a practice known as *dure* (두레).

Small-scale academies created by dissident scholars afforded space for individuals to develop their intelligence and original thinking, often in a group context that existed in opposition to established powers. These were not places for *yangban* to study for civil service examinations and to become high-ranking government officials. Focused around particular scholars, *seowon* constituted an important source of a "reasoning public" and were places for individual self-cultivation of knowledge. Far from seats of power in well-chosen settings of natural beauty, Neo-Confucian scholars (*sarim*) venerated sages and sought to enlarge individual understanding of proper behavior.

Autonomous of government control, they were part of a public sphere, or mid-level institution of civil society.[58] Rural scholars often functioned as intermediaries between state and people, and were a vital component of traditional society.[59] In the sixteenth century, waves of literati purges were carried out by conservative forces whose heredity wealth and power were threatened, but it appears that these attacks strengthened *seowon* influence in the seventeenth century.[60] By 1700, private academies, or *seowon*, are thought to have been so widespread that there were some six hundred in all—more in Korea than in all of China.

In Gwangju, longstanding forms of mutual aid for everything from home repairs and agricultural labor to music, dance, and theater survives to this day, where neighbors and friends gather to make *kimchi*, buy fresh oysters at the seashore as part of informal, nonprofit cooperatives, or gather in neighborhood councils to solve pressing issues. Activists reminded me that even under the harsh terms of decades of dictatorships, oppositional zones proliferated outside state control. People spread word of the movement's ideas and planned actions by taking food to neighbors' homes (사발통문) in order to whisper news and organize events.

Voluntary civil groups were of tremendous importance before and during the Gwangju People's Uprising of 1980, including the Women's Pure Pine Tree Society, Nok Du Bookstore, Wildfire Night School, Clown Theater Group, and the Artists' Council. During the halcyon days of liberated Gwangju, general assemblies of tens of thousands of people (on three separate occasions 100,000 or more) gathered around the circular fountain in front of the provincial capital to freely deliberate their future.[61] While some favored immediate surrender of the weapons used to liberate the city, others vociferously defended their right to bear arms. Compromises were worked out in public. The three demands formulated at these mass rallies (punishment of top military officials responsible for the killings, compensation for the dead and injured, and an official apology) were finally won after years of struggle. The daily citizens' assemblies, unlike the representative government of the 1871 Paris Commune, provides a vivid embodiment of Habermas' description of undistorted communication.

One of the leading American Koreanists, Bruce Cumings, insists that civil society did not reawaken until elections of 1985.[62] He also does not consider the long history of scholars' schools and counterpublics as components of civil society. Indigenous traditions like *seowon* remained invisible to the first Americans who came to Korea after the Korean War, especially government functionaries who arrived under the auspices of the US State Department or Peace Corps, as did Cumings. One of their teachers was Gregory Henderson, who spent more than eighteen years in Korea or Washington as a chief architect of US policy. Like many of his contemporaries, Henderson simply transposed categories developed to explain feudal Europe to Korea,

where he found "a society lacking in strong institutions or voluntary associations
between village and throne; a society that knows little of castle town, feudal lord and
court, semi-independent merchant societies, city-states, guilds, or classes cohesive
enough to be centers of independent stance and action in the polity . . . a society
characterized by amorphousness or isolation in social relations."[63] Precisely those
dimensions identified by Henderson as missing can be located in Korea's past, in Jang
Bogo's semi-independent merchant society built by slaves who freed themselves, in the
class politics of the farmers' movement (*Tonghak*) at the end of the nineteenth century,
and in indigenous political formations such as federations and confederations.

Henderson neglected to include Confucian means of dissidence like *bibangmok*
(the tree where people could hang anonymous notes of protest), *kwondang* (when
students of high Confucian academies went on strike to call attention to grievances),
and *sinmungo* (the drum which could be beaten to request legal action).[64] Instead he
centrally located "persistence of the pattern" of the "vortex" of centripetal power
sweeping everything toward the center. Although he regards this dynamic as uniquely
Korean, similar centralization can be found in France, where power is vested almost
exclusively in Paris. In fairness, Henderson asserted that the pattern of the vortex "in
overt form can be detected in the period from 1880 to 1910; its transformation and
expansion" could be traced from the late Japanese period to the Americans' first two
decades.[65] Curiously, he failed to note that this was precisely the period of increasing
concentration of capital and simultaneously when Koreans struggled mightily against
Japanese and US power, a true "vortex"—but one propelled by foreign imperial forces.

Henderson well understood that countervailing powers traditionally existed
within the Korean state, specifically that a:

> top council, called *hwabaek*, determined the (nonhereditary) succession to the
> throne and sometimes exercised a veto over the king's decisions. Reflecting the
> importance of each element in the central council, discussion was supposed to
> produce unanimity, and 'it was the custom that any single disagreement
> brought the termination of the discussion on the specific issue.'[66]

Henderson's description of power would have made any European monarch blush
with anger at the notion that any high councilor's disagreement could essentially veto
top decisions. One can only wonder what Tudor monarch Henry VIII might have
been compelled to do with his first five wives.

For generations before the penetration of modernity, traditional networks
wielded power as much through cooperative dissidence as through competitive
violence. As far back as the fifteenth century, several kings unsuccessfully attempted

to expand the use of coins and paper currency. Despite severe punishment for refusing to do so, people quietly resisted, and the royal efforts failed. Apparently, people preferred to use grain and cloth as media of exchange and to live without banks—which they did until the 1880s.[67]

Precisely this difference with the West is an essential reason why Korean everyday life continues to be so attractive to foreigners and Koreans alike. Koreans know better than most how to thrive and prosper within groups, to excel at simultaneously offering individuals praise and criticism. When they emigrate to the United States, Korean small businesses use a unique method of lending money to each other to expand operations. These civil resources are not simply financial since they derive from generations of living with trust for each other in a social system where honorable action and righteous deeds are arguably more important than profitable maximization of individual financial gain.

Confucian economic transactions were thought to be best consummated when both parties were fairly treated. Rather than each individual seeking to maximize economic gain, as in the West, both sought to find the fairest bargain. Unlike Europe where "free" individuals principally sought profitability in commodity relationships, consideration of honor ("saving face") and family esteem were significant mitigating factors that helped to curb the worst excesses of the West. Neither China nor Korea may have constituted a bourgeois society, yet their social formations were another type of civil society whose contours have been left largely unexplored because of Eurocentric bias.

Islamic Civil Society

In Islamic society, the strength of group ties (*assabiyeh*) is such an important dimension that it was the main variable in Ibn Khaldun's materialist philosophy of history, written five centuries before that of Karl Marx.[68] Social regulation of what Hegel called "civil wrong" was thereby achieved by non-state civil constraints. The paramount influence of *assabiyeh* enforced solidarity through moral and ethical prohibitions even when state power was distant. So important is the group for Arabs that poetry is written to be performed in public rather than read privately in books.

Religious prescriptions are yet another layer of regulating behavior. Islamic duty to give to the poor is widely observed, especially during Ramadan, when fasting for 30 days serves to help people remember the less fortunate. The bonds among the community of the faithful (*ummah*) make it possible when needed to find a place to spend the night simply by asking for the hospitality of fellow believers. Individual property is not regarded with the same sacrosanct boundaries violently enforced in the West. Conservative philosopher Al Ghazali told us the story of Fath al-Mawsili, who took what he needed without asking permission from an absent brother of the faith. When the owner returned and was told what had happened, he was delighted. Compare with John Locke's *Second Treatise* where preservation of individual property is the goal of government, the same reason Hobbes called for a *Leviathan*. Elsewhere, al Ghazali asks: "Does one of you put his hand in the pocket or purse of his brother and take what he needs without permission?" If the answer is no, "Then you are not brothers!" To be a brother in God, "you have no greater right to your pounds or pence than I have."[69] The contrast with European possessive individualism could not be more acutely expressed.

Prescriptive aspects of Islamic culture have long been criticized by Europeans. It is often said, sometimes rightfully so, that society does not protect individual freedom of expression. Images of Mohammed were—and are—prohibited in most Islamic cultures, as is the depiction generally of the human figure. Western journalists' "right" to caricature Mohammed in extremely pejorative contexts serves to embellish claims of European superiority, evidenced by "freedom" to produce and market almost anything, including pornography.

Numerous counterexamples can be given to dispel the myth that intellectual freedom did not exist in Islamic society. Averroes (also known as Ibn Rushd, 1126-1198) stressed the role of science and philosophical speculation over faith, of individual reason and dialectical change over group conformity and eternal religious doctrine. Born in Cordoba, the pluralistic capital of Arab Spain where three monotheistic religions coexisted, his first 17 years were lived in a democracy. For 40 years, from 1106-1145, he tells us that Cordoba was "almost completely democratic" before it turned into a tyranny.[70] Known as "the commentator" for his extensive notes on Aristotle ("the philosopher"), Averroes challenged the cosmology of all three religions. He wrote a critique of Ptolemy and asserted that the planets rotated around the sun. As a result, he faced a ban on his works in his home city, his books were burned in public, and he suffered mobs' insults when he appeared in public. Before he died, however, he again found praise and acceptance.[71]

His books helped to invigorate scientific thought, notably influencing Galileo at Padua and laying the groundwork for the European Enlightenment. As his writing gained popularity in the West, however, a Papal edict prohibited uncensored versions in 1231, and his ideas were condemned by the bishop of Paris in 1277. Nonetheless, Thomas Aquinas quoted Averroes more than 500 times in about 1250.[72] In 1320, Dante's *Divine Comedy* placed Averroes in the same group with Socrates, Plato and Aristotle. For centuries, Averroes' cosmology remained anathema in Europe, so much so that in 1543, Copernicus placed his own manuscript proving heliocentrism under his deathbed so it would only be discovered when it was too late for his body to be tortured.

Compare Averroes' life to that of Giordano Bruno, burned at the stake in Rome in 1600 for breaking with religious cosmology and doctrine, to Galileo, forced by the threat of torture to recant his beliefs in 1633. In Amsterdam, Spinoza was ostracized by his fellow Jews in 1656 (with the support of the Calvinist theologians) for his opinion that reason, not scripture, was key to truth. All these European champions of the Enlightenment were influenced by Averroes.

European censorship persisted even into the eighteenth century. When Frederick the Great died, his successor Friedrich Wilhelm II proclaimed censorship in 1788 and circumscribed Immanuel Kant from writing anything about Christianity. One of the great philosophers of the Enlightenment, Kant had proclaimed "Have courage to use your own reason!" Yet he obeyed the King's order for as long as the monarch lived.

Concluding Comment

The time is long past when Western "superiority" can be justified through such notions as the "White Man's Burden," "Manifest Destiny," and "*mission civilisatrice.*" Yet, more subtle forms of bias persist, while at the same time, what was civil society in the West has turned even its promises into their opposite. The antagonistic structure of bourgeois society, in which individual selfishness drives a constant process of expanding wealth and state control, contrasts sharply with Asian societies, where group is central and stability desirable.

Is the Asian model better suited to lead the world in the twenty-first century? China's authoritarian system has lifted more than five hundred million people out of severe poverty, accounting for more than half of global reduction in absolute deprivation. That may be precisely why the 1% in the West view China as such a threat. Let's hope that history does not repeat itself, that the solution to the Great Depression of the 1930s—World War 2—does not prove again the means by which the 1% will attempt to salvage their dying system. We can create better societies, more "civil" ones in the future than anything humans have created in the past, provided we first give ourselves the chance to understand each other in our own.

NOTES

1   Originally presented to the International Herbert Marcuse Society, University of Salisbury, November 14, 2015. Substantially reworked thanks to encouragement and critical comments from Jack Hipp and Alda Blanco.

2   Herbert Marcuse, *Reason and Revolution: Hegel and the Rise of Social Theory* (Boston: Beacon Press: 1960), hereafter *Reason and Revolution.*

3   *Secret History of Procopius,* Translated by Richard Atwater (New York: Civici Friede Publishers, 1927) 138.

4   Actually, hundreds of principalities existed counting ecclesiastical ones and those of imperials knights. Alexander Grab, *Napoleon and the Transformation of Europe* (New York: Palgrave Macmillan, 2003) 22.

5   Perhaps most importantly of all, Western Europe's dire status as world backwater helped motivate it to

grasp modern world supremacy. For discussion of the "law of retarding lead" see L.S. Stavrianos, *The Promise of the Coming Dark Age* (San Francisco: W.H. Freeman, 1976) 181-185.

6   Habermas, *Strukturwandel der Öffentlichkeit* (Frankfurt am Main: Suhrkamp, 1990).

7   See Jack Seltzer and Sharon Crowley (editors), *Rhetorical Bodies* (Madison: University of Wisconsin Press, 1999) 227. At the end of the twentieth century, the CIA and National Endowment for Democracy began to fund and organize "civil society" groups to mobilize protests against governments not valued by the US. Some of the color revolutions were clearly the work of the government agencies. Covert and overt politicization of civil society is further evidence of its structural transformation. See Sarah E. Mendelson and John Glenn (editors), *The Power and Limits of NGOs: A Critical Look at Building Democracy in Eastern Europe and Eurasia* (New York: Columbia University Press, 2002) 5, 191–92.

8   William A. Callahan, "Comparing the Discourse of Popular Politics in Korea and China: From Civil Society to Social Movements," *Korea Journal* (Spring 1988), 281-2.

9   See Susanne H. Rudolf and Lloyd I. Rudolf, "The Coffee House and the Ashram: Gandhi, Civil Society and Public Spheres," in *Civil Society and Democracy*, ed. Carolyn M. Elliott (Oxford: Oxford University Press, 2003), 377-404.

10 William T. Rowe, "The Problem of 'Civil Society' in Late Imperial China." *Modern China* 19.2 (April 1993) 139-157, quoted in Callahan, "Comparing the Discourse of Popular Politics in Korea and China: From Civil Society to Social Movements," 287.

11 For more details, see my talk, "Rethinking Samuel Huntington's Third Wave," Brown University, Program in Modern Greek Studies, March 24, 2010, available at https://www.eroseffect.com/articles/huntington.pdf

12 Habermas, *The Inclusion of the Other: Studies in Political Theory* edited by Ciaran Cronin and Pablo De Greiff (Cambridge: MIT Press, 1998) 176. Hereafter Inclusion.

13 Inclusion, xxxvii.

14 Inclusion, 171, 175.

15 Inclusion, 178. Surprisingly, on the next page he bemoans the fact that "The UN does not yet have its own military forces…"

16 Inclusion, 184 (italics in the original).

17 Inclusion, 185.

18 See the recent post by Keven Rashid Johnson, *Our Deadly Bread: Coronavirus And Deadly Diet In Indiana Prisons* (2020) http://rashidmod.com/?p=2819 (accessed June 19, 2020).

19 Newton first proclaimed "revolutionary intercommunalism" on November 18, 1970 in a speech at Boston College. See David Hilliard and Donald Weise (editors), *The Huey P. Newton Reader* (New York: Seven Stories Press, 2002) 160-175. Twenty-one years later, Bookchin first enunciated his very similar notion on April 3, 1991. See "On Libertarian Municipalism," https://theanarchistlibrary.org/library/murray-bookchin-libertarian-municipalism-an-overview accessed June 19, 2020). Abdullah Ocalan, *Democratic Confederalism* (London, Cologne: Transmedia Publishing, 2011). Ocalan has also freed many Kurds from the illusion that a nation-state will lead to freedom.

20 No misunderstanding: UNICEF and human rights protections are blessings to millions of people because of the excesses of corporate greed and government brutality. It is no coincidence that the international arms market exists alongside hundreds millions of starving human beings. Structural solutions to such problems, however, lie beyond the purview of a confederation of nation-states.

21 Inclusion, 183.

22 Habermas, *Knowledge and Human Interests* (Boston: Beacon Press, 1972).

23 Such instances of global uprisings are what I named the "Eros Effect." See Jason Del Gandio and AK Thompson (editors), *Spontaneous Combustion: The Eros Effect and Global Revolution* (Albany: State University of New York Press, 2017).

24 Jack Goody, "Civil Society in an Extra-European Perspective," in *Civil Society: History and Possibilities*, eds., Sudipta Kaviraj and Sunil Khilnani (Cambridge: Cambridge University Press, 2001), 153.

25 *Reason and Revolution*, 211. The quotation from Hegel is from *Philosophy of Right*, §246-8. Note that the Knox translation of Hegel is different than Marcuse's. See *Hegel's Philosophy of Right* translated and with notes by T.M. Knox, (London: Oxford University Press, 1967 and Clarendon reprint 1975) 151-2. For Hegel's text in German, see https://hegel.net/hegelwerke/Hegel1821-Grundlinien_der_Philosophie_des_Rechts.pdf (accessed May 11, 2020).

26 *Reason and Revolution*, 164

27 *Reason and Revolution*, 206; *Hegel's Philosophy of Right* §245, translated and with notes by T.M. Knox, (London: Oxford University Press, 1967 and Clarendon reprint 1975) 150.

28 *Reason and Revolution*,174.

29 *Reason and Revolution*, 16.

30 *Reason and Revolution*, 197

31 *Reason and Revolution*, 213; Hegel, *Philosophy of Right*, §253.

32 In 2019, police killed 1,098 people in the US. See https://mappingpoliceviolence.org (accessed June18, 2020).

33 Keynes, "Economic Possibilities for Our Grandchildren," http://www.econ.yale.edu/smith/econ116a/keynes1.pdf (accessed June 15, 2020).

34 *Eros and Civilization: A Philosophical Inquiry into Freud* (Boston: Beacon Press: 1955). While mechanistic Marxists insist on the dependence of the "superstructure" on the "economic base," Marcuse would ask, where does psychology fit into that model?"

35 Marcuse, "Cultural Revolution," in Douglas Kellner (editor) *Towards a Critical Theory of Society* (London and New York: Routledge, 2001) 136. This is Volume 2 of Marcuse's selected papers, and this essay had never been previously published. Emphasis and parenthesis are exactly quoted here as they appear in Kellner's edited volume.

36 Marcuse, Cultural Revolution, 136-137.

37 Ibid.

38 John Keane, *Global Civil Society?* (Cambridge, UK: Cambridge University Press, 2003) 31. On the next page, Keane continues his commentary on Europeans' views: "Civil society was impossible in Muslim society."

39 See Thorkild Jacobsen, "Primitive Democracy in Ancient Mesopotamia," *Journal of Near Eastern Studies* 2, no. 3 (1943): 159-172.

40 Romila Thapar, *A History of India* (Harmondsworth: Penguin Books, 1966), 53. See Goody, "Civil Society," 156.

41 Kim Dae Jung, "Is Culture Destiny? The Myth of Asia's Anti-Democratic Values," *Foreign Affairs* 6, 189-194.

42 Gordon White, Jude Howell, and Shang Xiaoyuan, "Market Reforms and the Emergent Constellation of Civil Society in China," in *Civil Society and Democracy,* ed. Carolyn M. Elliott (Oxford: Oxford University Press, 2003), 266-267.

43 E. Balazs, "The Birth of Capitalism in China," in E. Balazs (ed.), *Chinese Civilization and Bureaucracy: Variations on a Theme* (New Haven: Yale University Press, 1964).

44 Marcuse, *Reason and Revolution* (Boston: Beacon Press, 1960) 197.

45 G.W.F. Hegel, *The Philosophy of History* (New York: Colonial Press, 1899) 18.

46 In his last great project, *Capital: A Critique of Political Economy*, Marx's Eurocentric model of the system considered capitalists and workers. By his own admission in a note to Engels, he could not solve the problem of expanded reproduction in volume 2. If only Marx had been more attentive to Hegel's insight that civil society would produce colonialism, he might have found the solution. It was left to Rosa Luxemburg to introduce the third person—people outside the core of the system—and thereby complete the puzzle. She understood that capitalism was imperialist from the very beginning, that it continually needs to absorb peripheral peoples and new arenas of life into profitable relationships. Rosa Luxemburg, *The Accumulation of Capital* (New York: Monthly Review Press, 1968).

47 Karl Wittvogel, *Oriental Despotism: A Comparative Study of Total Power* (New Haven: Yale University Press, 1957).

48 Peter Kropotkin, *Memoirs of a Revolutionist* (New York: Dover Publications, 1971) 76, 82, 310.

49 Bruce Cumings, *North Korea: Another Country* (New York: New Press, 2004) 118.

50 Edward Friedman (editor), *The Politics of Democratization: Generalizing East Asian Experiences* (Boulder: Westview Press, 1994) 14.

51 See the discussion in Jürgen Habermas, *The New Conservatism: Cultural Criticism and the Historians' Debate* (Cambridge, MA: MIT Press, 1990) xvii.

52   See, for example, John Girling, "Development and Democracy in Southeast Asia," *The Pacific Review* 1, no. 4 (1988) 332.

53   Lucian Pye, *Asian Power and Politics: The Cultural Dimensions of Authority* (Cambridge: Belknap Press, 1985).

54   See Larry Diamond, ed., *Political Culture and Democracy in Developing Countries* (Boulder: Lynne Rienner Publishers, 1993).

55   See my 2-volume book, *Asia's Unknown Uprisings* (Oakland: PM Press, 2012and 2013). Asian uprisings overthrew eight dictatorships in nine places, as uprisings suddenly erupted in a wave of popular enthusiasm for democracy in the Philippines in 1986, South Korea in 1987, Myanmar in 1988, Tibet and China in 1989, Taiwan, Nepal and Bangladesh in 1990, and Thailand in 1992.

56   See John Ehrenberg, "Civil Society," *New Dictionary of the History of Ideas* (New York: Scribner's, 2004).

57   Larry Diamond, Marc Plattner, Yun-han Chu, and Hung-mao Tien (editors), *Consolidating the Third Wave Democracies: Regional Challenges* (Baltimore: Johns Hopkins, 1997) xxx. Yet as Muthiah Alagappa notes, NGOs and civil society can also be impediments to democratization. Muthiah Alagappa (editor), *Civil Society and Political Change in Asia: Expanding and Contracting Democratic Space* (Palo Alto: Stanford University Press, 2004) 185.

58   JaHyun Kim Haboush, "Academies and Civil Society in Chosun Korea," in *La société civile face à l'État: dans les traditions chinoise, japonaise, coréenne et vietnamienne* (Paris: École-française d'extrême-orient, 1994). See also John Duncan, "The Problematic Modernity of Confucianism," in *Korean Society: Civil Society, Democracy and the State*, ed. Charles Armstrong (London: Routledge, 2002).

59   Cho Hein, "The Historical Origin of Civil Society in Korea," *Korea Journal* 37, no. 2 (Summer 1997).

60   Lee Sang-hae, *Seowon: The Architecture of Korea's Private Academies* (Seoul: Hollym, 2005) 14-15.

61   For the numbers of people who attended general assemblies during the days of liberated Gwangju, see *Asia's Unknown Uprisings: South Korean Social Movements in the 20th Century*, 185.

62   He accused Park Chung-hee of "shutting down civil society" in 1961, a curiously static notion of civil society. Bruce Cumings, "Civil Society in West and East," in *Korean Society: Civil Society, Democracy and the State*, edited by Charles Armstrong (London: Routledge, 2002) 23-24. Cumings went on to say that South Korea "…still falls short of either the Japanese or the American models of democracy and civil society…"

63   Gregory Henderson, *Korea: The Politics of the Vortex* (Cambridge, MA: Harvard University Press, 1968), 4.

64   Chung Chai-sik, "Confucian Tradition and Nationalist Ideology in Korea," in *South Korea's Minjung Movement: The Culture and Politics of Dissidence*, ed. Kenneth Wells (Honolulu: University of Hawaii Press, 1995), 71.

65   Ibid., 5.

66   Ibid., 22.

67   James Palais, (Seoul: Institute for Modern Korean Studies, Yonsei University, 1998) 10, 17.

68   See my article "Individual and Group: Comparative Cultural Observations with a Focus on Ibn Khaldun," *Journal of Biosciences* (Indian Academy of Social Sciences) 39(2), March 2014, 327-332.

69   Al-Ghazali, *On the Duties of Brotherhood*, translated by Muhtar Holland (Woodstock, NY: The Overlook Press, 1976) 24.

70   *Averroes on Plato's Republic*, translated by Ralph Turner (Ithaca: Cornell University Press, 1974) 133.

71   Paul Kurtz, "Intellectual Freedom, Rationality, and Enlightenment: The Contributions of Averroës,' in *Averroës and the Enlightenment*, edited by Mourad Wahba and Mona Abousenna (Amherst, NY: Prometheus Books, 1996) 30-32.

72   Dominique Urvoy, *Ibn Rushd*, translated by Olivia Stewart (Cairo: The American University in Cairo Press, 1991) 27, 33.

Ibn Khaldun: Dialectical Philosopher for the Twenty-first Century[1]

IN THE CONTEMPORARY world, groups have achieved preponderant power over the lives of all of us, enmeshing us in webs of nation, race, and gender and stimulating an expanding range of investigations into collective behaviour. In our historical epoch, scientists examine afresh individual ontogeny amid the role of groups. No less than contemporary social research, new natural science investigations pose the question: Is genuine individual autonomy possible?

Beginning in the seventeenth century and more so in the eighteenth century, European autonomous individualism began to flower. Men and women[2] made unique contributions as they penned masterpieces of art, music and philosophy, wrote magnificent novels, and dared to espouse political tracts declaring freedom of the individual. In the eighteenth century, European and American revolutions won new freedoms and rights. Today, past accomplishments are systematically eroded as governments claim for themselves new powers, including even the right to decide without due process matters of life and death.[3] Such vast historical changes compel us to consider the categories of individual and group viewed over time. Their relationships are not fixed but vary with the rise (and decline) of socially created forces.

Before we assume the parallel character of natural and social phenomena, questions need to be posed about the validity of positivism (the idea that the rules and methods of natural science can be applied to society). Can we rely upon scientific methodology that explicitly extends relationships and laws observed in the natural world to human phenomena? Humans have made history. We have overthrown the rule of kings and queens (or accepted it), but we are not blindly compelled simply to accept royal rule as our only option. Can the same be said of bees? Going further, water boils at 100 degrees Celsius at sea level everywhere in the world. Can any similar constant be uncovered with regard to human relationships? Are any two human beings exactly alike? Are there constant patterns to human interaction that can be compared with the rate of acceleration at which an object falls to earth or to the precise combination of atoms that form specific molecules?

Despite the best efforts of sociologists to postulate "iron laws" and of philosophers to assert that "history repeats itself," in certain respects society is characterised by change rather than by stasis.[4] When change occurs, its character is sporadic and uneven. It is not like the precise repetitive patterns exhibited by some natural phenomena.[5] Governments, religions, and even languages change over time, leading many thinkers to conclude that a sharp distinction must be drawn between *Geisteswissenschaft* and *Naturwissenschaft*—between the humanities and natural sciences.[6]

In the following pages, I discuss the views of Ibn Khaldun (1332—1406 AD), a fourteenth century Islamic philosopher for whom group identity or *assabiyeh* (translated as "group feeling" by Franz Rosenthal) was the critical element in his understanding of society. Because he was convinced of both the need for investigation and for faith, Ibn Khaldun differentiated between the physical world and the divine world, insisting that philosophy could comprehend history but not divinity:

> Man is composed of two parts. One is corporeal. The other is spiritual, and mixed with the former. Each one of these parts has its own perceptions, though the (part) that perceives is the same in both cases, namely the spiritual part. At times, it perceives spiritual perceptions. At other times, it perceives corporeal perceptions. However, it perceives the spiritual perceptions through its own essence without any intermediary, while it perceives the corporeal perceptions through the intermediary of organs of the body, such as the brain and the senses. (Ibn Khaldun, 1986, Vol. 3: 253).

Each of these different parts of human beings was integrated into a whole. Yet for him, change constituted a dividing line between divinity (which "lasts and persists") and the ephemeral fate of the corporeal dimension: "Time wears us out…". Ibn Khaldun understood the realm of spirit as prior to and influencing the world of the body:

> …there is something that exercises an influence and is different than bodily substances. This is something spiritual. It is connected with the created things, because the various worlds must be connected in their existence. This spiritual thing is the soul, which has perception and causes motion. Above the soul…is the world of angels. (Ibn Kahldun, 1986, 1:195)

For Ibn Khaldun, the soul had form and substance since its existence materialized in the exchange of "potentiality for actuality with the help of the body and (bodily) conditions." (Ibn Khaldun, 1986, 1:214). A central issue in Ibn Khaldun's philosophy of history was the possibility for human beings to understand forces beyond their control. He sketched an historical process, which in the final analysis, was not simply a history of external events but rather that of human beings becoming who they in essence are. As such, he offers valuable insights into the character and conduct of our species.

Across and even within cultures, changing meanings of group and individual will be noted. I will observe variable valuations and formulations of group and individuals in Islamic, East Asian, and European cultures. The broad sweep of my cultural comparisons is necessarily philosophical rather than based upon a numerical sampling of behavior.

Ibn Khaldun's Perspective

Despite his decidedly disinterested attitude to his own life, Abu Zayd Abdel Rahman Ibn Khaldun was a veritable fountain of original thought. In 1377, in the short period of five months, he wrote the *Muqaddimah* (or Prolegomena) while secluded at a palace of a sultan in what is today western Algeria (Enan, N.A., 1975, 51-52). Five centuries before Darwin uncovered evolution, Ibn Khaldun wrote that humans descended from "the world of the monkeys" through an ever-wider process in which "species become more numerous." (Ibn Khaldun, 1986, 1:195).[7] He attributed human racial characteristics to climate, thereby implying that all humans are related to each other.[8] By grounding his analysis in the universal relation of spirit and body, he also provided a basis for the history of our species, not simply for any particular sub-group—a universal history that is only today again emerging as national and ethnic ones prove insufficient in our globalized reality. Nearly half a millennium before Karl Marx wrote *Das Kapital*, Ibn Khaldun stated that "labour is the real basis of profit." (Ibn Khaldun, 1986, 1:303). Four hundred years before Auguste Comte named his new science of society as sociology, Ibn Khaldun unveiled a "science of culture." (Muhsin, Mahdi, 1957).

For Ibn Khaldun, group solidarity, or *assabiyeh,* played a critical role in the formation of kingdoms and societies. The root of the word is "nerve", the bond by which a group is connected. For him that was as much a gift of god as an historically conditioned phenomenon. (Goodman, L. E., 1972, 256).[9] The family is the first and most significant domain in which *assabiyeh* operates most naturally. "Compassion and affection for one's blood relations and relatives exist in human nature as something god put into the hearts of men. It makes for mutual support and aid…" (Rosenthal, Franz, 1969, 98).[10] For Ibn Khaldun, urban life explains why Arabs lost their group solidarity, "Later on, sedentary Arabs mixed with Persians and other non-Arabs. Purity of lineage was completely lost, and its fruit, group feeling, was lost and rejected." (Ibn Kahldun, 1986, 1:267). Extending his analysis, he maintained that the laws of *assabiyeh* would run parallel to those of history. He sought to explain if—and, if so, how—*assabiyeh* could be reconstituted at a new level beyond its original emergence.

While Ibn Khaldun emphasized group solidarity, a contrasting perspective on Islamic cultures can be found by examining the work of another Islamic philosopher, Averroes (also known as Ibn Rushd), who lived from 1126 to 1198—two centuries before Ibn Khaldun. Known as the "Commentator" for his extensive notations on Aristotle ("the Philosopher"), Averroes emphasized the individual rather than groups. For stressing the role of scientific and philosophical investigation—of the supremacy of individual reason over faith—he faced continual threats from his own fellow citizens in Cordoba. Approaching the end of his life, a ban on his work was issued, and his books were burned in public. He was insulted by a mob. Although reinstated as an esteemed scholar shortly before his death, his writings were prohibited at the University of Paris in 1210 and 1215. In 1231, a Papal edict was issued prohibiting uncorrected reading of his books, and in 1277 the bishop of Paris, concerned about Ibn Rushd's popularity among Parisian intellectuals, condemned his work. (Wahba, M. and Abousenna, M., 1996, 30-47). One result of such continual assaults on intellectual freedom was that during the same century that Ibn Khaldun lived, there was not one Christian Arabic scholar in Europe. (Southern, R.W., 1962, 88). Despite the repression of Averroes' thought, his life's accomplishments—especially the creation of a stratum of Latin Averroists, intellectuals who believed in reason over faith—helped stimulate the European Enlightenment. (Wahba, M. and Abousenna, M., 1996, 48).

Like Ibn Khaldun, Ibn Rushd owed his status in large part to his service as a jurist and interpretation of judicial doctrines. (Uvroy, Dominique, 1993, 109). Both men believed that individuals are corruptible while intellectual knowledge is eternally true—an illuminating product of human thought that each honoured in ways their anti-intellectual contemporaries did not. Each also understood the corruptibility of ruling elites as lasting through three generations. Ibn Rushd described the internal corruption of the Almoravids as beginning with rule by law, to the next generation's rule for love of money, and finally to the third generation's hedonism, during which the regime perished.[11]

Before and during Ibn Khaldun's life, various rulers rose and fell in the Maghreb (the land of the sunset across Northwest Africa). In the heartland of Arab/Islamic culture and learning far to the east, Baghdad had fallen to the Mongols in 1258. The Fourth Crusade had overrun Constantinople, another great centre of medieval learning, in 1204. Wholesale Venetian looting of the Second Rome not only included the most salient artifacts adorning contemporary St. Mark's Square but also libraries of books and hundreds of scholars and architects—all of which contributed to the Italian Renaissance generally dated to more than a century later.[12] The Mongols slaughtered 800,000 citizens of Baghdad, nearly extinguishing the magnificent intellectual legacy Baghdad's scholars could have passed to new generations.

Ibn Khaldun is likely to have known of the European cultural revival (the Renaissance) underway during his lifetime. Although he had faith that one day Constantinople would be an Islamic city (which it became in 1452), his own experiences convinced him of the need to ground scientifically his analysis of human beings in order to transcend the particular histories of any one group. His *Prolegomena* is an attempt to produce a history at a universal level, one that would not be situated in the narrative history of any particular ethnic group. In the fourteenth century, the Islamic world – particularly in North Africa – was in decline from its glorious past, and Ibn Khaldun attempted to understand the causes of the changes around him.

He sketched an historical process that, in the final analysis, was not simply a history of external events but rather that of human beings in the process of becoming their future. He comprehended specific actions as occurring within an internal and invisible rational structure through which external facts could be understood. For him, narrative history, i.e. the recounting of specific events, was inferior to philosophical history through which the inner causes and remote origins of events could be comprehended.

His view of human beings was unambiguously negative. "Man is ignorant by nature..." (Ibn Khaldun, 1986, 1: 215, 266). Royal authority, a "natural" quality of humans, was necessary to insure proper behaviour. (Ibn Khaldun, 1986, 1: 92). What of a trans- forming process through which humans might elevate themselves? For him, the unchanged individual might ascend to glimpse the realm of angels but could never be transformed into an angel. While history might have a direction, a perpetual cycle of growth and decay operated, a natural transition of three generations for dynasties. At best, Ibn Khaldun hoped governments would rule as uncorrupted representatives of divine laws, a belief that earned him a reputation as a harsh purist while he served as a judge in Cairo. He believed authority was one of the four attributes that distinguish humans from animals (the others being thought, labour and civilization), a view that flows from his perspective that individuals were "savage" and the mass "stupid."

Before we judge his authoritarianism too harshly, we should consider similar contemporaneous cultural prejudices in Western Europe that were subsequently challenged with the emergence of the ascendancy of the individual—notably during the Renaissance and Reformation. During these periods, individual entrepreneurs, no less than self-motivated artists and freethinking Protestants, embodied a new psychology— that of the individual bent on conquering the world. As Alfred van Martin characterized the enormity of the shift beginning with the Italian Renaissance, "Blood, tradition and group feeling had been the basis of community relationships as well as of the old domination. The democratic and urban spirit was destroying the old social forms and the 'natural' and accepted divine order. It thus became necessary to order the world starting from the individual and to shape it, as it were, like a work of art." (Von Martin,

Alfred, 1963, 2). Aesthetic principles of Renaissance art such as scientific perspective and realistic portrayal of light from the viewpoint of a solitary artist prefigured the preponderant future role of individual religious perspective in the Reformation, solitary scientific speculation in the Enlightenment, and principles of individual liberty in the American and French revolutions.

The Renaissance replaced previously dominant communal ideologies according to a perspective on the world individually visualized and organized on rationally calculable principles. The "crowd" became a derogatory word. Even in the declining period we call Romanticism, people escaped to the "tranquility of a private existence." (Von Martin, Alfred, 1963, 58). In a phrase, with the ascendance of western capitalism, *assabiyeh* was shattered. Capital as a self-expanding value permeated all membranes and distorted all relationships—including that most primal one to Ibn Khaldun—blood ties.

Despite Europe's claim to being modern, we can see the revival of blood ties and group identity in the first half of the twentieth century, when fascism reinforced ancient bonds: Mussolini sought to restore the glory of the Roman Empire and Italians, while Hitler's "master race" reshaped Germans' group identity. In both cases, an individual leader became all-powerful only because he represented the nation. The changing relationship of group and individual in both the East and West provide insight into the possibility of different formations of these universal dimensions. If indeed, East and West offer us different cultural productions of these same essential categories, what does this tell us about the character of human phenomena? At this juncture, comparing the behaviour of human beings to that of other life forms becomes again a vital question.

Individual and Group in the Work of Ibn Khaldun

For Ibn Khaldun, those groups with a strong sense of *assabiyeh* were destined to be strong and to rule—at least as long as they were able to maintain their sense of identity and solidarity. Thus, groups composed of blood relatives (as in the case of many Bedouin communities) have the strongest possible ties since they are based on kinship, while urban settings (in which settlers from many locales congregate and group homogeneity decreases) predispose urban dwellers to an eventual weakening of group feelings. Having committed himself to an understanding of political power as resting upon group strength, Ibn Khaldun went on to portray groups in stereotypical fashion. Not only did he formulate his notion of the individual and the specific nature of groups in rigid categories, but his philosophical framework precluded the self-conscious transformation of individual and group identity. Individuals and groups were tragically stuck in predetermined fates.

Although his own life was intricately interwoven with the great political and military dramas of his times, his autobiography (*al-Ta'rif*), supposed to be the "most elaborate autobiography penned by a Moslem intellectual," is "lacking in human interest." (Hitti, 1971, 242). He failed to mention his marriage to the daughter of a Hafsid general in 1345, even though she remained his primary wife until her death nearly four decades later in 1384. (Hitti, 1971, 241). His only mention of his mother is when she died from the plague along with his father.

It was not only Ibn Khaldun's autobiography that failed to touch upon his most intimate relations. The paramount significance of the group in both Arab and Islamic civilization appears to have blocked the emergence of the autonomous individual. The very word "Islam" means submission of the individual to god. Franz Rosenthal informs us that autobiography in general is "not highly developed" among Arabs. (Lawrence, Bruce B., 1984, 19). Even the name by which Ibn Khaldun has become known in history is not his own, but his father's. Arab patriarchy militates against the construction of autonomous individual identity today as much as it did 600 years ago, at least if we judge by the many names derived from Abu (father) and Ibn (Bin, or son). Further to the east and centuries later, a similar denigration of individuality can be seen in Stalinist communitarianism.

In evaluating the status of the individual in Islamic civilization, we might ask: While the group feeling of Muslims is surely one of Islam's noteworthy dimensions, what is the status of the individual? Is there a relation between the Arabic-Muslim prohibition of the human figure in art and Ibn Khaldun's understanding of the individual? Is *assabiyeh* a mechanical negation of the savage individualism of which Ibn Khaldun was so critical? Was his unwillingness to thematise rigorously the individual simply a reflection of the prevailing cultural values of his historical context?

Within an elaborate web of familial identities, strict social conventions, and cultural obligations, individuals in Islamic societies remain bound by collective forms whose power has long since been diminished in the West. Social community and cooperation exist within the *Ummah* (the community of Moslems) in ways that simply do not occur in everyday in much of the West. To be sure, individuals emerged in the Arab world, but he/she was dependent upon family ties and confined in life-options and social possibilities. Pedagogy in the Arabic world remains largely based on memorization and recitation, not individual creativity and imagination. Ibn Khaldun himself recommended memorization as the first step toward understanding poetry and for acquiring literary taste.[13] Even in love-poetry, "the realm of private sentiment, etiquette and courtesy reigned, and the poet's aim was to handle public images with grace and splendor." (Hodgson, 1974, Vol. 2, 303; Hourani, 1991, 75). Of course, one consequence of poetry designed for public recitation—not private reading—is the forging of group solidarity and shared experience. According to Bernard Lewis, other cultural links can be found: impersonality and collectivism are recurring features of Arab prose literature. (Lewis, Bernard, 1966, 142).

In a contemporary example of what might be considered savage individualism—individuals who sacrifice themselves through actions like the "revolutionary suicide" of car bombers—we find group feeling as a primary motivation. As with kamikaze pilots, one result of such actions is the destruction of the individuals who undertake them. Such actions embody subordination of the individual to the group—in this case, in the struggle to kill an externally defined enemy. The tragic effects of plundering the planet for individual greed and the imperialist conquest of peoples defined as "other" should be included at this juncture, as should the oft-neglected capacity of colonizers to unite their group identities at the same time as they divide their subjects and pit them against each other.

Individualism and Individuality, Collectivism and Collectivity

In exploring the future potential of human freedom, it is important to distinguish between individuality and individualism. The former refers to a harmonious relation between the single human being's inward life and group relationships with others while the latter denotes the individual as an isolated monad held in check by repressive groups (in which he/she may or may not claim membership). The determinate negation of individualism is the metamorphosis of individualism into individuality. Similarly, collectivism can be sublated into self-conscious collectivity. The transformation of groups who deem themselves superior to the rest of humanity requires an immanent self-consciousness that they are part of the human family, not simply an identity defined in opposition to external Others.

Ironically, the very scourge of the West—its savage individualism—may also contain a contribution to global civilization. Finding the good in the bad, we might simultaneously locate the seeds of autonomous individuality in the West (understanding the role of the individual in history as forging rights and imagination) alongside the pursuit of wealth and power. Similarly, a contribution of Islamic civilization is the potential of a universal group feeling and cooperation among human beings that transcends racial, ethnic and even gender divisions—a force so strong that it overnight transformed Malcolm X. (X, Malcolm, 2001). A dialectical sublation of Islamic group feelings synthesized with the determinate negation of Western individualism might result in an individuality that is simultaneously that of an autonomous thinking person who is part of a species-cognizant group.

REFERENCES

Enan MA 1975 *Ibn Khaldun: His Life and Work* (Lahore, India: NP)

Goodman LE 1972 "Ibn Khaldun and Thucydides," *Journal of the American Oriental Society* **92**:2 250-270

Hitti PK 1971 *Makers of Arab History* (New York: Harper and Row)

Hodgson M 1974 *The Venture of Islam* 3 volumes (Chicago: University of Chicago Press)

Hourani A 1991 *Islam in European Thought* (Cambridge: Cambridge University Press)

Ibn Khaldun 1986 *The Muqaddimah: An Introduction to History*, translated from the Arabic by Franz Rosenthal, 3 volumes (London: Routledge and Kegan Paul)

Lawrence BB (ed) 1984 *Ibn Khaldun and Islamic Ideology* (Leiden: E.J. Brill)

Lewis B 1966 *The Arabs in History* (New York: Harper and Row)

Mahdi M 1957 *Ibn Khaldun's Philosophy of History* (London: Allen and Unwin)

Rosenthal F 1969 "Ibn Khaldun: the Muqaddimah," in N.J. Davord (ed.), *Bollinger Series* (Princeton University Press, 1969)

Southern RW 1962 *Western Views of Islam in the Middle Ages* (Cambridge, USA: Harvard University Press)

Uvroy D 1993 *Ibn Rushd (Averroes)* (Cairo: The American University in Cairo Press)

Von Martin A 1963 *Sociology of the Renaissance* (New York: Harper and Row)

Wahba, Mourad and Abousenna M (eds) 1996 *Averroes and the Enlightenment* (Amherst, NY: Prometheus Books)

X Malcolm and Haley A 2001 *The Autobiography of Malcolm X* (New York, Penguin Books)

NOTES

1   Originally published in *Journal of Biosciences* (Indian Academy of Social Sciences) 39(2), March 2014: 327-332.

2   Although generally unknown, female artists in seventeenth Century Europe made significant contributions. Judith Leyster (1609-1670) apprenticed to Frans Hals, was a member of the prestigious Painters' Guild, and taught male students. Most of her work was attributed to men. Anna Maria Sybilla Merian (1647-1717) produced volumes of flower engravings as well as drawings of insects, which became significant resources for the subsequent classification of species. After moving to Surinam, she produced *Metamorphosis Insectorum Surinamensium*, considered one of the world's best books of biological illustration. Rachel Ruysch (1664-1750) received more for her art than Rembrandt did for his work. See *The Guerrilla Girls' Bedside Companion to the History of Western Art* 1998 (New York: Penguin Books) 40-43.

3   Cf. speech delivered by Dr. Martin Luther King, Jr., on April 4, 1967, at a meeting of Clergy and Laity Concerned at Riverside Church in New York City. See http://www.hartford-wp.com/archives/45a/o58.html

4   Robert Michel's *The Iron of Oligarchy* is the classic example here, and Karl Marx followed in his teacher G.W.F. Hegel's footsteps by declaring, "history repeats itself." Depending on the level one deals with, of course, for in other respects, "the more things change, the more they stay the same", and we can look at the

issue of individuality vs. groups across history. To that extent, we deal with the same questions, which is among the reasons for studying history.

5   And not necessarily unlike the long periods of stasis punctuated by change claimed for biological evolution. See http://en.wikipedia.org/wiki/Punctuated_equilibrium.

6   Such critics of positivism also oppose the notion that history has precise and repetitive cycles. They understand every event in history as unique, an insight noted long ago by Heraclitus of Ephesus and reinvigorated more than a millennium later by G.W.F. Hegel.

7   To be sure, his theory had no precise notion of natural selection or branching evolution. Ibn Khaldun's "evolution" was just the Great Chain of Being, not a unique notion at the time and derived from Aristotle.

8   In contrast, the polygenist Lucilio Vanini (1585-1619) asserted that "negroes" descended from apes because of their skin color while other races did not.

9   Following Galen, Ibn Sina (Avicenna; 980-1037) had identified nerves as the consolidators of perceived pain in the muscles: as unifying agents as it were, analogous to group solidarity.

10   The work of Peter Kropotkin on mutual aid should be considered in this regard.

11   From a longer perspective, we understand today that the decline of Islamic world was due in no small reason to European discovery of sea route around Africa and establishment of direct trade with China and the East. The excision of merchant profit in the Middle East led to its precipitous decline, one which, intellectually at least, has yet to be reversed by the creation of a handful of oil-rich oligarchic states in the twentieth century. Evidently, the variegation of social life produced by robust forms of economic activity creates intellectual and artistic possibilities that the mere acquisition of wealth cannot. Thus, hopes to stimulate a revival of "the golden age of Islamic intellectual civilization" through the translation, publication and discussion of classical philosophical texts appears to be of less value than hoped for. Amid a dearth of original thinking in the contemporary Arab/Islamic world, we have a plethora of scholars who are obedient employees of foundations, religious or secular, which provide endowed chairs at universities.

12   There is debate as to the beginnings of the Renaissance. Some scholars refer to the Renaissance of the late Medieval period beginning about 1100—a period of the early Crusades, the building of monumental cathedrals, the founding of the Hanseatic League, the rise of towns and the development of Gothic art. Kenneth Clark called this period Western Europe's first "great age of civilization" and traced its beginning to around the year 1000. See Kenneth Clark's *The Gothic Revival* (1928). A major contribution to the rise of Italian power and its Renaissance was the Venetian-sponsored Fourth Crusade's sacking of Constantinople in 1204. Some scholars date the beginning of the Renaissance to Florence in 1401 or to when Greek scholars fled Constantinople in 1452 following the Ottoman conquest of the city. One can also argue that the period from 962, the crowing of Otto as Holy Roman Emperor, to 1452 (i.e. the High Middle Ages), was qualitatively a different world from the Renaissance. It included the Crusades, the Lateran Council and the heyday of Scholasticism. Even in the time of Bracciolini (who discovered the Lucretius manuscript that helped inaugurate Christian humanism in 1417), the Church's control over life made the notion of an individual almost incomprehensible. Curiosity was sin then.

Unpacking My Library

Fro Alda, who loves books as much as I do

TODAY IS January 23, 2016, my first-born's 31st birthday. Exactly one month ago, I arrived in Ocean Beach after leaving here 33 years ago and moving to Boston, where I had a distinguished career as a professor at Wentworth Institute of Technology. Having retired from my job with sufficient funds to move back to San Diego, I hired a moving company to transport what was left of my earthly possessions. After weeks of delay due to a broken axle in Kansas, a huge moving van finally arrived, delivering 5300 pounds of belongings to my door, more than half of which were books and bookcases, the remainder mainly papers and framed art.

The movers left after setting up my bookcases in the long hallway leading from my apartment entry door. I thought it would be an easy matter to unpack my books. Recalling with a smile Walter Benjamin's beloved essay, I happily began. A few exhausting days later, I had filled all my bookcases, 21 feet long by 7 feet high of them, but only a fraction of my books were unpacked. Fortunately, friends came to my assistance. In the process of unpacking and moving my boxes of books, I had developed a severe case of sciatica. David Zebra and Harold helped arrange the remaining boxes of books, creating a wall dividing my living room. As they effortlessly moved box after box, the barrier become so wide that I could not even get to my couch on the far wall.

The sheer quantity of books that I moved from Cambridge to Ocean Beach staggers my mind. And that does not include 700 books I donated to a university library in Guyana, the 475 books on Korea I donated to the Harvard's Yenching Library, or some 200 books on Vietnam I had put aside for the Vietnam vets center at UMass. I can still visualize the happy face of the person who came to pick up these books. As soon as he realized they were written by the "enemy" (members of the National Liberation Front in southern Vietnam and Foreign Languages Publishing House in Hanoi), he gasped and said "This is what we've been missing." My generosity even came to include my ex-wife, mother of my children, to whom I delivered several shelves of books about Palestine. In addition, I calmly gave at random many books to friends when they expressed interest in them or even when I saw their eyes light up as they encountered them—not to mention students who came to my office and found some source of inspiration as they gazed at my collection. They left with smiles as they cradled their gifts. This society may be ridding itself of books, but there are still some of us holdouts who treasure them. Rather than hoarding them, keeping them in private, now is the time to share them, discuss their ideas, and inspire people to produce more.

Today, after Harold helped me assemble three new IKEA bookshelves—9 feet wide and 6 shelves high—I filled them quickly yet still, more than a few boxes remain unpacked. By now, you may have the impression that I have been overwhelmed by the sheer quantity of my books—and you would be right, although it would be more correct to say that the books possess me. My aching back has not yet returned to normal, and my life is still centered on completing the job of moving to San Diego one month to the day after I arrived. Some days ago I complained to one of my friends in Boston that although I had quit my job, I had less time than ever, in large part because I have not yet unpacked my library. And I thought I was going to have time—finally—to read many of the books I had not yet had the opportunity to enjoy.

Nonetheless as I gaze with wonder over my wonderful library (the only thing on earth that I missed as I circumnavigated planet earth twice from 2013 to 2015), I note that these books carry my experiences with them. Some of them were with me when I left Ocean Beach in 1983. They then accompanied me on my move to Boston and have returned with me. I'm think thinking particularly of several volumes by Adorno, *Negative Dialectics* and the unreadable *Philosophy of Modern Music*, both of which I stole from the bookstore at the University of California, San Diego. There is a story here. In 1974, I helped found a bookstore, the Left Bank, today a Starbucks on Newport Street in OB. We started the store as a communal enterprise with zero money, well next to zero money, in fact so close to zero money that it became my task to steal books from corporate bookstores to stock our shelves. Fortunately not all the books I put on display found willing buyers. These two remained behind, and I managed to keep them for myself. As I cradle Adorno in my hands, I remember with a smile how the workers at the university bookstore warned me, laden with more than half-a-dozen books hidden inside my clothes, that the police were coming to arrest me. They encouraged me to evacuate quickly, to avoid arrest, but also not to take all—only some—of their books so they would not continually have to reorder them.

On my next shelf, I spot my nineteenth-century edition of Hegel's *Philosophy of History*. Twice, I have enjoyed reading it slowly. I recall my dilemma when I first discovered it in a used bookstore in San Diego. It was way over my price range. Although long since erased, the penciled price inside the cover still remains legible: $6.50—an exorbitant sum for me in the 1970s. It would have been the easiest matter to conceal and take it, but my strong sense of ethics—only to take from corporate stores—held firm. I have never regretted spending the money on such a treasure.

Paris, May 1968.

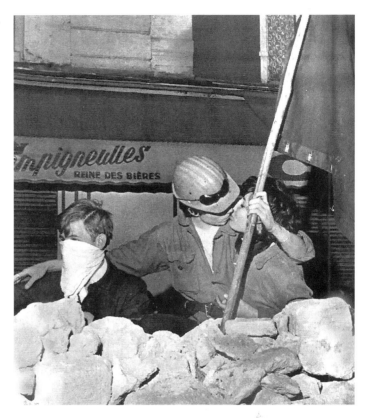

A few books have even made trips with me from Berlin, where I lived from 1979 to 1981, to OB then to Boston and now back home to California. My five volumes of Rosa Luxemburg's *Collected Works* (unavailable in English) were successfully smuggled out of East Germany. My friend Reiner, with whom I had a standing arrangement to exchange books for blue jeans, then a scarce and valuable item in the East. The problem was to get my goods home. I could simply wear jeans and carry an extra pair or two in my suitcase, but getting books back across was a major endeavor. In his wisdom with border issues, Rainer had craftily inscribed them: *"zur Erinnerung an einen guten Freund, für eine beiderseitig gesehene Sache, um das Ziel des Sozialismus in der ganzen Welt durchzusetzen."* ("In memory of a good friend, for a mutual vision, to achieve the goal of socialism in the whole world." And, of course, he dated it: July 6, 1980. I recall crossing the border on the East Berlin side of Checkpoint Charlie, where the guard stared for what seemed an hour at Rainer's inscription. He was trying to find a way to confiscate the books, yet somehow Reiner's phraseology succeeded in averting the guard's grasp.

One prize possession which traveled with me from East Coast to West Coast, then back to the East Coast and now again to Ocean Beach, is Wiktor Woroszylski's *The Life of Mayakovsky*. In 1972, I came down with dysentery while visiting Vermont. My friend Denise Levertov took me in so I could heal. Laid up for more than a week in her library, I discovered Mayakovsky—and much more. As I pull Woroszylski's thick volume down from the towering top shelf, Mayakovsky's slender volume, *How Are Verses Made?*, falls out with it. Inspired by that book, I penned a poem to my fallen comrade Ronnie Brazao in 1972. I still mourn his loss. I wonder, if he had used a larger caliber handgun, might it have been the heroin dealer, not Ronnie, who perished that morning? But Ronnie had no desire to kill anyone, only to rid the Bay Area of the dope that would be the scourge of the movement.

One of my most important sections of my library, one that I return to tie after time, is an entire shelf of books by my teacher and friend, Herbert Marcuse. I smile as I spy the five new volumes of his selected works which Doug Kellner edited. Reading the papers and essays in them has brought me renewed energy and galvanized new ideas. Just below them is a shelf that I never could've imagined would exist: my own published books in English, more than 12 volumes in all, as well as six volumes in Korean, and one apiece in Greek, Spanish and Russian.

I pause to count boxes. So far I have I have unpacked 96 of them and only three remain. My friend Jack Hipp, who packed them in Cambridge, labeled these last three George Lukács, Karl Marx, and MR, for Monthly Review School. Seeing them, I recall vividly when I was living at Red House and read *History and Class Consciousness*, Lukács' masterpiece from 1923. I had purposely delved directly into the text before reading his infamous preface from 1966 in which, under pressure from Party orthodoxy, he recanted so many of his brilliant conclusions. Today however, in 2016, Lukács' importance to me—and not only to me—is a pale imitation of what it was.

At last I reach the box marked Marx. Inside I'm delighted to find my three volumes of *Capital* which also have made the trip from Ocean Beach to Cambridge and back to Ocean Beach. Heavy tomes, I perused them along with Rosa Luxemburg's *Accumulation of Capital*, in which she completed the missing pieces of Marx's systemization of the consequences of expanding capitalism. My good German friend Markus was staying with me in Cambridge one day when the couch where he slept fell off one corner. I am reminded of the sheer amazement on Markus's face when he discovered that I was using those three heavy volumes to replace the broken leg of the couch. "Georgie," he screamed, "you've discovered a use-value for *Capital*!"

Next, I encounter my 3-volume *Selected Works* of Lenin. These very books had accompanied me in 1970 as I sat in prison, where I graduated from MIT. They, too, have made many long journeys from Cambridge to Ocean Beach, back to Cambridge and then again to OB. They still bear the prison guard's handwritten entry of my inmate number, #42987. Holding Volume 2 in my hands, the memory of reading it in 1976 returns to me. I had set aside a block of time to study the two revolutions of 1917, and was engrossed with Lenin's threat to resign from the party Central committee if they did not call for the second insurrection. Suddenly three fellow activists arrived at Red House and immediately began to pressure me to go to the airport with them. They needed to rent four cars for a delegation to attend the Puerto Rican national convention in Chicago and were one driver short to pick up the rentals. With only very seldom periods of time to read, I refused to leave my concentrated study of Lenin. They finally persuaded me by promising I could read at the airport. Once we arrived, they left me to read, and I stood using one of the high counters to support the heavy book. Out of nowhere, I suddenly felt a gun in the small of my back. "Move and you're dead" a low voice intoned. Not knowing if it was a joke, I turned to see two brown-shirted police handcuffing me as they arrested me for armed robbery.

The four of us were taken to El Cajon and held in jail overnight without even being permitted phone calls. I refused to cooperate at all with the police, especially with their continuing inquiries about the bank vault combination I had concealed in my wallet. It was the combination to the empty vault at the Left Bank bookstore, a meaningless set of numbers since the vault was empty except for the checkbook of our perpetually empty account. On principle, I refused to cooperate with my tormentors. The cells were cold, we were not given our constitutionally mandated phone calls, and I didn't appreciate being arrested for nothing more than reading a book at the airport. The jailers finally put me in the rubber room to try and persuade me to talk.

Years later, this apparently nonsensical set-up was clarified when we discovered that Bill Joyce, one of the local organizers of that convention, was a paid FBI informant. It was a sad discovery since along with it came the revelation that some of my "comrades" knew of his affiliation with the FBI, of how he and his wife were taking photos of everyone who entered and left Red House. These "comrades" had discussed the matter and decided not to tell us—the targets of the FBI surveillance—because we were "not working together." When I asked them what that meant, they remembered that our study group had discussed *Revolution and Evolution in the 20th Century* by James and Grace Lee Boggs while theirs had focused on the Weather Underground's *Prairie Fire*. They had been told of the Joyce's FBI work by their older son, then a member of the Free School, who believed that if he told Frank, we in Red House (who were his pals), would know. What do children know that such finely educated "comrades" do not?

Eventually, I received some money for the false arrest in El Cajon. Although not a lot, it was enough to rent an apartment right on the water in Ocean Beach, where I lived happily for 2 years while I wrote my dissertation on the global movements of 1968. For the first time in my life, I was able to focus deeply.

The evening on which I sat in El Cajon jail's rubber room, Herbert had been expecting me as we had made an appointment for me to pick up his house guests from Paris, Andre and Doreen Gorz. Despite anything I said to explain my absence to Herbert, he remained upset. Even when I told him that Stanley Aronowitz had vouched for my presence in his seminar at the exact time when the bank robbery had taken place, which is how we were released, Herbert asked me twice if I was sure I had not robbed a bank.

My failure to show up or even call had infuriated him, so months later, when I had proof of the injustice done to me, I rushed to tell him we had won a suit for false arrest. When I told him I had received money from the court's decision, Herbert asked how much. He scoffed at what he considered the paltry sum I had received. "You've sold your rights cheaply," he said. As I recall the sum was $750, not an considerable sum at the time since it allowed me to pay the first and last month's rent and security deposit to move into my own place.

Yes, I love these books, and not only for what the words and ideas inside them, not only for their valuable lessons and intelligence to pass on to future generations. Each volume brings with it the stamp of time of its place in my life. Each can rekindle long-forgotten memories, in a magic circle not only of acquisition but also of experience. Goethe's thought suddenly returns to me:

"Was ich besitze, sehe ich wie im Weiten.
Und was geschah, wird mir zur Wirklichkeiten!"

"What I possess, I see in the distance.
And what happened becomes reality!"

In Defense of Picasso[1]

SIGNIFICANT EVENTS and personalities disappear for a time, only to reappear in new forms. So it is with the work of Pablo Picasso in Boston. Seldom discussed here for years after the cool reception initially afforded his art by the Brahmins of this city, suddenly Picasso's art and life have taken center stage in the cultural life of the Athens of America. Alongside the Museum of Fine Arts' blockbuster show, "Picasso—The Early Years, 1892-1906," Steve Martin's hilarious play, "Picasso at the Lapin Agile," played the Schubert Theater. If we add the pay-per-view screening of "Surviving Picasso" (also available in video stores), we find a veritable Picasso revival underway.

Ever since the Spanish Armada, Anglo-European superiority has become a matter of course in relation to Spain, to Spaniards and, for that matter, to anything Mediterranean. Boston's new rendition of the life of Picasso is no exception. These portrayals of Picasso do injustice to his politics and personality. Instead of a politically committed and aesthetically revolutionary human being, we are presented with a genius, an egomaniac who is both fawningly celebrated and hypercritically ridiculed. Stories of Picasso's sexual exploitation of women, of his crass use of them as toys, or in what amounts to the other side of the coin, of his dire misogyny and castration fears are freely promulgated. How do such stories originate and become fact among people who know nothing about his art?

Part of the answer can be found by watching Anthony Hopkins play the role of Picasso. We are at a loss throughout his performance to keep up with his numerous mistresses, ex-wives and lovers. Nor is Picasso's apparent collaboration with the Nazis ever explained. In fact, Picasso refused to collaborate. The film's jump cuts from one scene (and significant other) to another have something of the feel of Gabriel Garcia Marquez's *Hundred Years of Solitude*. At least Marquez provided a list of his characters and their relationship to each other! This film purposely seeks to confuse us, thereby assembling a collage of Picasso's politics and love life that is singularly distorted.

The crudest types of control—portrayed in one instance as Picasso kidnapping one of his wives when she tries to leave him—is how the filmmaker portrays the artist. This one-dimensional caricature obscures Picasso's aesthetic impact.

By age 25 (when the MFA show ends), Picasso had found a wealth of material to appropriate. Although he had experimented with many styles, he had not yet found himself. Almost by accident, the MFA show has assembled the raw material from which we can see the young man mature, but we have to know what we are looking for. This was a man of feeling, not a cold detached man always in control—the kind so beloved by the British and typified by their crown prince. After Picasso's best friend, Carles Casagemas, committed suicide in 1901, the young artist, struggling desperately to make a name for himself, brought nothing but blues to the canvas, as if he were possessed by some force beyond his control. At the time, he fretted that he might never emerge from this monochromatic compulsion. For years, he lost the ability to play with forms, deconstructing them and assembling them afresh with his own distinguishing touch, a talent so remarkable even at an early age that his father, an art instructor and something of a painter himself, is said to have given away his brushes after watching his young son complete one of his own unfinished paintings. Interpreting Picasso's blue period, I understand him to be deeply mournful and melancholic, not in the midst of an intellectually constructed aesthetic experiment.

How else can we understand why Picasso's ability to assimilate emergent forms and take them in directions even their originators never imagined? Evidence abounds in the MFA to show how he had already appropriated the avant garde styles of his day (as well of as those artists he admired from centuries before). We see him wrestle with the colors and symbolism of Gauguin, toy with the painterly transgressions of Van Gogh, imitate the exaggerated limbs of El Greco and even experiment with the fleeting moments so important to impressionists. His impressionist painting, "The Fourteenth of July" tingles the viewer's feeling of place. One is easily swept into the canvas, feeling the joviality of the event as though standing on a street corner. Picasso not only imitated master strokes from the past, he often surpassed their most brilliant accomplishments as easily as a child picking up a new toy. So why did he lose his touch? Why did he suddenly fall off the edge? These are unanswered questions in the MFA's presentation. The need to sanitize a bohemian artist, to make him acceptable to the viewing public, treats his blue period as chronological event or aesthetic choice, not as a deeply felt block. No mention is made of his numerous experiments with opium, hashish and different forms of sexuality. Invisibility is the status afforded the anarchist movements and popular uprisings in Andalusia, even though they had a huge impact on Picasso and his contemporaries.

Picasso's status as a member of a circle of outsiders—foreigners, misfits, homosexuals and marginalized intellectuals—in the art world of Paris at the turn of the century is similarly unthematized. His masterpiece, "The Funeral of Casagemas," is hung as part of his blue period, but we are left clueless that this man's suicide is what produced Picasso's melancholy—a depression obvious enough in his ghastly self-portrait hanging alongside "The Funeral of Casagemas." Without any deep understanding of Picasso the man, his art becomes analyzed formally rather than understood as autobiographical and substantive. Accordingly, one critic comments that in this particular self-portrait, Picasso "made himself appear far more mature and world-weary than he was at the age of 20." No matter that he painted himself recuperating from the suicide of one of his best friends, a fellow Spaniard with whom he had learned the ropes as a foreigner in France, a man many people believe was also his lover. Here is one example of how Picasso the man is buried beneath academic explanations of his art.

If the film version of Picasso vilifies him, the MFA's collection of his work presents a clean image, one so sanitized, however, that even this man whose entire youthful existence was an attempt to damn bourgeois society, to protest its sterility by living and painting differently, has been made acceptable to the same people who, in his own day, were precisely the ones he sought to disturb. It is no accident that review after review of the MFA show grovels at the feet of the great master, the show's curator and the paintings—even though many of the pieces in this show are clearly inferior pieces, ones rejected, even mutilated and discarded by Picasso himself.

The show in Boston initially opened at the National Gallery in Washington. Left out of most attempts to establish the pedigree of the MFA show by linking it to its Washington sister institution is any mention that over two dozen paintings hung in DC failed to make the trip to the Hub. And MoMA (the Museum of Modern Art in New York) agree to let only one of its Picassos travel to Boston. As a result, the leftovers hung in the MFA sometimes have the feel of a motley assortment of inferior paintings, many done on off days. Take the still life with flowers (done in Gosol in 1900) remarkable only for how out of place it seems alongside other pieces of the same period. Upon close examination, this painting reveals slash marks meant to mutilate it—probably by the artist who rejected its place in his aesthetic trajectory. And the cantankerous Lady in Blue was left behind in Madrid when Picasso returned to Paris in 1901.

There are a number of drawings and paintings worth more than a second look, extraordinary paintings in which his enormous talents and inspired subjects are brought together. None has more presence than his portrait of Gertrude Stein, lent at the last minute by the Metropolitan Museum of Art. Picasso labored for weeks trying to finish the canvas but could not come up with an appropriate face. He finally gave up and went on one of his rare trips. Upon returning, he quickly finished the face, only to have Ms. Stein complain that it did not look like her. Unruffled, he is said to have replied that with time she would come to resemble it.

Steve Martin's play captures more of the intellect of Picasso than either the film or the MFA show, but his caricature of Picasso is facile, and a superficial and unflattering portrait of the artist emerges. The story is short and sweet: Picasso and Einstein meet by chance in a Parisian bistro in 1904. After a few words of introduction, they recognize the similarity of the unique contribution each will make to the twentieth century. When Elvis shows up, they come to the conclusion that the twentieth century is an epoch to celebrate because men of culture will have more of an impact than men of power. We can overlook for the moment Martin's ignorance of the tremendous suffering caused by powerful men in this century. World War I alone had a horrific effect on humanity—among other things, destroying the utopian imaginations of several generations.

For all its intelligence and humor, Martin's play provides the same stereotypes of Picasso's character as the screen version. In Martin's script, Pablo meets a young female in the Lapin Agile, or at least he thinks he does, since it turns out they have already slept together. At another point in this one-act production, he asks if can have anything he wants simply by painting it, a query whose potentially magical implications are buried beneath the materialistic personality Martin created to utter them. While Picasso's character is not well developed, Martin's witticisms carry the entire production. His script reveals why this actor is so funny: he is able to write with the same facility with which he brings us to laugh at his screen antics. In his portrayal of Einstein, we encounter someone with a sense of humor whose intelligence and propriety are unquestioned, and it is Einstein's role (superbly performed by Mark Nelson) that is most memorable.

Why does Martin's play succumb to vulgar stereotypes? The prudish morality of Victorian England permeates the film's inner message as does the subtle preference for more gentile (read as English) forms of male domination. Picasso is portrayed as the kind of man for whom a woman—any beautiful woman—is the only thing of importance. For this sex maniac, all that matters in a woman is that she is young and infatuated with his genius. His unique abilities are little more than a vehicle for scoring with the opposite sex.

Fortunately, some of the paintings assembled in the MFA's show tell a different story. Anyone who could create these tender faces of human beings, who could paint torsos of so wide a variety with such sensitivity to the humanity of the body (not its nudity) can only be said to have the ability to cast a magical spell. With the wave of his hand, he could transform commonplace junk into works of art—as when a bull's head appears where before was a bicycle seat and handlebars.

NOTES

1   Originally appeared in *New Political Science* Vol. 20 No. 1 (March 1998) 91–95.

George Katsiaficas

by Victor Wallis. With permission from Clyde W. Barrow, ed., Encyclopedia of Critical Political Science, Vol. 2: Concepts & People. Cheltenham, U.K.: Edward Elgar Publishing, Inc., 2024.

BORN IN EL PASO, Texas, in 1949, George Katsiaficas grew up in the US Army. By the time he left home to go to college at MIT, he had lived more than half his life abroad, in Germany and Taiwan. In the US, he went to public schools in Brooklyn and Queens, New York, and finished high school at Baltimore Polytechnic Institute (a public inner city school).

Katsiaficas has been active in social movements since 1969. In 1970, in the midst of the nationwide student strike, he was graduated from MIT while in solitary confinement after being convicted of "Disturbing a School" for organizing anti-war protests. After his release from prison, he founded the Red Bookstore in Cambridge. Escaping continual arrests and prosecution in Cambridge for his support of the Black Panther Party, he moved to California, where he helped build a network of counter-cultural institutions in Ocean Beach, San Diego. He went on to lead an anti-police movement, founded another collectively managed non-profit bookstore, helped organize a food coop, and led study groups based upon the writings of James and Grace Lee Boggs. After driving a taxi for several years, he became friends with Herbert Marcuse and enrolled at UCSD, from which he earned his PhD in 1983.

With Marcuse's support, he received a Fulbright Fellowship and enrolled at the Free University of Berlin. In his doctoral thesis, he uncovered the "Eros Effect" to explain the global synchronicity of movements in 1968. His 1987 book, *The Imagination of the New Left: A Global Analysis of 1968*, was the first study to comprehend a globally unified uprising among the plethora of diverse social movements involving millions of ordinary people that had emerged simultaneously, rejecting dominant values such as national chauvinism, hierarchy, and individualism. In 2007 at a conference at Queen's University in Canada, he maintained that despite the relative quietude then prevailing, protests on a global scale were soon to erupt, a prediction verified by the subsequent Arab Spring, Occupy Wall Street, and Black Lives Matter movements. (See Jason Del Gandio and AK Thompson, eds., *Spontaneous Combustion: The Eros Effect and Global Revolution*, SUNY Press, 2017).

240

Portrait of the author on the Mekong River by Vietnamese artist Huynh
Phuong Dong.

For years, Katsiaficas taught at Boston's Wentworth Institute of Technology, a working-class college, during which time he was a research affiliate at Harvard University in both European and Korean studies. After his book on 1968 was translated into Korean and became something of a bestseller, he visited Gwangju for the first time in 1999. In 2007, he was awarded a Fulbright fellowship to Korea. He lived and taught at Chonnam National University in Gwangju, South Korea for many years. His research and writings have consistently challenged Eurocentric and traditional approaches to social theory. Inspired by the 1980 Gwangju People's Uprising, he devoted 13 years to completing his two-volume book, *Asia's Unknown Uprisings,* which places Gwangju at the center of a wave of Asian insurgencies that overthrew eight dictatorships in six years.

His second book, *The Subversion of Politics: European Autonomous Social Movements and the Decolonization of Everyday Life* (1997), analyzed post-1968 radical formations in Germany, Switzerland, Italy, Holland and Denmark. His writing about the German autonomous movement, with its emphasis on revolutionary politics, squatted housing and cultural spaces, and street militancy including black bloc tactics, was influential for many anarchists and other US-based radicals at that time.

Katsiaficas is a militant researcher, who lives amongst and collaborates with the people he writes about and sees his research as advancing global activism, not simply describing or analyzing it. Together with Kathleen Cleaver, he edited *Liberation, Imagination and the Black Panther Party*. His latest book, *The Global Imagination of 1968: Revolution and Counterrevolution* (PM Press), discusses Sixties' movements in more than fifty countries and outlines global waves of uprisings subsequent to 1968. During his international sojourns, he has been active in liberation struggles in Germany, Lebanon, Korea, Greece and other places. His books have been translated into Korean, Russian, Greek, and Spanish.

He was editor of *New Political Science*, 1998-2003, Chairperson of the Caucus for a New Political Science, 1989-1991, and founded a book series for the Caucus. Honors include the Kim Dae-jung Scholar's Award at Chonnam National University; being made an Honorary Citizen of Gwangju; and the Charles A. McCoy Career Achievement Award presented by the Section for a New Political Science of the American Political Science Association (2011).

BIBLIOGRAPHY

The Global Imagination of 1968: Revolution and Counterrevolution (Oakland: PM Press, 2019)

Asia's Unknown Uprisings: Vol. 1 South Korean Social Movements in the Twentieth Century (Oakland: PM Press, 2012).

Asia's Unknown Uprisings: Vol. 2 People Power in the Philippines, Burma, Tibet, China, Taiwan, Bangladesh, Nepal, Thailand and Indonesia, 1947-2009 (Oakland: PM Press, 2013).

South Korean Democracy: Legacy of the Gwangju Uprising (London: Routledge, 2006) edited with Na Kahn-chae.

Confronting Capitalism: Dispatches from a Global Movement (New York: Soft Skull Press, 2004) edited with Eddie Yuen and Daniel Burton-Rose.

Interviews with the Shimingun, 2 volumes of interviews with participants in the Gwangju Uprising published by May 18 Institute (Gwangju, South Korea: Chonnam National University Press, 2003) in Korean.

The Battle of Seattle (New York: Soft Skull Press, 2002) edited with Eddie Yuen and Daniel Burton-Rose

After the Fall: 1989 and the Future of Freedom (New York: Routledge, 2001)

Liberation, Imagination and the Black Panther Party (New York: Routledge, 2001) edited with Kathleen Cleaver

Latino Social Movements: Theoretical and Practical Perspectives (New York: Routledge, 1999) edited with Rodolfo Torres

The Promise of Multiculturalism: Education and Autonomy in the 21st Century (New York: Routledge, 1998) edited with Teodros Kiros

The Subversion of Politics: European Autonomous Social Movements and the Decolonization of Everyday Life (New Jersey: Humanities Press, 1997; Oakland: AK Press, 2006).

Vietnam Documents: American and Vietnamese Views of the War (New York: M.E. Sharpe, 1992).

Introduction to Critical Sociology (New York: Irvington Publishers, 1987) co-authored with R. George Kirkpatrick.

The Imagination of the New Left: A Global Analysis of 1968 (Boston: South End Press, 1987).

EPILOGUE

Dimitrios Roussopoulos

IT WAS MID-JUNE, 2007 at the conference "New World Coming: The Sixties and the Shaping of Global Consciousness" where George and I linked up. The conference took place at Queen's University, Kingston, Canada; I was a keynote speaker on the opening panel. Given who I was largely surrounded by, I sharpened my axe like a razor's edge.

My comments focused on the sixties slogan, "the personal is political." I expressed irritation and anger at the academic Left, who, I pointed out, having largely left behind radical activism, focused instead on buying a house in suburbia, having a family with one or two cars, and a cottage out of town. I reminded all present of the work ethic that those of us in the field shared.

For most, the activist uniform was the blue jeans first brought north by the activists who went down south in the US to help. Peanut butter and jelly sandwiches were the common diet on the run, in an atmosphere filled with anti-war demonstrations of all kinds, sit-downs, sit-ins, and teach-ins from coast to coast.

One could feel the discomfort in the packed room at these words, as one person told me when we were leaving the hall after a pointed discussion period. I had let a romping fox among the chickens. Most of the rest of this conference I spent with George and a group of activists who where weathering the hot air surrounding us during the rest of the event. A book was eventually published of most of the proceedings, but my commentary was neglected. The book in question was largely ignored.

George and I bonded best together thereafter in Athens. Either we meet in a nice taverna, Rozalia, around the corner from his apartment in Exarchia, or in another taverna I favoured, down the street from a small hotel in the old Plaka. After the warmest hugs and kisses, a longstanding Greek tradition, we would get down to discussing our mutual experiences since we last saw each other.

Thereafter we often were part of what George called our "road show" where we were speakers at the same conferences. One particularly memorable one was at the most northern university in Lapland. We were in the capital of Lapland's 21 municipalities, Rovaniemi. The cycle of changing lights sets the pace for life in this part of the world, the mythical northernmost region of Finland. There we stood during a reception, a few meters from the Arctic Circle, tasting Arctic char and sipping vodka while at the same time launching radical verbal missiles among those present.

What were some of these missiles then—and still today? In a post-Revolutionary period, it is no longer possible to put a limit "in practice" on the affirmation of a right to engage in politics. On the contrary, it is more than ever a necessity and there is a universal capacity to do so. There is a paradox here. Freedom can only be won by those who generally are living with a lack of freedom. In various places it is the 99%. We can give a name to this situation. What is needed is the democratic revolution or, again revolutionary democracy. There can be no democracy as we understand it without all its roots in society as a whole... Democracy as we embrace it is not primarily in terms of institutions or procedures whose radical openness (with a concomitant and unpredictable turbulence) nevertheless derived from the essence of the revolution at its founding moment. And whose development once again is thrown up in its turn—the matter of institutions and procedures. All of this has to be learned. We humans are not born democrats. We must recognize that becoming democrats is an educational process that takes several years of practice and results in a certain level of maturity.

George is not only an activist; he is the kind of activist who is also a teacher. What he sees in the field, he researches further and extrapolates helpful insights about what is, and where we could and should go. The gap between life and knowledge has grown wider. Those who rule choose not to understand those who think and act differently. In the midst of unpresented knowledge, popular ignorance is widespread, and those on top are the exemplars who rule the great cities of the world. Amidst the sciences enthroned as never before, new religions are born every day, and old superstitions recapture lost ground. The working person finds a sick choice between a scientific priesthood mumbling unintelligible pessimism, and a theological priesthood mumbling incredible hopes.

In this situation the function of the teacher/activist is clear. Such persons should not be ashamed of teaching the people, and not only the activists. Those jealous ones who guard their knowledge from all have only themselves to blame if their exclusiveness and their barbarous terminology have led us to the edge. Others who love life enough humanize their teaching. Between us we might build up a society which is eager to learn from geniuses, and therefore ready to produce more. George has advanced our understanding much, and has done his best. It is, however, a prologue, because the people write the rest.

The title of this book, *Eros and Revolution*, is full of meaning. Igniting a revolution is one goal—sustaining it, protecting it from being devoured by the Jacobins, Bolsheviks and other authoritarians, is another. And helping to put in place the inspiriting democratic practices as well as the community and workplace institutions that constitute the engines of a social revolution is another. George contributes insights to all of these branches of radical change.

So George, grow stronger, my comrade... as you stand unshaken, that we may know that the many beside you will fathom more.

Ask your local independent bookstore
for these titles or visit blackrosebooks.com

Subverting Politics:
Autonomous Social Movements Today
Marcos Ancelovici & Francis Dupuis-Déri, eds

Paperback: 978-1-55164-800-2
Hardcover: 978-1-55164-802-6
eBook: 978-1-55164-804-0

Take the City:
Voices of Radical Municipalism
Jason Toney, ed.

Paperback: 978-1-55164-727-2
Hardcover: 978-1-55164-729-6
eBook: 978-1-55164-731-9

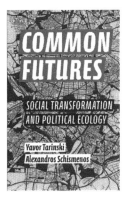

Common Futures:
Social Transformation and Political Ecology
Yavor Tarinski and Alexander Schismenos

Paperback: 978-1-55164-773-9
Hardcover: 978-1-55164-775-3
eBook: 978-1-55164-777-7

Montréal: A Citizen's Guide to City Politics
Mostafa Henaway, Jason Prince,
and Eric Shragge eds.

Paperback: 978-1-55164-779-1
Hardcover: 978-1-55164-781-4
eBook: 978-1-55164-780-7

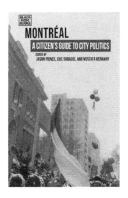